The John D. and Catherine T. MacArthur Foundation Series on Digital Media and Learning

Families at Play

Connecting and Learning through
Video Games

Sinem Siyahhan and Elisabeth Gee

The MIT Press
Cambridge, Massachusetts
London, England

This book was set in Sabon by Westchester Publishing Services. Printed and bound in the United States of America.

Library of Congress Cataloging-in-Publication Data

Names: Siyahhan, Sinem, author. | Gee, Elisabeth, author.
Title: Families at play : connecting and learning through video games / Sinem Siyahhan and Elisabeth Gee.
Other titles: Play 2 Connect | Play to Connect
Description: Cambridge, MA : The MIT Press, 2018. | Series: The John D. and Catherine T. MacArthur Foundation series on digital media and learning | Includes bibliographical references and index.
Identifiers: LCCN 2017024949 | ISBN 9780262037464 (hardcover : alk. paper)
Subjects: LCSH: Video games--Social aspects. | Family recreation. | Communication in families. | Intergenerational communication.
Classification: LCC GV1469.34.S52 S59 2018 | DDC 794.8--dc23 LC record available at https://lccn.loc.gov/2017024949

10 9 8 7 6 5 4 3 2 1

To our mothers . . .

Contents

Series Foreword

The John D. and Catherine T. MacArthur Foundation Reports on Digital Media and Learning, published by the MIT Press in collaboration with the Monterey Institute for Technology and Education (MITE), present findings from current research on how young people learn, play, socialize, and participate in civic life. The Reports result from research projects funded by the MacArthur Foundation as part of its $50 million initiative in digital media and learning. They are published openly online (as well as in print) in order to support broad dissemination and to stimulate further research in the field.

Preface

Although most video gaming takes place at home, family learning and communication around video games, for the most part, has been ignored in education and communication research. At the same time, despite being increasingly accepted as a context for teaching and learning, video games continue to be a source of skepticism and concern among many parents due in part to the negative portrayal of video games in mainstream media. This book is an attempt to broaden the conversation and discourse around video games by focusing on what this medium could do for families.

Although I played video games while growing up, it wasn't until the first year of my doctoral program, where I studied family learning in the context of museums, that I discovered video gaming as a means to support families. A serendipitous observation of rich conversations among parents and their six-year-olds around a glass-blowing simulation game at an exhibit gave me the idea to design video games for families and planted the seed for this book.

I am indebted to Michael Downton, a fellow graduate student, for helping me run the first Family Quest after-school program for families in the fall of 2007. As part of this program, families played through different educational games using Quest Atlantis, a three-dimensional, multiplayer online teaching and learning platform. I spent the next three years growing Family Quest from an after-school program into a stand-alone virtual world within Quest Atlantis where families played the games I developed. My advisers, Joyce Alexander and Sasha Barab, should be recognized for providing guidance and encouragement to pursue an area of research outside of the traditional boundaries of the learning sciences. Many ideas and some of the work presented in this book are drawn from my dissertation work, which was supported by a fellowship I received from Indiana University.

Elisabeth and I met while I was a faculty member and fellow at the Center for Games and Impact at Arizona State University (ASU). Through our collaboration, we were able to expand the research on families and video games in new and exciting ways. A grant from the Joan Ganz Cooney Center at Sesame Workshop and the Heising-Simons Foundation allowed us to document how families with diverse backgrounds engage in intergenerational play around video games in the context of their homes. Chapter 2 of this book focuses primarily on the findings of this work.

During the three years I spent at ASU, Juli James was generous with her time and played a pivotal role in connecting Elisabeth and me with families and promoting our work. We would also like to thank students who assisted us across different projects, including ASU undergraduate students Luz Pacheco, Cinthia Manjarrez, Brianna Shuttleworth, Rafael Varelas, Ben Pincus, Rebecca Hoffman, Alex Cope, and Michelle Capriles-Escobedo; and graduate students Kelly Tran, Anna Cirell, and Earl Aguilera. In addition to helping us collect data, Kelly and Earl also compiled appendix B, the list of video games and descriptions provided at the end of this book.

We are deeply appreciative of the parents and children who took the time to share their experiences and participate in our gaming activities, and—in some cases—invited us into their homes. This book would not have been possible without their openness and willingness to spend time with us. We are grateful for the chance to meet and get to know these families over the years, and we are humbled to share their stories with others through this book. Finally, we would like to thank the teachers and the school, library, and museum administrators who recognized the need to support intergenerational play around video games.

Portions of chapter 2 were previously published as "Understanding Gaming and Gender within the Everyday Lives of Mexican-American Family Homes," in *Diversifying Barbie and Mortal Kombat: Intersectional Perspectives and Inclusive Design in Gaming*, edited by Yasmin Kafai, Gabriela T. Richard, and Brendesha M. Tynes (Pittsburgh, PA: Carnegie Mellon ETC Press, 2016). Portions of chapter 4 were previously published as "Using Activity Theory to Understand Intergenerational Play: The Case of Family Quest," *International Journal of Computer-Supported Collaborative Learning* 5, no. 4 (December 2010): 415–432.

Sinem Siyahhan
March 27, 2017
San Marcos, California

1

A New Perspective on Games and Families

As researchers who have spent a number of years studying the educational uses of video games in and outside of schools, we almost always find ourselves stymied whenever we are asked, "How much video gaming is bad for children?" This is a difficult question to answer for two reasons.

First, our focus has been on discovering the opportunities around video games for teaching and learning. We are mostly interested in understanding the more positive aspects of video games in our studies. We play, study, write about, and discuss video games to understand and enhance the potential of this medium for learning, social interaction, and well-being. Given this disposition, we find the question naturally unidimensional and limiting in revealing the "big picture" of what video games are and can do for children and families.

Second, we believe context matters in understanding the role video games play in our lives. We do not perceive video games, or any medium for that matter, as inherently good or bad. People, young and old, bring different tendencies and dispositions toward their gaming experiences that require more or less monitoring, regulation, and self-reflection on the part of the individuals. For instance, Nancy, a mother of two, takes two completely different approaches when it comes to monitoring her children's gaming because of the individual differences she observed between her son and her daughter:

I don't ever have any issues with my daughter because she balances so many other things on her plate. It's never an issue; I'm seeing her doing her homework, I can see her doing these other things. But with my son is different from my daughter because I think he plays too much. He doesn't like to read; even, like, trying to push him into some other reading, it's very hard to find things that he enjoys reading and I think part of it's just the grade he's at. He finishes his work fast but he very seldom does homework so then I feel like, "Are you sure you don't have homework?" and I don't really trust his responsibility on that either, so I don't ever have an issue with my daughter but sometimes I do with my son; he plays too much.

In addition, what kinds of or how much gaming is perceived to be positive or negative can vary according to families' values and the role that games play in family life. Consider the following exchanges we witnessed at a conference between two mothers who were both professionals in the field of video games development and research.

When discussing her children's technology use, Katie mentioned that her eleven-year-old son was not allowed to play *Call of Duty* (a first-person shooter game where players take on the role of a soldier during World War II) because she found the game violent and inappropriate for her son's age. At the same time, she loved watching the television show *Game of Thrones* every week as a family. Linda, a bit surprised with Katie's choices, preferred having her eleven-year-old son play *Call of Duty* rather than watch *Game of Thrones* because she found the depiction of women as sex objects and the nudity and violence in the show disturbing.

Here we have two parents with very different beliefs about the same video game and its suitability for their child. We share this anecdote to demonstrate how video gaming in the context of families is complex and situated within a set of family norms, values, beliefs, and culture.

Despite the complexities surrounding video game play and its effects, we are often asked by parents and educators how much video gaming is good or bad for children. Many parents we've talked to over the years have expressed a deep concern about their children's video gaming. In addition to the time their children spent video gaming, parents also worried about the content of the video games their children played. Often these concerned parents were mothers who did not play video games with their children. Although these mothers might play games like *Candy Crush* on their smartphones or *Farmville* on Facebook, they did not see themselves as "gamers" and often perceived video games to be a waste of time. The following excerpt echoes the sentiment of many parents, and mothers in particular:

I'm not into gaming myself. He's tried to get me involved, but I'm just—no interest. I've tried to limit his time on the game because I think it does consume him if I let him. But it's really hard to do. I stay on it constantly. You know, limit it, and then I start slacking, and then I have to go back to limiting. He'd be on it 24/7 if I let him, so that's the only challenge for me.

Parents like this mother tended to focus on restricting and regulating their children's video gaming by reinforcing strict rules around the amount of time and the content of their children's video gaming. By so doing, they hoped to shield their children from inappropriate, violent, and sexual content. Video games like *Grand Theft Auto* naturally triggered anxiety and a sense of urgency among parents when their twelve-year-old children asked them to buy the game for Christmas, or they discovered that their child somehow had played and developed a deep knowledge of the game unbeknownst to them. Parents expressed interest in learning more about strategies, tools, and resources that could help them better evaluate the appropriateness of the content of video games and select more educational video games for their children. However, even parents who were successful in finding educational video games for their children struggled to get their children to play these games. When Zoe, a mother we interviewed during a home visit, lamented that her children never played the games she bought for them, her three children unanimously shouted, "Because they are boring!"

We also met a small number of parents who joined their children's gameplay. Some parents had played video games in their own childhood, while others discovered video games later in life with their children. Across various studies we have conducted, fathers reported playing with their children and knowing about video gaming more often than mothers did. This is consistent with national survey findings, which suggest that although playing video games is one of the most popular daily activities among youth, only 33 percent of parents play video games with their children.[1] Furthermore, intergenerational play around video games is divided along gender lines, with more fathers than mothers playing video games with their children.[2] It appears that little has changed in the last three decades since Edna Mitchell's ethnographic study of fifteen families' use of the first game consoles, where she found that fathers were more involved and interested in video gaming than mothers.[3]

This gender gap is worrisome for a number of reasons, in particular due to the potential of gaming as a gateway to a broader interest in computing. Over the last several decades, the gender gap has widened in the information technology (IT) and computer science (CS) fields, both in higher education and in the workforce.[4] Many scholars argue that the roots of this gender gap in the workforce are at home, with more boys exposed to computing early on through playing video games and hacking. Although girls play video games at the same rate as boys, the kinds of games they tend to enjoy playing are different, and they are less likely to engage in activities such as modifying the game that can enhance their interest and skills in computing.[5] Coupled with the persistence of gender-stereotypical beliefs (including those held by parents) around video gaming, this difference can dissuade girls from continuing to play video games and developing their skills.[6] Parents play a major role in implicitly and explic-itly communicating gender-stereotypical messages around video games. As their children's role models, parents set examples through their attitudes, behaviors, and interactions with their children around video games.

We also encountered a different group of parents who enjoyed playing video games—even the ones that involved violent content—with their children. These parents were knowledgeable about the games their chil-dren played and monitored how much time their children spent playing video games. They also talked about games with their children, mentored them to improve their skills, and introduced new games as their children advanced as gamers. For these parents, monitoring the time and content of video games was not the goal of their engagement with their children around video games. It was a natural outgrowth of spending time together with their children around a shared activity that they both enjoyed. They exhibited what Lynn Schofield Clark calls "participatory parenting," in which parents are actively involved in the activity of play with their chil-dren as coparticipants.[7]

This approach to video gaming is fundamentally different from medi-ating children's video gaming by making rules that serve the sole purpose of reducing the negative effects of video games. It shifts the focus of inter-action with children around video games from telling them what not to do to engaging them in rich conversations that promote family connec-tion, communication, and learning around video games. Here's Abigail, a mother of three daughters, ages three, five, and thirteen, whose family experiences around video gaming we detail in the next chapter, talking about playing *Halo* with her children:

For me, my kids playing *Halo* is no different than playing outside and com-ing up with scenarios that seem kind of violent like our kids . . . they could be outside playing Nerf guns and pretending to shoot each other and die. I can go outside and play Nerf guns with my kids and we can be playing in the neighbor-hood. And I don't get questioned about that, but I get questioned about *Halo*. To me, it is no different. It is just a different space but what we are doing is the same kind of thing. So, I wouldn't take them out to a strange neighborhood with a bunch of people I didn't know and play Nerf guns. So, I don't do that online either. But I would if my family was visiting and we all had a Nerf gun and played outside in the neighborhood and played together, we would do that just like we play *Halo* together. My kids don't play with strangers online. That is not appropriate for their age. We structure it as family time so my husband and I are there with them playing.

In this book, we focus on experiences of parents like Abigail who play video games with their children, with the goal of highlighting the aspects of these experiences that are valuable for families. Before we tell their stories in the next few chapters, we review some of the common concerns and issues that continue to dominate popular discussions of video gaming, particularly for children. How video games and gaming are portrayed in the media, for example, continues to be problematic in reinforcing misperceptions about the nature and effects of gaming. We address these concerns up front in order to contextualize the experiences of families shared throughout this book around video games. Rather than discussing specific strategies for parents around video games, this book will synthesize findings from different research projects and conversations we have had with parents over the years to draw the attention of parents, educators, game designers, and researchers to the potential of intergenerational play around video games for families.

Our Contribution

In the last decade, the ubiquity of digital media technologies has sparked an interest among researchers from different fields in taking a closer look at how children and youth use these technologies for a variety of purposes, such as socializing, civic engagement, self-expression, learning, and media production. The primary goal of this work is to use what we learn from these practices, which often take place outside of school, to better serve the learning and developmental needs of children and prepare them for successful participation in civic life and workforce in the twenty-first century. Through detailed qualitative research studies and surveys, many scholars have documented the networked, connected, distributed, and diverse nature of children's use of social media, the Internet, mobile phones, and video games.[8]

These studies contributed significantly to our understanding of how children's practices with and around new media are embedded within a broader social and cultural ecology. They provided a holistic picture of youth culture and new media practices and drew our attention to youth-driven, interest-focused, peer-based groups, networks, and institutions, and the role of adult mentors within these spaces in supporting youth. While these accounts of young people's experiences with digital media technologies involved a glimpse of their interactions with parents at home, we have yet to give our undivided attention to understanding families and video games.

At the same time, there is a growing body of research on parenting in the age of digital media technologies. Many surveys on this topic have focused on parents' reports of their children's digital media use, their perceptions of different digital media technologies, their attitudes toward monitoring their children's digital media use, and parenting styles and strategies around digital media technologies.[9] More recently, qualitative studies have documented family life in the twenty-first century from the view of parents, detailing the anxieties, tensions, changes, challenges, and opportunities families experience around children's use of digital media technologies to provide a broad and balanced view of how the new media landscape is impacting families.[10] Similar to research on youth culture and practices around digital media technologies, in the studies on digital media technologies in the context of families, video gaming is subsumed under the broad umbrella of digital media technologies and practices, and constitutes only a small portion of children's and families' experiences around digital media.

When we look at the literature on video games, the number of studies on families and video games continues to be relatively small, compared to the broader scholarship and commentary on video games as a technology as well as a cultural phenomenon and medium for learning. Some game designers and researchers have looked at patterns of parent-child coplay around different video games in home and lab settings, and tested games with parents, grandparents, and children to assess engagement and enjoyment.[11] Others have written about children's video gaming experiences to inform and educate parents about the potential of video games for learning.[12] These efforts aim to debunk some of the misconceptions parents might have about video games, legitimize children's video gaming as a productive activity, and provide recommendations to parents about how they can guide their children toward more optimal gameplay. Finally, as we will discuss in more depth later in this chapter, research on video games in education has focused on helping educators understand the teaching and learning that occurs around video games and bring children's interest in video games into schools, and not so much on using video games as a tool and a context to build stronger connections between home and school.

This book is unique in several ways. First, we intentionally narrowed our focus to understanding how families interact and connect around video games without the cautionary note about limiting gameplay. Rather than providing a holistic picture of digital media use within which video gaming emerges as a practice of young people only, we put video games and families at the center of our inquiry. We see this focused approach as bringing more clarity to the important role video games play in family life and complementing the broader ecological approaches previously utilized by others. Although this deep and selective focus might have its shortcomings, we believe there is much to be gained from a detailed description of the experiences of families around video games and a larger discussion around the affordances of video games for family connection, communication, and learning.

Second, the cases we share in this book are sampled from five different research projects that spanned a decade and involved both naturally occurring family interactions and designed family experiences around video games. Appendix A at the end of this book describes each project in detail. In writing this book, we also drew on our conversations and informal interviews with parents at events, workshops, meetups, and gatherings. Collectively, these varied sources of information and perspectives have enabled us to paint a picture with broad strokes of the actual and potential ways that families might productively and beneficially engage with gaming. We don't claim to have the definitive word on families and gaming, and we hope that readers will consider what we have to say along with other perspectives. Indeed, we hope to spark greater interest among educators and scholars in understanding and supporting family gameplay, and look forward to future work in this area.

Finally, instead of prioritizing children's practices and culture, we emphasize the experiences of families as a unit. This differs fundamentally from other research and commentary that treat parents as guides who structure and provide social support for children's experiences with video games and remain at the periphery of learning. To us, families must be understood in their own right, each with its own unique dynamics and shared history. Families are the first and most important social groups with which children interact, and we feel that the role of gaming in family relationships, culture, and mutual learning has been neglected. Our goal is to shift the larger societal conversation about video games away from a singular focus on their effects on children as individuals and toward a greater appreciation for their role in the lives and learning of families as a whole.

The Debate over Screen Time

One popular topic associated with digital media technologies, including video gaming, is "screen time." The term was originally introduced sometime between the 1960s and 1970s, when television became a household technology in the United States. It was extended to include computers and game consoles as these technologies have taken their place in families' homes. And, more recently, it includes time spent using handheld devices such as cell phones and tablets across different settings such as the home, doctor's offices, and restaurants, as well as while traveling.

The recent change in the American Academy of Pediatrics' (AAP) media guidelines on screen time—which recommend no screen time for children under the age of two, and up to two hours of high-quality screen time per day for older children—has once again fueled a public debate and conversations around screen time. Many have critiqued the recommendations as unreasonable or unattainable given that research suggests children across different age groups are already consuming media for much more than two hours a day. Others have commented on the recommendation's focus on the quantity rather than quality of screen time, noting that not all screen time is equivalent in its effects.

Since television was first introduced, pediatricians, developmental psychologists, and communication scholars have been concerned with reducing the negative effects and amplifying the positive effects of media on children. Now that television has become ubiquitous, researchers have turned their attention to the behaviors of parents at home to understand the relationship between media and sociocognitive development of children. Given that television viewing most commonly takes place within the home, and parents are the ones who socialize and spend the most time with children at home, they are positioned to be key influences on the effects of media on children. Parents play a role in children's television watching through the strategies that they employ at home. These strategies are referred to as "parental mediation strategies" and include restrictive mediation (setting up rules around television), active mediation (talking to children about television), and coviewing (watching television with children).[13] Over the years, this body of research has disproportionately focused on reducing the negative effects of media and the parental mediation strategies that are effective in accomplishing this goal, rather than exploring the positive effects of media and the role parents play in realizing them with children. After many years of neglect, the latter area of research is now beginning to grow with the emergence of new social and digital media technologies and new practices around them.

However, while the new media landscape is far more diverse today than it was forty years ago, there still is a tendency to treat all information and entertainment screen media as equivalent. The notion of an optimal or harmful "media diet" is widespread. Parents are urged to limit media consumption and create "screen-free zones." The following statement that was only recently removed from the AAP's website would scare any parent: "Studies have shown that excessive media use can lead to attention problems, school difficulties, sleep and eating disorders, and obesity. In addition, the Internet and cell phones can provide platforms for illicit and risky behaviors."[14] However, there is no definitive point at which media use becomes excessive, and two hours of television viewing is not the same as two hours of video gaming. Furthermore, reports of daily screen time (an average of nine hours per day even for adults) typically do not take into account simultaneous or overlapping media use, such as messaging with a friend while watching a video, thus creating potentially exaggerated representations of screen time. Even the AAP has begun to acknowledge that the term "screen time" is increasingly obsolete, as the use of mobile devices in particular has begun to permeate our lives.[15] While there is no doubt that disproportionate media use can be harmful for children as well as adults, "turning it off" is not the best or only strategy.

Research on Negative Effects of Video Games

Research on the negative effects of video games is as old as video games themselves, and spans more than twenty years. Although findings from this research are not to be completely dismissed, they need to be weighed against the growing research on the positive cognitive, social, and emotional impact of video games on children as well as adults. The pendulum of public opinion and media portrayals of video games seems to swing from balanced to negative whenever there is a school shooting in the United States.[16] These devastating events are almost always reported along with the information that the shooters were players of violent video games. From there, public condemnation of video games extends to blaming video games for other societal issues such as mental illness and obesity.

One important fact about the research on negative effects of video games is that most studies conducted in this area are correlational. These studies do not establish cause-and-effect relationships between variables such as playing video games, increased aggression, and committing violent crimes or other behaviors for which video games are often blamed. Correlational studies suggest the coexistence of two different phenomena, but cannot establish that one causes the other. The relationship may be completely spurious, or there may be another variable that causes both. This is a particularly obvious issue in research on diet and health. For example, studies may show a positive relationship between eating yogurt and longevity, leading to claims that eating yogurt will add years to your life. However, it may be the case that people who ate yogurt during the study were wealthier and more likely to get good health care, or perhaps they also were more likely to exercise regularly. Unless all of these other kinds of influences are controlled, it's impossible to establish cause and effect. As another example, in 2010, juvenile arrests for violent crime hit a thirty-year low while sales of violent video games increased substantially over the same period.[17] It might be just as plausible to attribute the decline in juvenile crime to violent video games, though just as inappropriate.

A number of controlled studies in which children play video games indicate that aggressive behaviors and thoughts are increased directly after playing violent video games.[18] However, there is no evidence that these short-term changes lead to actual violence or any lasting tendencies toward aggressiveness.[19] Furthermore, these studies may not take into account other factors; for example, one possibility is that competition, not violence, leads to an increase in aggressive feelings.[20] In addition, the real-life context of play is quite different from playing games in a laboratory setting, and other influences, such as interactions with peers and family, may play an important role in moderating the effects of any kind of gameplay.

In summary, multiple factors need to be taken into account when evaluating claims about the negative effects of video games on children. The nature of the research informing these claims needs to be examined critically, at a minimum. In addition, the attributes of individual children and the context of their gameplay will moderate any potential effects. With that, we now briefly review three common concerns we have heard from parents regarding video games.

Antisocial Behavior

One of the first questions parents typically ask is whether playing video games can lead to antisocial behaviors such as violence and aggression. This is one of the most prominent and persistent concerns about video games, resulting in the establishment of a regulatory body, the Entertainment Software Rating Board (ESRB), in 1994. The ESRB assigns ratings based on age appropriateness to video games and mobile apps sold in the United States and Canada.[21] The ratings are intended to help parents decide which games are appropriate for their children, and include E (for everyone), EC (for early childhood), E10+ (for everyone age ten or older), T (for teens; age thirteen and older), M (for mature; age seventeen and older), and AO (for adults only; age eighteen and older). Ratings reflect the kind of violence, sexual content, and language in the game.

Many parents worry because children either play or watch others play video games that are rated inappropriate for their age group. Contrary to common belief among many parents, however, the relationship between playing violent video games and exhibiting antisocial behavior continues to be unclear. Although there has been exponential growth in the number of children between the ages of ten and seventeen who play video games, as we noted earlier, there has been a steady decline in the number of children arrested for violent crimes since the 1980s. Similarly, in Japan, the second-largest game market after the United States, crime levels are four times lower than in the United States.[22] Finally, while factors that contribute to antisocial behaviors vary, stressors at home and personal traits are far stronger predictors of antisocial behaviors among children than playing video games.[23] At best, playing violent video games may be a risk factor that contributes to antisocial behaviors in addition to other factors but cannot be solely responsible for antisocial behaviors.

Addiction

Anything that is engaging and pleasurable has the potential of being addictive, and video games are no exception. Although the American Psychiatric Association has not recognized video game addiction as a condition, a small proportion of video game players demonstrates the behavior of addicts, playing excessively and compulsively.[24] What counts as excessive or compulsive video gaming? Research suggests that those who devote so much time to video gaming that they ignore personal hygiene, deprive themselves of sleep, or are unable to perform daily tasks such as going to school or work are at risk of video game addiction.[25] We stress that while 97 percent of children ages twelve to eighteen play video games daily,[26] only a small portion of this population is at risk of addiction.[27] Many children can play video games for an hour or two every day and still manage their schoolwork, chores, social life, and family life. Furthermore, obsessive gaming may be a symptom of some other issue in a person's life. For instance, addictive gaming behaviors may be exhibited by a person dealing with depression, anxiety, or stress who uses video gaming as a coping mechanism.[28] More research is needed to understand what counts as video game addiction (if such a thing exists) and risk factors that may contribute to it. At the same time, it is just common sense that doing anything—including reading books and exercising, not just playing video games—to an extreme is unhealthy.

Obesity

Another concern of parents is that video gaming is to blame, at least in part, for children's lack of exercise and weight gain. Health trends in the United States suggest that a high percentage of adults and children are overweight and that there is an obesity epidemic facing the nation.[29] There are many factors that have contributed to the increase in obesity among children and adults alike, and it is unclear to what extent video gaming or "screen time" in general has contributed to this trend. Overconsumption of sugary, fatty, and generally unhealthy foods is certainly a contributor, and a generally inactive lifestyle can also be a factor.[30] The amount of time that children spend in sedentary behaviors has increased in recent years, with a particularly noticeable growth in time spent watching TV and playing video games, and in recreational computer use. Even though children spend more time watching TV,[31] video game play is often singled out as a particular problem, perhaps because of the assumption that it is replacing more physically active forms of play. There is a correlation between obesity and sedentary behaviors, but as we discussed above, such correlations do not explain why such relationships exist. For example, parents' increased concern over children's safety has led to greater restrictions on their outside playtime, potentially leading to an increase in both sedentary behavior and obesity. Research on video gaming is scarce, but one study indicated that there was no relationship between time spent video gaming and increased weight or body mass index.[32]

Notably, video games have also been promoted as a means of helping children to be physically active and lose weight. Games such as *Dance Dance Revolution* and *Wii Sports*, as well as "exergames" created specifically for physical fitness, can keep children and adults active even while in front of a screen. Research suggests that these games may be just as physically intense as, if not more than, children's typical outdoor play.[33] And in our work, we've found that such games can be appealing activities for families to engage in together.

Disruption of Family Life

There has been a considerable degree of concern expressed in popular publications—such as Sherry Turkle's *Alone Together*[34] and *The Big Disconnect*[35] by Catherine Steiner-Adair and Teresa H. Barker—that digital media promotes forms of communication that have adverse effects on face-to-face relationships, particularly in the home and among family. Turkle argues, for example, that while communication might be more frequent, it is more shallow (e.g., brief text messages) and allows people to avoid deeper intimacy and emotional connections. Similarly, Steiner-Adair and Barker suggest that digital media technologies consume family life, and parents are losing a meaningful connection with their children as a result. The claim made in these books is that digital media technologies have made us less social and more disconnected from one another, and are fundamentally threatening the core family unit. This concern resonates with the general public, due to ongoing concerns about changes in traditional family structures and persistent anxieties about how our lives are increasingly affected by digital media. Images of families sitting at a dinner table, seemingly ignoring each other while checking their phones, are quite powerful in conveying the message that digital media use is a problem.

When these snippets of everyday experiences with technology are put into sociocultural and historical perspective, however, such reports become less alarming and appear to be a more natural response to the integration of technology into our daily, work, and family lives. Various technologies have long been part of family life, and how families use technology varies considerably. Families have been watching television during dinner since the 1960s. Families with two working parents often cannot share family dinners regardless of the technology available at home. The many images from the 1950s of people reading newspapers during bus rides while ignoring fellow passengers perhaps underscore how we romanticize the past in our society. These images are no different than images of people using their phones on the bus today. In both cases, people are immersed and consumed by a piece of technology (see figure 1.1). Yet, the images of people using their smartphones evoke more anxiety over human communication than newspapers do.

A common solution offered by many to the invasion of the Internet, smartphones, and other digital media technologies in our daily lives is

Figure 1.1
People using media on the train

"unplugging" or "cutting the cord." These attempts to remove digital devices from our daily lives ignore the meaningful and rich context within which people use their devices. The Internet and mobile devices permit families to communicate more frequently and across greater distances. Siblings and friends engage in various types of teaching and learning in and through video gaming.[36] One advantage of using a smartphone today over reading a newspaper on the train four decades ago is that people continue to socialize with friends and family through online chatting, social media, and games using their smartphones while riding the train. People are not passive consumers of digital media technologies, but rather active agents in constructing the purpose, value, and meaning of using digital media technologies in their lives. Furthermore, as many images from the 1950s show, our relationship with "disruptive" technology precedes smartphones, and it is hard to make claims about whether we are less connected to one another because of digital media technologies.

Framing of Video Games in Education

Educators did not pay much attention to video games until computers were introduced into many schools in the United States during the 1990s. Even then, it took another twenty years for video games to be taken seriously as an important tool for teaching and learning in education. It is only in the last decade that we have experienced an exponential growth in the number of studies that have investigated video games as an educational technology medium. More recently, the educational potential of video games has been recognized at the national level through initiatives such as White House Apps for Healthy Kids Challenge and the National STEM Video Game Challenge. In March 2011, President Barack Obama called on educational software developers to design better games and apps for education:

I am calling for investments in educational technology that will help create . . . educational software that's as compelling as the best video game. I want you guys to be stuck on a video game that's teaching you something other than just blowing something up.[37]

While it is exciting to see video games acknowledged as a compelling medium for teaching and learning at the national level, this quote also captures the tension that exists in the uptake and framing of video games in education. Since the inception of video games, entertainment and educational games have been defined and perceived as two different genres, with learning reserved for the latter. In her book *Engineering Play*, Mizuko Ito describes the entertainment genre as kid centered and intended to be consumed at home, while the educational genre supports children's academic content knowledge and is intended to be consumed in schools.[38] Although these distinctions are driven more by market economies than the actual learning that takes place while playing these genres of games, they continue to shape the way parents and educators think about the relationship between games and learning, and how video games are talked about and discussed in the public sphere.

From this perspective, a game like *Math Blaster*, in which players solve abstract math problems that are remotely related to the game narrative, has educational value by default whereas a game like *Halo*, in which players solve problems to survive in a complex immersive world, has no educational value because it was not intentionally designed to support academic learning. Statements like the one made by President Obama perpetuate the idea that video games are of value only if they are intentionally designed to be "educational." The goal should be to discover the "secret sauce" that makes entertainment games engaging for children and use them to better design the games that have overt educational agendas.

Although this is certainly an important area of research and development, we believe reducing the value of video games in education to this narrow focus undermines the power of video games as a medium for teaching and learning as well as supporting family communication, connection, and learning. This framing also ignores the many studies that have documented how learning takes place in a wide variety of ways around entertainment games. As we will discuss further in chapter 3, associating learning only with schools and with video games that are intentionally designed to teach academic content limits the possibilities of what parents and children can do around video games, and how they can engage in learning together

Evolution of Games as a Medium

Drawing upon Johan Huizinga, Douglas Thomas and John Seely Brown identify knowing, making, and playing as fundamental practices that define what it means to be human.[39] Humans have a long history with games; the first board game, Senet, dates back to 3100 BC. Since then, games have evolved as a cultural medium. The games humans designed and played have become more sophisticated and diverse with respect to their content, mechanics, and purpose as humans developed new tools, technologies, and ways of thinking. Today, people around the world play all kinds of games, including but not limited to video games, for a wide variety of reasons.

Video games first entered our lives in the form of "arcade games" with coin-operated machines installed in public spaces like shopping malls, restaurants, and amusement parks. The baby boomers, now in their sixties and seventies, were between the ages of ten and thirty at this time. The first commercially successful game to be played on coin-operated machines was *Pong*, developed by Atari in 1972. The same year, the first commercial home video game console, the Magnavox Odyssey, was developed and sold 350,000 units. Between the late 1970s and early 1980s, the number of companies that developed games blossomed, and it is during this time the games we still remember today, such as *Space Invaders*, *Pac-Man*, and *Donkey Kong*, were released. Limited by the available technology, these early games fell into the action genre, using simple game mechanics that tested the speed and skill of players.

Up until the end of the 1970s, television defined people's experiences with media at home. Owning a television set was common, and families gathered around the television to watch their favorite shows. By the beginning of the 1980s, however, video game consoles and personal computers started to enter homes at a rapid pace. At the same time, these technologies were fairly expensive, and not all families were able to afford them. Arcade games were still the dominant means of playing video games, although they were gaining a bad reputation due to their shooting mechanics, addictive qualities, and the fact that they were primarily targeted at boys. During this time, the game industry experienced an oversaturation of game companies and it crashed, with many companies going bankrupt in 1983. Despite this financial crisis, video games had already become part of popular culture in the United States.

By the mid-1980s, the game companies Nintendo and Sega dominated the home video game console market and games like *Tetris*, *Super Mario Bros.*, and *The Legend of Zelda* were released. The designs of these three quite different games are significant milestones in the evolution of video games as a medium. *Tetris*, a puzzle game, engages players in spatial reasoning to rotate and match geometric shapes. *The Legend of Zelda*, by contrast, is an action-adventure game embedded within the coming-of-age story of its main character, Link, who is on a quest to find and rescue Princess Zelda. One of the most popular games of all time, *Super Mario Bros.*, is a side-scrolling platform game that engages players in fun gameplay that involves jumping and running in a vibrant, colorful world. All of these games have stood the test of time as they have been rereleased repeatedly across different platforms as technology evolved, allowing multiple generations to enjoy playing these games. *The Legend of Zelda* and *Super Mario Bros.* have become franchises, expanding and improving the story line, game mechanics, and graphics with each new installment in the series. Parents who participated in our projects often shared their memories of playing *Super Mario Bros.* and *Tetris* while growing up and when their children were younger.

Generation X-ers, who are now in their late thirties to early fifties, were between the ages of ten and twenty-five in the early 1990s. This era was marked by the rapid increase in the presence of personal computers in homes and workplaces in the United States. The simulation game genre emerged around this time, notably with *SimCity* and *Civilization* published in 1991 for the PC. Unlike other games that came before, this genre involved open-ended gameplay in which players built cities and civilizations. These games were more complex and required more time commitment from players than other games. With this genre of games, video games as a medium started to move from entertainment to self-expression.

By the 2000s, the game industry was dominated by companies like Nintendo, Sony, and Microsoft. This era marked a transition from 2-D games that were more targeted to children to 3-D games that targeted adult or more mature gamers. Video games such as *Halo* and *Grand Theft Auto* were first released around this time. Since the debut of the iPhone in 2007 and iPad in 2010, the graphics and the core mechanics of video games have evolved yet again. So-called casual games became wildly popular, partly through their integration with social media sites such as Facebook. Smartphones and tablets of all sorts put games within reach of a wide potential audience, and this shift in audience as well as format pushed game design in new directions. While early games made for touch screen technology were often clunky and frustrating, designers have learned to utilize the features of these devices in innovative ways. As we write this book, *Pokémon Go* has become a worldwide phenomenon, drawing in millions of players with its creative use of augmented reality to make the real world into a game platform. On the console side, the release of platforms with sensor technology, such as the Nintendo Wii in 2006 and Kinect for the Xbox in 2010, led to games that get players out of their seats to dance, play virtual guitars, hit virtual tennis balls, ski down virtual slopes, and otherwise engage in a more physical way with video games.

Today, people of all ages can play video games across different platforms including game consoles, smartphones, tablets, and computers. Depending on the devices available to them, they can play video games in the comfort of their homes or on the go. They can progress through multiple games at the same time or play different kinds of games depending on the devices they use, the people they are with, and what piques their interest.

Intergenerational Play

Our society tends to associate play with children and work with adults. Although the idea that play is the domain of children dates from antiquity, it became popular again at the turn of the twentieth century.[40] Until this time, children worked alongside adults on farms and later in factories. During the first several decades of the twentieth century, however, public schools opened, school attendance became mandatory, and laws established a minimum age of employment and maximum hours of paid work for children. Efforts to remove children from the workforce altogether to provide them with education were in full swing around the 1930s. At this time, many psychologists, educators, and advocates studied and wrote about the importance of play in children's lives, the relationship between play and work, and the value of play in education, especially during early childhood.[41] Susan Sutherland Isaacs, who shares similar ideas with such famous child psychologists as John Dewey, Jean Piaget, and Lev Vygotsky, defined play as a child's work.[42] The role of adults in children's play was to create the environment for children to play in but not necessarily participate in the activity with them.

This conceptualization of play has dominated our thinking since the early twentieth century. We are enculturated into understanding work and play as mutually exclusive and age bound. Children as young as three years old can sort activities into different categories of play, work, and learning.[43] They perceive their interactions with peers and toys as play but activities with adults as work. Furthermore, despite the emphasis on the importance of play in education, young schoolchildren perceive the tasks they do at school as work, not play.[44] This separation of work and play in our society is antithetical to the embeddedness of play in human experience and undermines the function of play in our lives. It also reinforces such counterproductive messages as "work is not fun" and "play is mindless work or a waste of time."

Despite these long-held societal beliefs, play is increasingly becoming central to innovation, imagination, and experimentation in the twenty-first century. According to the new media literacy scholar Henry Jenkins, the capacity to experiment with one's surroundings in the form of play is a skill that is important in the new media landscape shaped by social, online, and mobile technologies.[45] In their book *New Culture of Learning*, Thomas and Brown argue that the twenty-first century is marked by constant change, and play is the basis for cultivating imagination and innovation not just for children but for adults as well:

Children use play and imagination as the primary mechanisms for making sense of their new, rapidly evolving world. In other words, as children encounter new places, people, things, and ideas, they use play and imagination to cope with the massive influx of information they receive . . . Historically, the pattern had been that as children grow up and become more proficient at making sense of the environment in which they live, their world seems to become more stable. Thus, as a child grows and becomes accustomed to the world, the perceived need for play diminishes. Today, however, children and adults alike must continue to deal with an ever-changing, expanding world. A child playing with a new toy and an adult logging onto the Internet, for example, both wonder, "What do I do now? How do I handle this new situation, process this new information, and make sense of this new world?"[46]

Beyond providing a venue for imagination and experimentation, playing games has cognitive, social, and emotional benefits for both adults and children.[47] According to Janet Murray, by creating *joint attentional scenes*, games provide "understanding of the self both as an agent and an object within a community of intentional agent-objects" and help "develop the ability to shift perspective from one's own point of view to the point of view of others, to imagine what someone else is thinking, to see oneself from the point of view of the other" while engaging those who play in teaching and learning simultaneously.[48] Games allow for adults and children to make connections, share perspectives, experiment with new roles, and learn from one another. They also help parents to learn how to effectively communicate and provide assistance to their children.[49]

Gaming is actually a common activity among families. Families have been playing sports games (e.g., soccer), board games (e.g., backgammon), and card games (e.g., Go Fish) together for decades if not centuries. While they value playing with their children, parents may hold different values about playing video games with their children. Although playing games is a common activity among families, parents' engagement with video gaming has been consistently less frequent.

Several recent studies suggest that engaging in intergenerational play around video games can have a positive impact on family relations and children's well-being. Researcher Sarah Coyne and her colleagues found that female teens between the age of eleven and sixteen who played video games with their parent(s) had higher levels of connection to their families than those who did not play video games.[50] In a case study with two families in Silicon Valley, Heather A. Horst found that fathers bond with their sons over video games.[51] In an earlier study, Pål Aarsand observed that the "digital divide" between generations—that is, children being more adept and skilled than their parents and grandparents around technology—is a resource for intergenerational interactions in the context of video games and families; adults can use their status as "learners" to have conversations and otherwise engage with their children.[52]

At the same time, although we have a sense of the potential benefits of families playing video games together, only a small proportion of families engage in the type of game activities that would allow them to experience these benefits. Furthermore, we know relatively little about the kinds of family interactions around video games that support family connection, communication, and learning. Not all families collaborate and interact productively around video games. While video games can be a context for family learning and connection, more research is needed to understand what design element(s) in video games can create opportunities for mutual engagement and promote collaborative problem-solving experiences among parents and children.

In addition to its direct benefits for families, when facilitated at an institutional level, intergenerational play around video games can be a vehicle for building a sense of community. Educators have already been implementing activities like family nights and open houses to increase parental involvement in their children's schools by promoting connectedness, belongingness, and inclusiveness. Similarly, educators can integrate intergenerational play events around video games into their current offerings to bridge student learning across home, school, and after-school settings.

Organization of the Book

Because the relationship between video games and families is a topic that has received little attention, we wrote this book with a broad audience in mind. Parents, educators, game designers, and researchers will benefit from reading our book. Throughout the book, we share the experiences of different families with both young and older children around video games and discuss how their experiences connect with the themes of this volume. Specifically, we focus on the diverse ways video games support family connection, learning, and communication. Although these themes are intertwined in that families communicate, connect, and learn simultaneously when playing video games together, we dedicated a chapter to each. In the next three chapters, we foreground each theme and illuminate the opportunities for families around video games. These chapters draw upon our research projects and are structured around cases of different families. In the last two chapters, we discuss the practical implications of our work for parents, educators, and game designers. We provide an overview of each chapter below.

In chapter 2, we share the cases of five families to demonstrate how parents and children use video games to connect with each other and extended family members such as cousins, aunts, and uncles who live far away. We discuss the power of video games for bringing family members together, strengthening family relations, and creating a sense of closeness. We juxtapose our observations of families connecting around a shared interest of playing video games with the popular angst over technology creating an emotional disconnect and distance between family members.

In chapter 3, we take a deeper look at how learning and teaching take place when families play video games together. We introduce several key ideas about how video games are similar to and different from books, other media, and other forms of play in their opportunities for teaching and learning. Although research on teaching and learning around video games is extensive, we know little about how families' interactions around games might promote learning, or more broadly, how families might incorporate gameplay into the wider learning ecology of the home. Furthermore, the broader literature on learning in the home tends to position parents and other adults as experts and teachers. We identify ways that all family members can take on varied roles in teaching and learning interactions around video games and contribute to the collective development of valued knowledge and skills.

In chapter 4, we shift our focus to how intergenerational play around video games is a vehicle for socialization. Traditionally, parents are conceptualized as the ones who socialize children into different ways of seeing, doing, and being in the world. Although parents are their children's first role models and teachers, they also develop different understandings of the world through interacting and communicating with their children. Therefore, socialization in the context of families is bidirectional in that as much as parents influence the way children think about themselves and the world, children also affect their parents' understanding of themselves and the world. Using specific examples, we describe how intergenerational play around video games is a stage for self-expression, negotiation of individual and family identities, and making sense of the world.

In chapter 5, we offer a new vision for how to think about families in the twenty-first century. Specifically, we push back against the traditional paradigm of the parent as the more knowledgeable person (or expert) and the child being the less knowledgeable person (or novice) in the family relationship. We revisit Seymour Papert's notion of "family learning culture" and how families as communities of practice can utilize the different expertise that both young and old bring to shared activities.[53] We offer video games as a fruitful context for families to form, develop, and sustain their learning culture as well as develop skills that are valued in the workplace and for civic engagement in the twenty-first century. We suggest four different ways parents can engage with their children around video games to support a family learning culture at home.

Finally, in chapter 6, we discuss the practical implications of our work for educators and game designers. We believe educators and game designers, as the creators of learning environments, are key players in helping families use video games to enhance and maintain family connection, learning, and communication. Through the activities they design, educators can facilitate positive and productive social interactions between parents and children around video games, and connect learning in the home to school learning. As content producers, game designers are well positioned to design game experiences that take into account the social dynamics that are unique to families and invite families to become collaborative problem solvers.

In the beginning of this section, we stated that we wrote the book with a broad audience in mind. Our approach is rather unusual, given the diverse needs and interests of such different groups, and the challenge of accommodating these differences in one text. However, we believe that the topic of families and video games by its very nature crosses the boundaries of theory, research, and practice. The paucity of research on the one hand and the visible lack of conversations in the public sphere around this topic on the other compelled us to write this book. By so doing, our goal is to promote the study and understanding of families and video games in their own right, as well as the design of video games and game-based experiences for families. To this end, we synthesized findings from different research and design projects we conducted throughout the last decade, and connected these findings to themes and concepts drawn from the work of others in a form that we hope is meaningful for everyone. That said, here we describe the relevance of this book for different audiences, to highlight its potential value for each type of reader.

Researchers

In this book, we share findings from a collection of studies that utilize a wide range of research methods, as opposed to reporting the results of one large study. There are a small number of studies that focus on families and video games. Researchers in education, communication, and human–computer interaction will find it useful to learn about the social dynamics, learning arrangements, and interaction patterns of families around video games. Surveys and ethnographies are common research methods used to understand the experiences of families with video games and digital media technologies more broadly in the current research landscape. In this book, we also share findings from projects that employed design-based research approaches. We believe the time is ripe for more research addressing not only naturally occurring family interactions around video games but also exploring ways to bring families together using video games and optimize the time they spend to achieve positive outcomes. We hope this book will inspire researchers to conduct studies that contribute more basic and applied knowledge in this area.

Parents

Although this book draws upon our research with families, we believe parents have much to gain from reading this book. Rather than telling parents what their children are doing with and around video games and what they should be doing to support their children, we report the experiences of families who actually play video games together. The cases we present are stories of other families that parents can relate to, draw upon, and apply to their own context. We see our role as a conduit to bring stories to light that otherwise have not been visible. Parents who are looking for suggestions will find chapter 5 particularly useful in learning about how to participate in intergenerational play around video games, and unearth the potential of this technology for their family learning and well-being.

Educators

This book is relevant to educators in two ways. First, understanding what families do with and around video games can inform educators in designing learning experiences for children and families at their institution. Too often, the family context is treated as a "black box" in education because it is out of educators' reach; educators interact with children and families at their institutions without much knowledge of what is going on at home. Second, educators play a key role in supporting productive use of video games at home. Many educators have already integrated video games into their curricula in schools and activities in libraries and museums. To enhance the impact of these efforts on children' learning trajectories, connections should be made across children's school, family, and personal lives. To this end, in chapter 6, we review specific strategies that will allow educators to create intergenerational play experiences that connect children's learning across different contexts.

Game Designers

Although we list them last, game designers have as much to gain from reading this book as any other readers. From a design thinking perspective, the first step in developing a product for consumers is to understand the users. This step, also known as "empathizing," prompts a closer look at what users do, want, need, and value and can challenge preconceptions and biases of the designer. The family cases we share throughout this book are, in a sense, profiles of a particular group of video game users. The game industry is increasingly paying more attention to families as users, and understanding their experiences will allow game designers develop new insights into how to engage this group with video games. Second, the cases we share draw upon observations of intergenerational play around commercial, off-the-shelf games and games that were intentionally designed to elicit collaborative family interactions. Together, these observations inform design heuristics that will be useful for game designers when developing video games for families. We discuss these heuristics and what the game industry can do to support families in chapter 6.

2

Strengthening Family Relations

The ubiquity of the Internet, cell phones, and social media has raised questions regarding the impact of such media on family closeness. Too often, these media have been conceptualized as a threat to family cohesion and bonding. In fact, as we discussed earlier, research has focused primarily on how using technology takes away from the time families spend together. However, recent studies suggest that technology is well integrated into positive family routines. Many families consider technology to be a tool that facilitates staying connected and creates a sense of closeness and togetherness.[1] Parents use cell phones to check in on their children, send them reminders, and coordinate activities while on the go during the day. Grandparents utilize video conferencing tools such as Skype to talk to their grandchildren and share experiences with them as if they are in the same room. Families also use social media sites such as Facebook to share life events through pictures and written posts and keep in touch with extended family members who live far away.[2]

In this chapter, we discuss how video games promote family connection and communication, similar to other digital media technologies. Although video games are not intentionally designed to connect people, they provide a context for shared experiences that facilitate a sense of closeness and togetherness. Many parents in our study observed both their young and older children connecting with friends, cousins, and other family members through playing online games. Here is David talking about how his son keeps in touch with his friends through playing video games:

My fourteen-year-old really likes *Halo* a lot, but I can't say that he gets to keep it for very long at a time [*laughs*], so he'll have it for a couple of days and then he'll do something and won't be allowed to play it for a couple of days. And he likes the social part of it as much as anyone; he's got a headset so he can talk to his friends back in Chicago. All of his friends are back in Chicago, so they get to have party games where they talk to each other about their day and stuff like that where they're blowing stuff up. And I sit down and I've played each one of those things with them.

Compared to other communication tools such as cell phones and video conferencing, video games afford connection and closeness through a different mechanism. When families talk or FaceTime on the phone, family members voluntarily share information and experiences they have had outside of the call. For instance, a grandmother may have a conversation on the phone with her grandson who lives far away while cooking dinner for herself and her husband. If the call involves a video camera, the grandson watches his grandmother cook, and she may even involve him in the process of cooking by telling him what ingredients she is using. However, while the grandson can see what his grandmother is doing, he cannot participate in the act of cooking because he is not physically in the same room with his grandmother. Furthermore, when the grandmother asks about school, the grandson may or may not share information about what he experienced that day. Depending on what he chooses to share with his grandmother, the conversation between the two may or may not lead to a deeper sense of closeness.

Conversely, when playing video games in the same room or in the same virtual world when living at a distance, family members are jointly engaged in an experience, similar to playing a board game or going to a library or museum together. Conversations are impromptu, organized around doing something collectively, and responsive to the environment. Research suggests that doing things together promotes a sense of closeness. Families are often told that they need to spend time with each other and do things together, such as eating dinner, taking a vacation, and exercising, to build and maintain intimate and healthy family relations.

Although playing video games as a family shares the same mechanism through which other nondigital activities promote connection between family members, video games are often portrayed as widening the generation gap between adults (parents and grandparents) and children rather than bringing them closer together. People rarely perceive visiting a museum or playing board games as an activity that divides the old and the young in the family. Playing video games, however, is an activity that parents are encouraged to regulate and limit but not necessarily join. In fact, research studies and commentators erroneously lump video games in with other technologies and practices that parents need to monitor (texting, using social media, etc.).

Such an approach is predicated on the belief that all forms of digital media engagement are one and the same. However, a child texting with her friends to organize a get-together, browsing through her friends' posts and pictures on Facebook, and playing video games for thirty minutes are very different activities. In the case of texting, the child uses written communication to coordinate with other people to achieve the goal of getting together with her friends. Browsing pictures and posts by friends on Facebook does not require much mental effort from the child. In the case of video gaming, the child is actively thinking about how she is going to make progress and accomplish the goals of the game. She might have to persist if she tries a strategy and fails to perform the tasks. Needless to say, we believe that playing video games has a unique set of affordances that are more similar to face-to-face activities that families do together than they are to activities that involve digital communication technologies.

Parents tend to perceive playing video games as their children's activity. It is difficult to avoid viewing video games as primarily a children's domain. Almost all children, without their parents' prompting, become interested in playing video games. Children can stay focused for long periods of time while playing video games. They can fail multiple times but will persist to pass a level. Children do not need to be encouraged to play video games. They are intrinsically motivated and self-driven when it comes to video games. Children push themselves to develop new skills by experimenting with one game and moving on to another, constantly looking for something new and challenging.

From an *interest-driven learning* perspective, an approach that has gained momentum among educators in the last decade, children's interest in playing video games is a golden opportunity for learning. Interest creates motivation to learn, which plays an important role in academic success.[3] Interest is also the engine for persistence and perseverance in the face of challenge and failure during the learning process.[4] When children are interested in doing something, they also enjoy talking, reading, and learning more about the topic.

Things in the environment pique our interest all the time. For example, observing the birds nesting in the backyard of his house, a child becomes interested in learning more about birds. He starts observing the birds every day and searches online for information about hatching and nesting. But once the baby birds mature and fly away, his interest in birds disappears. This type of spontaneous engagement with a topic prompted by circumstances, known as "situational interest," can be an entry point to developing an expertise in a domain if it is sustained over time.[5,6] Our situational interests tend to dwindle once conditions change in the environment. However, in some cases, they stay with us. In our example, a different scenario would be that the child retains his interest in birds even after the birds leave the nest. His experience motivates him to watch experts talk on YouTube, go hiking so that he can bird-watch, and even pursue ornithology as a career in the future.

It is notoriously difficult for a situational interest to transform into an intrinsic motivation to learn about a topic.[7] From an interest-driven learning perspective, children's interests must be cultivated and fostered for children to engage in meaningful learning experiences that allow them to develop specialized skills and expertise. What is the role of parents in this framework? Their role is to "broker" resources, experiences, and opportunities for children to continue to pursue their own interests and goals. Brokering takes many forms. Let's go back to our earlier example of a child becoming interested in birds as a result of observing a bird's nest in his backyard. What could a parent do to support the child's situational interest so that the child's interest can spark learning? The parent can ask the child questions every day to help the child make sense of his observations. Later, the parent can buy a book about birds for the child to read. Noticing that her son is searching online for information about birds, the parent might decide to take the child to a natural history museum to get more information about birds. Later, long after the birds have flown away, the parent might encourage the child to use his experiences with the birds as an inspiration for an essay assignment or science project in school.

Out of many ways parents cultivate children's interests, participating in activities together with the child is perhaps one of the more direct ways to create family closeness. The parent bird-watching with the child and developing knowledge about the topic along with the child is different than providing tools and opportunities for the child. In the former case, the parent is an active participant or colearner, not just a provider. All forms of parental brokering are important. However, we argue that participation in activities together around a shared interest is quite powerful in supporting closeness and strengthening social relationships.

First, participation in activities around shared interest creates an opportunity for families to spend quality time together. Second, people enjoy sharing their interest and passion with others, including family members. It makes us feel less alone and more connected. Finally, while individualized learning arrangements enable children to pursue their interests, we know from research that deep and meaningful learning takes place when children engage in social interactions with others, including peers, parents, and other adults. In chapter 3, we will introduce a broad definition of learning as embedded in social interactions, histories, values, identities, and cultures, and detail what learning looks like when parents and children engage in intergenerational play around video games. In this chapter, we discuss the benefits of having and sharing an interest in video games and the kinds of connections family members make around them.

Games as a Context for Horizontal and Vertical Connections

Strong and productive social relationships not only support the socio-emotional well-being of adults and children but also are at the core of culture, identity, and learning. In recent years, propelled by interest-driven learning principles, the concept of *connected learning* has captured the networked and multigenerational aspect of children's lives in the information age.[8] Connected learning reflects the belief that today's technology can coalesce children's interests, peer culture, and academic success through experiences that stretch across different contexts of formal (e.g., school) and informal settings for learning (e.g., home, libraries, museums). We found in our research that video gaming sits at an interesting intersection in the context of family life. Playing video games is one of the many nondigital and digitally mediated activities children do around an interest that is personal to them. We refer to the connectedness of children's video gaming to other activities associated with a common interest as *horizontal connections*, to highlight the connections across different spaces and domains. For example, a child might play a video game about soccer, watch soccer matches on TV, and practice playing soccer in her backyard. At the same time, children's video gaming can be a linchpin in the family system that bonds multiple generations. We refer to the connectedness of children's video gaming to shared interests among family members as *vertical connections*, to highlight how games can bridge age and social differences. For example, that same child might play the soccer video game with her teenage brother, watch the soccer match with her mom, dad, and grandfather, and kick the soccer ball around with her sister and uncle.

As a further example, children's interest in playing video games can be used as a launchpad for developing knowledge and expertise in a domain. For example, a child's interest in playing *Zoo Tycoon*, a simulation game in which players assume the role of a zookeeper, can inspire naturally or be leveraged by adults to encourage the child to learn more about animals in real life. Perhaps the child starts reading a book on animals, or an adult takes the child to a real zoo, connecting gaming horizontally with other experiences. While this is how we traditionally conceptualize the role of video games within the framework of interest-driven and connected learning, the opposite is also true. Children's interest in a topic drives a constellation of activities including playing video games. This kind of horizontal connection between video games and other activities around a personal interest is important for parents to note. Children's video gaming can either be a precedent for developing an interest in a topic or a manifestation of children's interest in a topic. Attuning to children's video gaming better positions parents to support interest-driven and connected learning experiences and make their children feel like their interests are valued in the context of family life.

The second form of connection video gaming affords is vertical. Children not only develop close relationships with people within their own generation, such as peers, but also bond with people across generations—siblings, parents, grandparents, aunts, and uncles—through gaming. Having a shared interest is important in promoting a sense of affection, togetherness, and belonging among family members. It also creates a context for generational continuity when the older generation that grew up playing video games introduces children to video gaming. For example, a mother who played *Pac-Man* in the arcade in the 1980s can share her memories, achievements, and experiences with her son who enjoys playing action-adventure games. The parent can download *Pac-Man* on a cell phone or bring it up online for her son to explore and share his perspectives about the game that she used to enjoy playing. This is similar to the excitement parents feel about sharing music and movies with their children to help their children learn a bit more about them beyond their roles as parents. As such, video games provide opportunities for cultural exchanges in which parents and children develop new insights about each other. These experiences create positive memories that are cherished by family members throughout their lifetimes.

The next sections of this chapter share the experiences of five families that come from different socioeconomic, educational, and cultural backgrounds. They also vary with respect to the number and the kinds of gaming devices they own. What is common among these families is the important role video games play in bonding family members who live together and far apart. By sharing the experiences of these families, our goal is to demonstrate the diversity of the ways in which video games might support vertical and horizontal connections, and how families are actively using gaming to enhance family relationships and shared interests in their own particular situations.

The Livingstone Family: Creating a Family Culture of Gaming

We start with the Livingstones, who exemplify the development of what we call a family culture of gaming. In general, family culture consists of the values, beliefs, traditions, forms of interaction, and rules that characterize a particular family. For the Livingstones, and families like them, gaming becomes an important aspect of their overall family culture, or part of who they are as a family. Gaming is a regular and valued activity for the family as a whole, and a concrete reflection of their sense of belongingness with each other. Here we'll describe the Livingstone family and how their family culture of gaming developed.

The Livingstone family included parents Abigail (age thirty-five) and Victor (age thirty-eight), and their four children: Isabella (age thirteen), Emma (age five), and twins, Mia and Sophia (age three). Isabella was Abigail's daughter from a previous relationship. Abigail, an Asian American, held a master's degree and worked part-time in marketing and communications when we met her. Victor, a Caucasian, also held a master's degree and was working at a company in the information technology department. The family lived comfortably in a two-story, four-bedroom house in the suburbs and had an annual household income between $90,000 and $99,999. The family had an Xbox and a Nintendo Wii hooked up to the television in the family room where either the kids or the entire family played video games together. Victor had a desktop computer in his office where he played online multiplayer games such as *Borderlands* that he enjoyed but found inappropriate for his kids to play. He and Isabella each owned a Nintendo DS. Abigail had an iPad that she used to play games and lent to her kids for gaming as well. Both parents had smartphones and occasionally used them for gaming.

Her parents described Emma as the most interested in playing video games in the family. According to Abigail, Emma played video games two to four days each week for an hour or two at a time. She played games from a wide range of genres: *Scribblenauts*, *Minecraft*, *Happy Action Theater*, *Candy Crush*, and *Mario Kart*. Her gaming arrangements changed depending on the game, the device, the day of the week, and the time of the day. Abigail also enjoyed playing the game *Scribblenauts*, so whenever Emma played the game on her mother's iPad Abigail tried to join her. Emma could spend hours building things in *Minecraft* by herself. She usually played the game on the Xbox but occasionally she played the game on her mother's iPad in the car or at the doctor's office. Because of its simple player actions and user-friendly controls, *Happy Action Theater* allowed Emma's twin sisters and grandmother to play with her in the family room. *Candy Crush* is a single-player game, but family members took turns playing the game on the iPad while waiting for dinner or driving long distances for vacation. Although controlling the wheel could be challenging for the younger children, the entire family gathered in the family room to play *Mario Kart*.

Of the many games Emma and the family played alone and together, one game stood out the most with respect to its affordances for family connection and communication: *Halo*. The family had a long history with this game. Victor first started playing the game with his younger sister, Mary, while growing up. When the siblings became adults and moved to different states, they continued playing the game to stay in touch. Abigail joined them in playing the game when she married Victor. Later, when Mary married her husband John, he joined the game as well. Before Emma and Nick (Mary and John's son) were born, the two couples played *Halo* online together several times a week. They found this to be a great way to spend time together as a family since they lived far apart and did not have the opportunity to do activities that would require more proximity, such as going out to dinner. Emma and Nick were born around the same time. The parents included the children in their gameplay and shared their passion for playing video games.

When Emma and Nick were babies, they sat in their bouncy chairs in the living room while their parents played the game. Later, as toddlers, Emma and Nick played with their toys on the floor alongside their parents. Because their parents used voice chat while playing, Emma and Nick could hear each other and knew that the people they heard were their extended family. Around the time that Emma and Nick were three years old, they started to participate in actual gameplay. First, they sat on their parents' laps with their hands on top of their parents' hands using the controllers and mostly watching their parents play. Once the children mastered the use of the controllers, the parents gave them their own controllers. This allowed Emma and Nick to run around in the virtual world with their avatars while their parents completed missions in the game. Eventually, the children developed enough understanding of the game to play alongside their parents and complete missions. The two families alternately competed and collaborated in the game. The time the families spent together playing *Halo* was marked with laughter and playful interactions between parents and children (see figure 2.1). For instance, Emma's parents teased Emma by saying things like, "Emma, you just killed Aunt Mary!" Emma looked forward to playing the game with her

Figure 2.1
The Livingstone family playing *Halo* together

cousin, aunt, and uncle, and would ask her parents when they could play the game again.

Abigail perceived playing video games with her extended family as an important part of building close relationships and family bonds:

We really enjoy playing together . . . I feel like we have a friendship in addition to being a family. We don't Google Chat or Skype with them. We don't seek this way to connect out. We see them once a year when we visit my husband's family. And he might call them once in a while, but that is for a particular thing, whereas through video games it is more organic. Like, "What are you doing? Let's play together"–type of thing. We don't seek out interactions separate from that. I guess if [Mary and John] weren't there, [Victor and I] would still play with other people, but we have something in common with Mary and John that we really enjoy doing. I guess there are other technologies that would facilitate communication but we are not interacting like we do when we play together.

Overall, video gaming—and play more broadly—is a big part of who the Livingstones are and what they value as a family. Over the years, their gaming arrangements with their extended family changed as new games attracted the interest of different family members, children grew older, and the families felt more pressed for time. As a result, they played *Halo* together less frequently. However, the cousins continued the tradition of playing video games together and bonding over games with the game *Disney Infinity.* The parents used text messaging to schedule time on weekends for Emma and Nick to play online together. While these "play-dates" were initially set for Emma and Nick, their younger siblings joined the duo to play the game as well. Similar to *Halo*, the game *Disney Infinity* allows players to utilize voice chatting while playing, so all the cousins could hear each other and talk while playing.

The Contreras Family: Building on Shared Interests through Gaming

Creating a family culture of gaming is certainly not the only way that families can make video gaming a positive aspect of family life. For the Contreras family, video gaming provided an avenue for father and son to deepen their relationship through a shared interest. In this case, the shared interest was in *Star Wars*, a pop culture phenomenon that spans generations in its appeal. Gaming was also a way for the son to enhance his relationship with his brother, though in this case the common interest was gaming itself.

Our focal child in the Contreras family was four-year-old Gerardo, a middle child of Yesenia (age thirty-eight), a second-generation Mexican, and Tom (age thirty-nine), a Caucasian. He had three siblings: a twin brother, Gabriel; an older half-sister, Valeria (age seventeen), from Yesenia's first marriage; and a younger brother, Eduardo (age two). All family members were born in the United States, and spoke English as their primary language. When we met the Contreras family, Yesenia worked for sixteen hours each week as a therapist and Tom worked full time as an engineer. The family lived in a spacious two-story, four-bedroom house in a sprawling suburban development and had an annual household income of over $100,000. The family owned a Nintendo Wii connected to the television in the family room. In addition to this game console, Gerardo and Gabriel each had their own iPads that they used to play games. Gerardo also owned a Nintendo DS, which the family kept in the car for him to use while traveling. Valeria owned an iPod Touch that she used to connect with her friends and play games. Both parents owned smartphones they used occasionally to play games.

Despite his young age, Gerardo was described as the "gamer" of the family. According to Yesenia, Gerardo's game time had to be limited or he would play video games all day long. This was best captured by a photo Yesenia showed us of Gerardo falling asleep next to his iPad while playing games. One difference Yesenia noticed between the twins was that Gabriel would play games on his iPad for a while, get bored, occupy himself with other toys, and then pick up his iPad again later. Gerardo, however, would not stop playing until she reminded him to do so. Yesenia also noticed that while Gabriel responded to other people while playing, Gerardo would become so immersed in the game that he stopped responding to others.

Despite these challenges with Gerardo's gaming, Yesenia realized that Gerardo was developing a constructive mentoring relationship with Gabriel through gaming. For instance, Gerardo provided assistance when Gabriel became frustrated while playing games. He would also play a difficult part for Gabriel and make suggestions about what to do in the game. Gabriel often spent hours watching his twin brother play games on his own iPad. In fact, Gabriel spent more time watching Gerardo play than playing the games himself. Thus, even though the brothers had quite different gaming skills, they were still able to spend time with each other in a positive way.

As we got to know Gerardo over a period of six months, it became clear that one game he enjoyed playing the most was *Lego Star Wars*. At a first glance, given the content of *Lego Star Wars* (while less central and more benign than in *Halo*, the game does involve killing and fighting), one could argue that Gerardo should not have played this game until he was much older. However, Gerardo's engagement with *Lego Star Wars* is a good example of the potential intersections among horizontal and vertical connections. The game expanded his existing interest in building (a horizontal connection) while simultaneously bringing him and his father together (a vertical connection) around a shared interest in *Star Wars*. According to his mother, Gerardo's interest in building first manifested through playing with Lego bricks and the significant amount of time he spent daily building complex structures in his room. Later, Gerardo discovered the EvanTubeHD channel on YouTube, where he could watch the seven-year-old boy Evan reviewing *Star Wars* Lego sets. To our surprise, Gerardo, who did not know how to read, needed no adult assistance to search for videos on YouTube. As he demonstrated to us during one of our home visits, he pressed the search box on YouTube and the letter "L" on his iPad, and then selected one of many keywords suggested by the YouTube search engine. Using this simple strategy, Gerardo explored YouTube and watched Lego videos by himself for hours. When he found the *Lego Star Wars* game on the Apple App Store and asked his mother to download it, Yesenia was not surprised. Out of many games Gerardo played over the years, *Lego Star Wars*, according to Yesenia, by far held Gerardo's attention and interest the longest.

Tom, the father, played video games on an Atari and later on a Nintendo console when he was young. After graduating from college, he stopped playing video games for a while until he moved in with his sister and brother-in-law, both of whom played online games. He invested significant time in playing online games and even made extra money trading and selling items. However, he stopped playing games as intensively once Gerardo and Gabriel were born because he did not have enough time. Still, Tom played games almost every day on his phone or on the iPad after the kids went to bed. He commented that his gaming was limited to casual games in the last few years but he still enjoyed playing games with his children, in particular, the *Lego Star Wars* game with Gerardo.

Every Saturday morning, Tom and Gerardo connected with each other through playing *Lego Star Wars* on the Nintendo Wii. The family purchased the game for the Wii to support Gerardo's interest in Lego. Tom, a *Star Wars* fan, did not care so much for the gameplay, but enjoyed being able to share his love of *Star Wars* with his son (as opposed to sharing his love for gaming). Tom even attached a toy sword to each controller to make the game experience more immersive, making it feel like the two were using lightsabers and pretending to be Obi-Wan Kenobi and Luke Skywalker. The time Tom and Gerardo spent together playing *Lego Star Wars* on Saturday mornings was considered special by their family. This time was marked with laughter but also moments of teaching as Tom coached Gerardo on how to beat enemies and explained the story line as they played together.

The Gastelum Family: Gaming as a Context for Engagement

In our next family, the Gastelums, the father also used gaming as a means of enhancing his relationship with his children. In this case, however, gaming was not tied to a shared interest, like *Star Wars*, and gaming itself was not an interest that the father shared with his sons. Instead, he created a context and routine through which he could engage with his children around an interest of theirs, with the goal of building deeper family relationships.

The Gastelum family consisted of Diana (age thirty-three), Hector (age thirty-two), Emilio (age four), Diego (age five), and Luis (age thirteen), Diana's son from a previous marriage. All of the children were born in the United States. Diana and Hector were born in Mexico and moved to the United States when they were in their late teens. Hector spoke only Spanish, but Diana was fluent in both English and Spanish. The family primarily spoke Spanish at home; however, the siblings spoke English among themselves. Diana was a stay-at-home mom and Hector worked sixty hours per week as a tile installer, with an annual household income between $20,000 and $29,999. The family owned three television sets:

one located in the living room, one in the parents' room, and one in Luis's room. They also owned an Xbox that they kept in the garage because Luis had stopped using it. Luis owned a smartphone, which he used to connect with his friends and play games. The other smartphone in the family belonged to Hector, and he used it mostly for work-related tasks. Among the low-income families who participated in our study, the Gastelum family had the least number of devices at home and played video games less frequently than others.

Emilio's play partner was his brother Diego, with whom he spent most of his time during the day. The two enjoyed playing outside and doing craft projects. The boys would wake up after Hector and Luis left for the day. A typical day involved such activities as having breakfast, playing outside, eating snacks, playing indoors with various toys, eating lunch, taking a two-hour nap, and watching an episode of a television show while their mother performed household tasks. The brothers' playtime was almost completely unplugged during the day, but this changed in the evenings once Hector came home from work. Over the previous year, Hector had developed a routine of allowing the two younger children to play games on his phone while he watched and chatted with them. Given that the family placed considerable value on unplugged activities, we were surprised to find out that anyone in the family would spend time playing video games together.

This was not the first time that Hector used video games as a way to strengthen relationships with his children. Before Emilio and Diego were born, Hector used video games to build a relationship with his stepson, Luis. Hector bought Luis an Xbox at a yard sale, and while Luis no longer played Xbox games when we spoke with him, he told us stories about how he, Diana, and Luis played games together. While growing up in Mexico, Hector played arcade games such as *Pac-Man* and *Street Fighter* and owned a game console, but then stopped playing games around age thirteen, like Luis. Hector did not have a persistent interest in playing video games as an adult; however, he saw video games as something his children enjoyed playing, and wanted to join them in exploring their interests.

Hector usually arrived home from work around dinnertime. Two to four nights per week, Emilio, Diego, and Hector played video games on Hector's phone for one hour while Diana prepared dinner for the family. Diana valued the time that Hector and the boys spent together, but she did not encourage her children's interest in video gaming outside of the routine that they had with their father. Although she played video games while growing up and played games like *Super Mario Bros.* with Luis when he was younger, Diana perceived video games as a waste of time and was concerned about her young children's screen time.

At the time of our study, Hector and the boys frequently played the game *Subway Surfers*. Hector did not find the game particularly educational but thought that his children were improving their mental and manual dexterity as a result of playing the game. He enjoyed watching his children develop their skills and was amused by how competent they were at dodging the trains and collecting coins—something that was challenging for him but seemed like second nature to them. Hector described himself as the "backseat driver" when it came to gaming with his children; he enjoyed watching his sons play games and have a good time. As we probed him further about his involvement, however, it quickly became clear that this was not a spectator sport for Hector. He did more than just passively observing his sons play video games; he interacted with them to help the boys become more competent at playing the game (see figure 2.2).

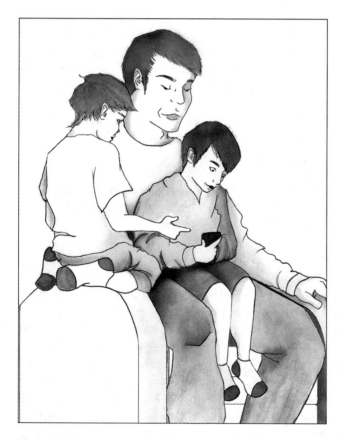

Figure 2.2
Hector Gastelum and his sons playing games

Hector often played difficult parts of the game for the boys, especially when he observed them becoming frustrated by their inability to pass an obstacle. He also strategized with the boys about how to score higher or perform better in the game. When we asked him if he played with or competed against his children, he said, "Neither. It is not like that. It is more like working together." Hector commented that he learned a lot about how his sons thought by watching them play the game. Unlike Abigail and Victor, who created a culture of family gaming, and Tom, who saw a particular game as a way to share his interest in a topic with his son, Hector provided the tool (his phone), created a context (allowing his children to use his phone after work and before dinner), and participated in his children's gaming as a way to support their interest while strengthening his relationship with them.

The Morgan Family: The Joint Evolution of Gaming, Interests, and Relationships

It's clear from our previous examples that the role of video gaming in family life changes over time, as do individual and shared interests and relationships among family members. For example, in the Livingstone family, gameplay with extended family changed as the children grew older and could play independently with each other. In the Gastelum family, although Luis no longer played games with his parents, video gaming together remained a fond, shared memory that reinforced their sense of closeness. In addition, we also saw how interests and family relationships can develop together through gaming, as Tom and Gerardo Contreras deepened both their relationship and their interest in *Star Wars* as they played *Lego Star Wars* together. Now we turn to another family, the Morgans, to look more closely at how family video gaming practices change over time, along with, for example, children's changing skills and interests and changes in relationships among family members. In fact, video gaming can create opportunities for parents and children to experiment with different roles and broaden as well as deepen their relationships.

The Morgan family consisted of Carol (age forty-two), Lily (age nine), and Alex (age sixteen). Carol, a Caucasian single mother, worked in higher education and had a household income between $80,000 and $89,999. The family owned several devices: two iPads, an iPod Touch, two laptops, a desktop computer, and a Nintendo Wii. However, computers were the primary devices for gaming because the family enjoyed playing massively multiplayer online role-playing games (MMORPGs).

Carol's parents were early adopters of technology. While growing up, Carol had an IBM PCjr, the first home computer that IBM developed in the mid-1980s, and a game console. She had always been interested in computers and started experimenting with programming at an early age. While she remembers playing *Super Mario Bros.* and buying *Nintendo Power* magazine, Carol described herself as having an affinity for computer games—in particular, online role-playing games (RPGs). Her earlier experiences included playing text-based online RPGs similar to *Dungeons and Dragons* on the computer. In the late 1990s and early 2000s, she moved on to playing the 3-D MMORPG *EverQuest*. In the mid-2000s, she began playing *World of Warcraft* (*WoW*), which she continues to play to this day.

Although Carol was always interested in computers and gaming, she did not discover these games herself; rather, a relative, friend, or colleague would introduce these games and invite her to play with them. Carol preferred playing with people she already knew rather than random people she met online in the game. She enjoyed extended conversations and discussions about different strategies with the people she knew within and beyond the game.

Lily, Carol's daughter, played *Minecraft, Roblox*, and *Animal Jam* on the computer at the time of our study. Lily also wanted to play *WoW* and asked for Carol's help to get started. Carol thought her daughter was too young for the game and did not consider *WoW* to be a kid-friendly game compared to the more age-appropriate multiplayer online games Lily played. At the same time, she was happy to slowly introduce the game to Lily, show her the more welcoming areas in the virtual world, and play alongside her. When she was younger, Lily watched her mother and her older brother Alex play the game together and wanted to be included in the experience. Lily adored Alex and looked up to him. In the past, Alex often coached and played video games with Lily, but when he became a teenager and a very advanced player, it was more difficult for him to find games that were enjoyable and challenging for both of them. *Minecraft* was the only game the siblings were able to play together. In a way, Lily's desire and effort to learn how to play *WoW* was an attempt to connect with her brother.

Like Carol, Lily felt that playing video games online was all about interacting and connecting with people that she knew personally. Her online gaming partners had always been her mother and her brother, although in the past two years her partner had been mostly her cousin, Jake (age nine), who lived in another state. Lily enjoyed the social interactions around online games but felt safer when she played with a family member. She and her cousin communicated through FaceTime on their iPod Touches while playing *Minecraft* and *Roblox* together. Unlike the Livingstone family, where playdates between Emma and Nick were coordinated by parents, Lily and Jake arranged their own playdates without any adult involvement. Jake did not own an iPod Touch but borrowed his father's to communicate with Lily. Lily was uncomfortable calling due to the risk that someone else would pick up the phone, so usually Jake would reach out to her. When they met for play, Jake and Lily often scheduled a time for their next meeting and discussed the tasks they would complete in the game in the meantime.

Alex played a level 100 character in *WoW* and more recently had begun to play the science fiction–themed MMORPG *Eve*. Alex started playing *WoW* by watching his mother play when he was six years old. By the time he was ten, he played the game with his mother and his father (who were together at the time). In the beginning, Carol took the lead, showing Alex around and coaching him in gameplay, similar to what she was doing in the present with Lily. Gradually the dynamics of their intergenerational play experiences around *WoW* changed as Alex improved his skills, eventually surpassing his mother's level in the game. Alex then took on a leadership role when he played the game with his mother, giving her guidance on what to do and showing her new places in the virtual world. Carol described the change and what it meant for her in this way:

Alex has Asperger's Syndrome and so he is very, very smart, but sometimes it is difficult to connect with him because he is just in his own little world at times. [Playing *WoW*] was a way to connect, and something to talk about, have a common ground, and something we could enjoy together. Computers and games have always been a big part of his world, and still are. What was neat is that I was showing him around, like, "Here's how you do things." It wasn't too long before he exceeded my level, and then he and I were running through instances together. He became the teacher. That was a really neat time because it was one of the only areas where I wasn't the one doing everything for him, and teaching him. As being the mother, you are the teacher, you are the guide. It was neat because it was this online environment where he really excelled and he knew . . . I remember very clearly going through this instance and he would say, "OK, stay on this side because these guys are going to come through and you have to watch out." He was very much guiding me about what I should do to survive, and it was a complete role reversal. In that online environment, he was almost the parent—maybe not the parent, but definitely the leader—and I was the follower. I remember noting that because it was interesting, and it was a good feeling because in his everyday life, those moments did not come around too frequently. I was kind of leading him, and it was neat to see him take the leadership role.

Eventually, other obligations began to interfere with Carol's gaming, and at the time we spoke, Carol played *WoW* sporadically with her children. Alex, however, persisted in playing *WoW*, and pursued new and more challenging games, such as *Eve*. More recently, Alex's father bought him a more powerful computer that supports gaming. Unlike Carol and Lily, who preferred to play with people they knew, Alex enjoyed playing with people whom he met online. By playing with and against other players, he was able to develop his skills and find new challenges within a game that he had been playing for six years. It took a long time for Alex to warm up to others in real life, and making friends at times could be challenging. In the game, however, Alex met new people and started playing with them all the time. He was also connected with people in the game whom he considered his friends. These friendships formed over many years of joint gameplay. Alex knew these people by their usernames, not necessarily by their real names, but because of their long history of playing together, they enjoyed a considerable degree of familiarity. They learned each other's style of communication and play and shared things about themselves while spending time together playing the game.

The Perez Family: Connections and Disconnections around Gaming

In the previous cases, we focused on the ways that gaming can enhance family relationships and be a focal point for the development and expression of shared interests. One reason we have stressed the potentially positive role of gaming is to provide a counterbalance to the often negative portrayal of gaming in popular media as something that interferes with connections among family members. In this last example, we look at the Perez family and examine how gaming might have both positive and negative effects on family relationships. In this case, the interest and connections that developed around gaming for some family members led to feelings of exclusion on the part of another family member.

The Perez family included parents Felipe (age thirty-one), an accountant; Zoe (age thirty-six), a stay-at-home mom; and their three children: Amelia (age seven), Matias (age nine), and Daniel (age eleven). Zoe's oldest son Ben (age nineteen), from a previous relationship, had recently moved out of the house and lived nearby with his girlfriend. The family had a household income between $60,000 and $69,999. All family members were born in the United States and spoke primarily English. The family owned three TVs, one of which was located in Amelia's room. The

Nintendo Wii and Xbox 360, as well as one of the three desktop computers, were located in the living room. The family also owned a PlayStation Portable (PSP) and a Nintendo DS, which Amelia won at a church event, but these devices were not being used at the time of our study. The Nintendo Wii was initially purchased as a Christmas present for Amelia but was used mainly by her mother for playing *Just Dance* and watching movies on Netflix. The Xbox belonged to the entire family, but it was often used by Amelia's brothers to play video games.

Felipe, like Victor Livingstone, started playing video games while growing up and continued to do so as an adult. Felipe mostly played games with his son Daniel because, compared to the younger Amelia and Matias, he was more capable of keeping up with the complex games Felipe preferred. At the time of our visit, the father-son duo was playing *League of Legends* and *World of Warcraft*. Since he worked full time, Felipe had limited time to play with Amelia and Matias, but he regularly engaged in conversations with them about the games they played and the progress they made. Daniel also had a busy schedule with soccer practice and academic responsibilities. When he had a chance to play video games, he played with either his father or his younger brother, Matias. As the middle child, Matias not only interacted with his older brother around games but also played an important role in Amelia's everyday experiences as her playmate. Matias played with Amelia, coached her on how to play, and read instructions and text in the games for her.

Over the years, playing video games became a shared interest among the members of the Perez household—except for Zoe. Felipe initiated the purchase of computers and gaming devices when he and Zoe began their relationship because of his own interest in gaming and his desire to connect with Ben. Once Daniel and Matias came along, gaming had already become a regular activity in the household and a means for the males in the family to bond. Initially, Amelia did not seem to be interested in playing video games because she did not like the content of the games that they played, such as *WoW*. At the same time, like Lily Morgan, she really wanted to be part of the gaming experience that her father and brothers shared, and felt left out. As she grew older, she developed better skills and more games became available for her to play by herself and with her father and brothers. Video games like *Roblox* and *Minecraft* provided opportunities for Amelia to connect with her brothers while games like *Spore* allowed her to pursue her interest in animals. When we spoke with Amelia, she mentioned that she really enjoyed being able to play more games with her brothers now that she was older. She was also aware of how her time spent playing video games affected her mother. Although she preferred other games, Amelia played *Just Dance* with her mother because it was the only game her mother knew how to play, and her mother was happy when Amelia spent time with her.

The first thing Zoe told us when we met was that she "lost" her sons to video games and she did not want that to happen with Amelia. She was concerned about the number of devices the family owned, and the number of hours her family spent playing video games. She was against the purchase of the devices and had reinforced the rule of not playing games on the family computer until her boys started sneaking out of their rooms to play games on the computer at night. Zoe experienced some criticism from her extended family members and friends who suggested that she was being "a bit too strict" about video games. She felt like she was constantly in a battle with her husband and kids, and finally gave up her resistance to their desire to play video games.

Zoe's stance toward video gaming was not always this restrictive. When she was younger, Zoe played games like *Mortal Kombat* and *Tomb Raider* on a game console with her then-boyfriend and with her oldest son Ben on weekends. Ben stayed with his grandmother during the week because Zoe worked long hours. Things started changing once Zoe was able to take care of Ben full time:

And I moved up here and got settled. When Ben moved in with me, I didn't know how to be a mom. I didn't know what a mom was, so I read every book. I did everything the book said I had to do. So I stopped doing everything. It was just . . . I had to be this mom and that was it. Which was not right, but that's all I knew, so, um, that's why—I always joked with people, "There's the mommy and then there's the real me." When my son was around, I was a completely different person. So, I mean, we had computers and he had his own computer. But I didn't really do any of that stuff. It was all about . . . I paid all my attention to him.

Zoe stopped playing video games herself and limited Ben's gaming to conform to the messages she received about how to be a "good mom" from the books she read about parenting. Ben was born when Zoe was sixteen years old. She finished high school and college as a single parent, and faced challenges to be able to provide for her son. It was important to her that she did the right things to ensure that her son had a good life. The books she read were resources for her to become the best mother that she could be for her children. Zoe expressed anxiety over how her children would grow up, and about failing as a parent by not protecting them. It is through this lens that she viewed video games, leading to her absolutist stance of not allowing any games in the house. That is, until she met Felipe, who eventually challenged her rules around video games.

Although Zoe acknowledged that she might need to be a bit more flexible where video gaming was concerned, she still had misgivings about playing video games as a family activity. She did not share her family members' interest in gaming, and felt isolated when everyone gathered around a game in the living room or talked about games. She wanted her family to spend time together on unplugged activities that she could join. Felipe enjoyed playing video games a great deal, yet he also supported his wife in pursuing unplugged activities for the family to find a balance in meeting the values, needs, and desires of different family members. Talking through their different perspectives on gaming, and adapting at least somewhat to each other's views, became a way that Zoe and Felipe grew as parents and strengthened their own relationship.

The Prevalence and Versatility of Video Gaming in Family Life

We began this chapter with an argument that video games provide unique and pervasive opportunities for social interactions and connections among family members. Video games offer families the potential for enjoyable shared experiences that can allow them to explore common interests and deepen their relationships with one another. We stressed the value of shared experience as a context for rich conversations and for mutual understanding. Expanding on the notion of connected and interest-driven learning, we suggested how video games can be connected to other activities associated with children's interests—what we call horizontal connections. We used the term vertical connections to characterize the ways that video games can foster connections among family members across generations.

The preceding profiles illustrate some of the many different ways that families can make these connections. There is not one "correct" or "best" way for families to incorporate video gaming into family life. Video games, even in a household like the Gastelums's where children's time with media is closely monitored, are prevalent in the everyday lives of most families. While the amount of time children spend on gaming and the kinds of games they play vary between different families, children do play video games regularly. They play video games on a variety of devices, including game consoles, computers, and handheld devices. Parents have their own histories, experiences, and preferences around video games. Some of the parents described in this chapter had their own practices around video games and invited their children to participate in these practices. In some cases, such as that of the Morgan family, both mother and father played games together at some point and involved their children in gaming as an activity for the whole family. In the case of the Livingstones, the family activity of gaming encompassed extended family as well. In other families, such as the Contreras family, one parent was the primary play partner, and gaming was a way to pursue a shared interest or simply provided a context for having a good time together. Some families, like the Gastelums, included stepchildren, and gaming was one way that the stepparent developed a positive relationship with their stepchild.

The gaming experiences of the families we shared in this chapter defy gender, racial, and cultural stereotypes that surround video games. MMORPGs are often associated with male players, while casual gameplay is associated with female players. Carol Morgan routinely played MMORPGs while Tom Contreras switched to playing casual games on his phone as an adult when he was pressed for time. People also tend to think that only men enjoy playing first-person shooter games. However, as we have shown with the Livingstone family, Abigail and her sister-in-law both enjoyed playing *Halo.* There is also research suggesting that different racial and socioeconomic groups have different preferences with respect to the genre of games that they enjoy playing. First-person shooter console games are often played in low-income and Latino families, while computer-based MMORPGs are played more often in high-income and Caucasian families.[9] These reported tendencies often obscure the considerable diversity within racial and economic groups. We found that families played all kinds of video games and used different devices. Victor Livingstone, Carol Morgan, and Felipe Perez had different income levels, education, occupation, and cultural heritage, and yet all played MMORPGs. The Livingstone family had a high income level and played first-person shooter games. Tom Contreras and Hector Gastelum came from different backgrounds, but their cell phones were their primary gaming devices. Intergenerational play around video games also occurred in families irrespective of their racial, cultural, and socioeconomic backgrounds.

The kinds of games that families played together were also diverse and did not always conform to mainstream assumptions about "family-friendly" games. Parents who played video games with their children took not just their children's age but also the gameplay situation into consideration when deciding whether they wanted to introduce a video game to their children. In the context of joint gameplay, some games that might seem too difficult or have mature content were deemed appropriate by parents. Four-year-old Gerardo Contreras was able to play *Lego Star*

Wars with the help of his father, who shared his son's interest in the *Star Wars* universe. Victor Livingstone played video games that were inappropriate for his daughter, Emma, with people he met online, but Emma played alongside him and her mother when they played *Halo* together as a family to connect with her cousin, aunt, and uncle. In chapter 1, we quoted Abigail, Emma's mother, who stated that she would never let her children play online games with strangers, but viewed *Halo* as being similar to playing with Nerf guns together as a family.

When parents already enjoyed gaming and actively pursued their own gaming practices, it seemed natural that they would engage with their children around games. Although it may seem difficult to find video games that both adults and children can enjoy together, our families were able to adapt gameplay in ways that involved family members of varied ages and skills. In addition, we saw in the case of Hector Gastelum that parents can join their children's gameplay even if they themselves do not have strong connections to games as adults. Hector enjoyed talking with his children as he watched them play, using this time together as an opportunity to learn more about his boys' interests and ways of thinking, and to support their problem-solving skills. In general, intergenerational play around video games can involve varied forms of talk and interactions that represent a very different kind of joint media engagement than parent-child coviewing around television. In chapter 3, we look more closely at how parents, even those who have limited familiarity with video games, can engage in conversations around games with their children to promote learning and connection.

It is important to keep in mind how family gaming activities change over time, as do all family routines and practices. Our families illustrate changes in who is actively playing, how often they play, and the role of gaming in each family's daily life. Many of our families had young children, and—not surprisingly—parents or older siblings were often involved in introducing them to games, helping them play, and playing together. As children grew older, they tended to form their own gaming routines with family members closer in age and skill level, such as siblings or cousins, independent from their parents. This is typical of many shared play activities in families. Both shared and individual gaming experiences change over time as people grow older, new games pique the interest of parents and children, and life events happen. For some families, time spent playing video games together becomes a fond memory that contributes to sense of shared identity and history. For others, gaming practices evolve as children and parents take on new roles. The relationship between Felipe and

Daniel Perez around *World of Warcraft* gradually transformed into one of colearners or equally contributing partners. At the same time, within the overall family ecology, Daniel Perez took on the role of a teacher in relation to his younger siblings, Matias and Amelia. By comparison, Carol Morgan's relationship with her son Alex shifted as Alex took on the role of a teacher over time, allowing her to see Alex's capabilities in a different light. In chapter 5, we further explore how video games can be a rich context for cultivating what we call a *family learning culture* that benefits all family members.

Last, we wish to stress the many different ways that children's interest in video gaming can be connected to other aspects of family life. As we noted previously, video gaming is sometimes a distinctive and persistent interest for children as well as adults. Video gaming can also be an impetus for pursuing a different sort of interest, or a reflection of that interest, making what we called horizontal connections. For instance, Lily and Amelia were both interested in animals, so they played *Animal Jam* and *Spore*. Alex was interested in science fiction, so he started playing *Eve*. Gerardo played with Lego bricks and the game *Lego Star Wars* as part of his interest in building. If parent and child both share a persistent interest in video gaming, they can play games together, talk about these games, and deepen their relationships through such activities as well, making vertical connections. However, families can also use gaming to connect with each other even if they don't all share the same kind of interest in playing video games. For Tom Contreras, the shared interest with his son Gerardo was not so much playing video games but a topic: *Star Wars*. Tom would have been bored simply playing *Lego Star Wars*, but because he loved *Star Wars* and wanted to spend time with his son, he found the experience enjoyable. In such cases, something else is the shared interest that is expressed through gaming, and the shared interest combined with the gaming experience is what builds relationships.

Finally, video gaming can simply be one of many activities that allow families to interact with each other. The motivation—or interest, in this case—can be primarily spending time with each other. Amelia and her mom liked to play *Just Dance* together for fun. Amelia wanted to play other video games to connect with her brothers. Hector Gastelum, as another example, was primarily interested in connecting with his children. By providing the opportunity for them to play video games on his cell phone and watching them play, he was able to create an enjoyable shared experience for all of them. Abigail and Victor Livingstone enjoyed playing *Halo*, but they played with their extended family primarily to stay in touch and also ensure that their children were able to get to know their relatives.

Redefining "Disconnect"

Some researchers have speculated that because the first-generation play-ers who grew up playing video games now have their own families, there are more parents playing video games with their children. We met very few parents who did not play video games when they were younger. Thus, in our research, parents who engaged in intergenerational video game play with their children tended to have played video games in their youth. However, not all parents who played video games growing up continued playing video games as adults, had a positive view of games, or played video games with their children. Diana Gastelum and Zoe Perez are exam-ples of parents who played video games as children but stopped playing as adults, and had concerns about the content of the games their children played and the time they spent playing. There are many reasons why par-ents stop playing video games themselves or did not play with their chil-dren. Like Diana and Zoe, many parents we spoke to found the content of most video games unappealing. They were also pressed for time, as other obligations took over their schedules, making it difficult to carve out time and space for playing video games. Mothers in particular associated estab-lishing rules and monitoring the content and the time their children spent playing games with good parenting. For these parents, intergenerational play around video games was not necessarily associated with good parent-ing because they believed that video gaming would expose their children to harmful content or encourage excessive screen time. These beliefs are reinforced by media portrayals of the so-called dangers of excessive gam-ing and by publications aimed at parents—particularly mothers—that equate children's potentially excessive screen time with negligent or unin-formed parenting.

In a number of the families we studied, parents held differing views about how much gaming or what kinds of games were appropriate for their children. Tensions between spouses as well as parents and children around the use of digital media, in particular around video games, are well documented in the literature. Conflicts between family members arise when family members have values, beliefs, and approaches that are oppo-sitional and meet the needs of one member while undermining the other. Video gaming has been cited many times as a source of conflict in the context of family life. A typical scenario looks something like this: One parent tries to limit the number of hours her children play video games, while the other parent, who perhaps plays video games himself, encour-ages the children to continue to play and explore. It is usually mothers who are worried and frustrated about their spouses' and children's gaming and want things to change around the house: perhaps more rules, less time playing, and more time for unplugged activities. Fathers more often accept their children's gameplay and dismiss their spouses' concerns over issues like safety, screen time, and content.

We believe the typical lens through which conflicts between family members around video games are interpreted in the literature and in popular media is problematic for several reasons. First, the description of conflicts around video games perpetuates stereotypical perceptions of women and men in our society. In the cultural subtext of the above scenario, mothers are protective, conservative, old-fashioned, and unimaginative. Fathers, on the other hand, are fun, playful, open, and youthful. These qualities are associated with two different domains, namely video games and parenting, that are stereotypically deemed masculine and feminine. The implicit message is that mothers are unfamiliar with video games yet are knowledgeable, concerned parents who reinforce the recommendations of experts who suggest restricting screen time, monitoring content, and unplugging. Fathers, on the other hand, while they are knowledgeable about video gaming, do not necessarily know how to parent since they are not doing what experts suggest parents should do with their children around video games. This conception positions video games and parenting as mutually exclusive domains, and both parents somehow become deficient.

The second problem is the conceptualization of video games and family life around the cited conflicts. Many commentators use instances of the above scenario to make arguments for how video games, and technology more broadly, invade family life, break families apart, and create a disconnect between family members. As we discussed in the first chapter, characterizations of technology as something that "happens to" people positions them as passive consumers of technology; however, people are active agents in deciding how they want to engage with technology. In the experiences of the families we shared in this chapter, family members used video games to spend time together and connect with one another. Adults and children played a wide range of video games alone and together with different members of their family. The configuration of who played what with whom and how changed over time as families confronted life events, their interests shifted, and they experienced developmental changes. Overall, video gaming in the context of family life is far more dynamic and multidimensional than how it is usually portrayed in popular media.

Research suggests that conflict between family members is common. In fact, conflict is neither unique to family life nor to the topic of video gaming. It is a natural part of social interactions and human communication. The interest-driven lens we introduced in this chapter offers a different interpretation of conflict around video gaming in the context of family life. Diana Gastelum and Zoe Perez neither shared their children's interest in playing video games nor did they use video games as a tool to advance a shared interest on a topic with their children. In the case of Zoe Perez, this led to feelings of isolation and disconnectedness from the rest of her family, who played video games together. Diana did not feel isolated or disconnected like Zoe because the time her sons spent playing games on their father's phone was limited to an hour before dinner, and Diana organized the rest of the day around unplugged activities. Furthermore, Hector and Felipe had different relationships with video gaming. Hector did not play video games outside of the time he spent with his children, while Felipe played games alone and with his older son, Daniel. Zoe was happy when she was able to connect with her daughter over *Just Dance*. There was no other game that all family members enjoyed playing. Others in Zoe's family shared an interest around multiple games, experimented with games, talked about video games, and helped each other with games. The disconnect in the family stemmed not so much from inherent attributes of video games but from a lack of shared interest among family members around video games. A similar conflict and disconnect could have occurred if all family members except Zoe were interested in football and spent time watching football, playing football, and talking about football.

Conclusion

Where does this leave us? Obviously, parents do not have to play video games with their children if they do not enjoy doing so. But to make informed choices, they need to know about opportunities that exist around video games for connecting with their children and learning new things together with them. This book is about those opportunities. Parents are encouraged to read books with their children. They are also encouraged to play with their young children. However, despite the growing body of research that debunks long-held misconceptions around video games, messages about children's media use that target parents are still skewed toward urging parents to take the role of a gatekeeper to protect their children from the negative effects of video games. Even if positive aspects of playing video games with their children are mentioned, they typically are not presented as strongly as the negative, and often get lost in the mix of providing a balanced view of the role video games play in family life. As we show in the next chapters, parents do not need to be expert gamers to be able to take advantage of the opportunities that are afforded by video games. Like Hector, many parents can start with the simple act of watching their children play video games with the intention of understanding what their children do, how they think, and what strategies they use when they play video games.

3

Family Learning and Video Games

School is often the first thing that comes to mind when we think of learning. We associate learning with classrooms, teachers, textbooks, and tests. We often forget that the family is the first educational context, the first setting in which we all learn. When we do remember the importance of learning in the context of families, we tend to focus our attention on early childhood and what parents can do to support young children's learning to better prepare them for school. However, the family environment is an important social context where learning takes place for adults and children of all ages, and perhaps the only context in which participation occurs over a life-span. In this social context, playing games has always been one of many activities family members do individually and together that engages them in learning.

How video games might support learning, for children as well as families, is a theme that runs throughout this book. Making connections with other family members through gaming, as we describe in chapter 2, often involves learning about and sharing each other's interests and passions. Playing games as a means of developing a shared family identity, as we will discuss in chapter 4, involves learning about each other's values, experiences, and perceptions of each other, and constructing a shared understanding of family traditions and heritage. In this chapter, we look more closely at how video games create rich and meaningful learning experiences for families and children in their own right. We draw on examples from our focus groups and family gameplay sessions to illustrate how gameplay can promote literacy development, particularly reading skills, and how parents can leverage gameplay to introduce literacy practices beyond the game. We also introduce the concept of "learning conversations" around games and explore how families can use such conversations to enhance problem-solving skills, promote collaboration, and cultivate patience and persistence among all family members.

As we stressed at the beginning of the book, learning happens through and around all kinds of games, not just overtly educational games. In this chapter, we discuss how games of all sorts can provide opportunities for learning, and how families can take more advantage of these potential learning experiences. One problem with many educational games is that they are based on a narrow conception of learning as the acquisition of information or isolated skills. Therefore, we begin by briefly describing how we understand learning as a foundation for the rest of the chapter's discussion.

A Broad Perspective on Learning

We often think of learning as something that happens in the head; that is, as a *cognitive process* divorced from the world. It is hard to imagine learning in different ways when schools are engineered with this view of learning in mind. Children often fill out worksheets, solve abstract math problems, write essays as a response to some random topic, and take multiple-choice tests—things that we never do in our personal or work lives. Children are perceived as unintelligent if they are not succeeding in school. As adults, we are often uncomfortable or even apologetic about doing poorly in school as a child.

Generally, we acknowledge that perhaps the way we learn in school is different than the way we learn outside of school. People came up with terms like "book smart" and "street smart" to identify the multiple ways we learn and the different origins of our knowledge. What does it mean to be book smart versus street smart? A book-smart person is someone who does well in school and has acquired knowledge from books and academic work. A street-smart person is someone who knows his or her way around in the world and has acquired knowledge from real-world experience. The former emphasizes learning as an individualistic and cognitive process independent from our surroundings while the later encapsulates the social nature and messiness of learning in everyday life. Often we treat these two kinds of "smartness" as mutually exclusive; there's the book-smart person who is inept in daily life, and the street-smart person who can't read a book. Unfortunately, society tends to place more value on being book smart; we associate book smartness with being "really" intelligent and perceive street smartness as inferior. However, this dichotomous view of intelligence, with its emphasis on a cognitive view of learning, is quite narrow and does not reflect how learning scientists now characterize the complex nature of learning of all sorts and across situations.

From this broader perspective, learning is fundamentally a *sociocultural process*, shaped by cultural traditions, language, and the social groups we belong to or aspire to join. We learn through social interactions with others around shared activities using tools that are specific to our culture and history. For instance, in Western culture a child learns the word "fork" not because a parent repeats the word multiple times before the child goes to bed or shows the fork and calls it "fork" but because the word "fork" comes up in the context of the activity of eating, where the fork is being used in culturally appropriate ways with other people. In Asian cultures, the child may not learn "fork" but will learn the meaning of "chopsticks" in the process of learning how and when to use them.

According to Lev Vygotsky, children internalize the meanings constructed through these interactions, and come to learn about the world and themselves.[1] Barbara Rogoff studied children's cognitive development in the context of families across different cultures and described children as "apprentices in thinking."[2] Children develop skills to solve problems through participating in culturally valued activities (e.g., cooking, reading, calculating) under the guidance of more experienced members of society (e.g., adults). Rogoff calls this process "guided participation."[3] By participating in culturally organized activities with more knowledgeable adults such as parents, children gradually move from being an apprentice to an expert as they adopt culturally valued ways of doing and thinking.

As an extension of this social and cultural process, learning also involves *doing*. John Dewey suggests that learning takes place when we do something (take an action) in the world, receive feedback (responses from others and things to our action) from the world, and do something with that feedback.[4] Frequently, learning through doing involves learning how to use "rules of thumb," tools, and other aspects of our environment to successfully perform tasks, even those that we tend to consider purely cognitive. For example, in her study of mathematics in the everyday lives of adults, Jean Lave found that people learned to solve complex arithmetic problems while in practical situations such as grocery shopping or dieting through a combination of strategies such as estimating the size of packages, dividing portions, and comparing products, while judging the adequacy of solutions in relation to the broader context of their past and future actions and goals (for example, how many people they had to feed or how many calories they had already consumed that day).[5] Notably, participants in her research often did not think that they were "doing math" because it was so embedded in their daily activities and routines. Learning through video gaming also involves learning through doing, including how to take appropriate action in particular settings and in relation to specific goals and mastering the use of tools and resources. Similarly, learning is so embedded in gameplay that players often don't realize how or what they are learning.

Finally, from a sociocultural perspective, learning is inherently intertwined with identity formation—a sense of who we are as well as who we are becoming as a person in the world. Learning is often motivated by a desire to become a particular kind of person, affiliated with a particular social group. For example, a child might want to learn how to ride a skateboard to be like her peers, or a homeowner might start to research arid gardening methods to be part of a broader environmental preservation movement. In turn, learning allows us to enact desired identities and relationships: the child who masters a complicated skateboard move can gain acceptance at the skate park, or the homeowner might become a neighborhood expert on arid gardening.

Let's illustrate the sociocultural view of learning with three examples. As a first example, consider a small child attempting to name the colors of her crayons. The child naming the colors of her crayons is building her knowledge of language and of the salient features of crayons (color). She is learning to "do" or engage in the activity of naming or labeling, an important practice in many other settings, such as school. She is learning to "be" a particular kind of person as well; someone who values such labels and perhaps enjoys learning new words. Why she is engaged in this activity and what she learns is also related to her social relationships. For example, it's likely that an adult or sibling introduced her to the color names, and encouraged her to repeat and remember the names. Someone gave her the crayons, assuming that coloring is an appropriate and desirable activity for a child. Thus, she is learning something about what is valued in her family and what she is expected to be interested in as a child and member of that family.

As a second example, consider the three-year-old whose mother is reading the *Pokémon* game text to him. He is learning about writing and its correspondence to spoken language. He is also learning about the relationship of reading to an activity he enjoys, and that reading is necessary, or at least helpful, to playing the game. He also is learning that "people like me"—that is, his mother—are readers. From a sociocultural perspective, his mother's engagement with his gaming may reinforce his enjoyment, his sense of belonging, and his feeling that playing games is appropriate and valued for him as a child. He might also come to dislike waiting to play until his mother is available, and thus be motivated to learn to read so he can play on his own.

This sociocultural perspective on learning can be applied to learning across our lives, not just in early childhood. As another example, consider the adult executive who bought a new smartphone, and is learning to use all of its features. He bought the phone primarily because his colleagues at work have been recommending it, and he wants to sustain his identity as a savvy tech user and as a member of his peer group. He experiments with some new features on his own, and looks up some tips on an online support forum. A colleague recommends some productivity apps that will reinforce his identity as an efficient and well-organized manager. His son downloads a couple of new games that he wants to play, and together they figure out game strategies. Thus, our executive learns to use the phone as a tool that supports his identity as a supportive and "with-it" dad, as well as his identity as a competent and up-to-date company leader.

Video Games and Learning

Over the last several years, parents have become more aware of the educational potential of video games. In 2014, the Entertainment Software Association reported that 68 percent of parents with children under the age of eighteen at home believe gameplay provides mental stimulation or education.[6] However, this broad finding does not indicate what specific kinds of learning or stimulation parents have in mind or what games they are using as reference points. Some video games still have a bad image in the public eye, preventing parents who are unfamiliar with games from seeing what youth might learn from them. Games that typically get the most media attention and advertising, such as the *Call of Duty*, *Fallout*, and *Grand Theft Auto* series, tend to feature violence, warfare, and crime. Though many of these games involve complex problem solving, coordination, teamwork, and strategy, it can be difficult for those who don't play them to see beyond the blood, gore, and destruction to find any educational value in playing such games. Other video games have less objectionable content but may seem trivial; catapulting birds at pigs in *Angry Birds* is oddly compelling but not overtly educational.

As we mentioned in the first chapter, learning is usually associated with video games that are intentionally designed to teach traditional academic content. This notion of game-based learning is linked to the cognitive view of learning we described earlier and limits parents' conceptions of what they can do to support their children's learning as well as engage in joint learning around video games. From this perspective, games are mere vehicles for delivering content, and often that content has little to do with the game itself. The game story, rules, and interactions exist only to motivate children to acquire facts or skills presented in the game—an approach often referred to as "chocolate-covered broccoli," where academic content (broccoli) is made more palatable by combining it with something more appealing, such as video games (chocolate). Examples of this approach include games that reward players for solving math problems by allowing them to shoot aliens or that require them to correctly spell a vocabulary word in order to reveal the next part of the game story. In such games, learning and gameplay are not meaningfully aligned; that is, a player's ability to solve increasingly more difficult math problems has nothing to do with his or her ability to successfully shoot aliens. Such games are designed almost always as single-player experiences to ensure that individual children are mastering the content.

This approach to game-based learning can be successful in helping children learn basic information or master basic skills. Games reflecting this approach may be more engaging than workbook drills, and it's likely that children will prefer any sort of educational game over more traditional instruction in school. As we've discussed, however, this narrow focus on isolated academic context does not utilize the full potential of video games to engage players in more expansive forms of learning. If we keep looking at video games that are designed to entertain—the majority of games children play—solely through the lens of a narrow view of learning that emphasizes acquisition of information, we may never see the actual learning taking place.

Our broader sociocultural perspective on learning offers a much different way to understand the potential of video games for learning, both for children and adults. What makes video games a powerful medium and differentiates them from books and television is their *participatory* and *interactive* nature. When we are reading a book or watching a movie or a television series, we are spectators of the story—we are the fly on the wall observing other people and their experiences. When we are playing a video game, however, we are not a spectator but a protagonist whose actions change the story line. We are active participants, not passive observers. Unlike books and television, video games respond or give feedback to the players' actions. This interactivity is important for players' immersion in the experience and crucial for learning.

Let's return to John Dewey's ideas about learning through experience. Earlier, we cited Dewey's conception of learning as a cycle of doing, receiving feedback through the results of our actions, and taking action based on the feedback. To take this a bit further, Dewey suggests that "mere activity does not constitute experience"; that is, an experience that one can learn from. Making connections between our actions and their consequences and using these connections to better understand how the world works and our ability to make desired changes is how learning occurs. Educational games, in which the player solves math or language problems divorced from gameplay or the game world, are what we would call mere learning activities, not learning experiences. The player does not receive meaningful feedback about why his or her answer is right or wrong, and does not have the chance to develop hypotheses about what might improve his or her future performance, aside from trying to memorize facts or skills.

In contrast, well-designed entertainment games (and some educational games) create a context in which players' actions are tightly coupled with the situation within which they find themselves and with the problem they are confronting, just like in the real world. For instance, in the *Halo* game series, players assume the role of a soldier who is in a war zone with the Covenant, a military alliance trying to eradicate the human species. Players can carry a limited number of weapons and grenades, and need to plan their strategy carefully in relation to a particular set of enemies and obstacles. The problem that the players face is authentic to the narrative context of the game, and their choices have a meaningful impact on successful pursuit of game goals. As another example, in recent versions of the racing game series *Mario Kart*, players can customize their kart to alter its performance, choose among characters with different driving styles, and collect items that can be used strategically to hinder opponents or enhance their own performance. The players' choices have meaningful consequences in the game, and through experimentation, players learn what combination of choices has the best result.

Of course, not all games have a plot or even a narrative context, but a close alignment between the game mechanic and the problem the players are asked to solve is still important. For instance, in *Tetris*, the core game mechanic is rotating objects that fall at increasing speeds and moving them sideways so pieces fit together to make a solid line. Players are not asked to calculate the ratio of red to green squares, for example, because that has nothing to do with the game's goal. Similarly, in *Angry Birds*, the game mechanic is hurling round birds (and yes, they are angry) using a slingshot to knock down targets (the green pigs that stole their eggs) from a distance. The player isn't asked arbitrary questions about the attributes of birds or pigs, since that information is irrelevant to achieving the game's goals.

Though none of these games are overtly educational, they require players to engage in learning to play the game successfully. The player must figure out how the game world operates, how to use tools and resources in the game to achieve goals, and how to adapt strategies to changing conditions in the game. As the educational scholar James Gee has argued, well-designed video games immerse players in virtual environments that are intentionally structured to support and sustain learning.[7] Although a primary goal of learning through entertainment games is to master the game itself, players may also acquire skills or perspectives that have value beyond the game. For example, adults and children can develop hand-eye coordination (in the case of *Halo*), strategic thinking (in the case of *Mario Kart*), spatial reasoning skills (in the case of *Tetris*), or an understanding of motion and gravitational force (in the case of *Angry Birds*). The games are not intentionally designed to teach these skills, but people learn as a result of trying to master the game.

Thus, learning happens through and around all sorts of games, not just from overtly educational games. Here's Peggy, a mother of two, describing the learning opportunities she sees around *Minecraft*:

It's very creative. They do have to think on that one. Because the thing that I think I find interesting is they have to collect different things, certain goals in order to build something you have to have, like wood and iron. And there are so many things that they have to collect. I think for problem solving and thinking, it's like: "Okay, I want to achieve this, what do I need? Okay, I need a dinosaur. Well in order to get a dinosaur what do I have to go and find? Okay, where would I have to go and find it?" So, yeah, problem solving like that. And then just the spatial value of going, "Okay, I want to build a building." I mean, like . . . he's got, like, little beds, and he's got this little kitchen, and he puts a waterfall in the middle and, you know, from a spatial, architectural perspective I really like it for that.

Learning through playing video games goes beyond developing particular skills and includes learning how to be a learner; that is, developing an openness to expanding one's knowledge and capabilities, and cultivating a set of dispositions, such as perseverance, that are valuable across one's life-span and in all areas of life and work. This also includes developing an identity as a learner, including a sense of one's strengths and limitations. For example, when Gerardo, the four-year-old gamer of the Contreras family, plays video games like *Lego Star Wars*, he learns to persist when confronted with challenges rather than give up. He also acquires an understanding that expertise requires trial and error, time, and patience. He becomes someone who is competent and can teach others, like his twin brother, Gabriel. His expertise in video games is recognized and valued by his family members, which in turn reinforces his sense of place and identity within the family and in the world. He learns that if he gets really stuck, he can reach out to others for help, like his father (who shares his interest) and online communities and resources (e.g., YouTube). Of course, Gerardo and other children like him are often unable to describe what they learned from playing video games in this way. In fact, we did ask Gerardo what he learned from gaming, and he didn't answer. But we know he is learning because he is actually *doing* all the things we described. So, while he may not be able to articulate verbally or write an essay on what he is learning through playing video games, he is demonstrating the dispositions of a good learner in action.

Last, as our previous examples suggest, playing and learning through video games are not isolated activities. Learning around video games frequently involves social interactions and resources that are distributed across people, texts, tools, and artifacts. For instance, when David's fourteen-year-old son Robert plays *Halo* with his friends who live in Chicago, he is not only staying in touch with them and meeting his social needs but also learning through social interactions with his friends while playing the game. Robert and his friends mutually undertake challenges that are often beyond the competencies of one person alone to succeed in the game. When sixteen-year-old Alex Morgan meets new people online in *World of Warcraft*, he is not only making friends (again fulfilling a socioemotional need) but also learning how to strategize and collaborate with other people and how to use the resources, tools, and artifacts available in the virtual world effectively in relation to the tasks that they need to accomplish in the game.

Learning goes beyond the game world to include other means of sharing information and interactions online, such as discussion forums, chat rooms, and walkthroughs posted on YouTube. Players also get together in the same physical space to play games, watch each other play, and otherwise interact around gaming. As we found in our own research, children's video gaming at home often involves interactions with family members including parents and siblings. For instance, Emma Livingstone (age five) and Amelia Perez (age seven) learned how to participate in gameplay, solve problems, and be a team player as a member of a group—the family—that cares about and values video gaming. Other family members modeled how to play the game, coached Emma and Amelia to improve their skills, and supported their learning process by managing the difficulty of the tasks in games. Learning around video games in the context of families is not limited to the social interactions during coplay. Family members also talk about games and gameplay outside of the actual coplay situation, exploring topics such as the design of the game and the underlying game mechanics, and how the game relates to other games as well as other kinds of experiences.

Gaming as a Constellation of Literacy Practices

A common concern expressed by parents and educators is that children's digital media use, especially video gaming, is replacing reading books as a key learning activity and form of entertainment. In reality, studies have shown that children's book reading has held steady or even slightly increased over the past decade, and that TV viewing consumes far more of children's time than video gaming,[8] but the concern remains, based on the following logic: Strong reading skills are considered to be a foundation for success in school and in other areas of life, and we develop these skills by engaging with a wide range of texts in and out of school. Playing video games does not involve much, if any, reading, and in fact can prevent children from developing traits or skills that are associated with being a good reader, such as the ability to interpret complex language, imaginative thinking, or concentration.

Reading books and playing video games are indeed very different activities, and the foundation for different kinds of learning experiences. However, both can be valuable opportunities for literacy development. We use the term "literacy" to shift the focus away from a narrow view of reading and writing to a broader set of abilities to make meaning of and create a wide range of "texts" that we encounter in our daily lives, including digital media. For a long time, literacy was equated with the ability to read and write and, like learning, was considered to be a set of purely cognitive ("in the head") skills. That is, learning how to read and write was viewed in terms of stages, involving developmental milestones and beginning with the ability to decode—to break down words into smaller parts.[9] The assumption underlying such a view is that everyone learns how to read and write the same way and anyone who strays from the stages of literacy development is deficient.

However, along with a broader view of literacy as constructing meaning using a variety of texts, we now understand literacy learning as more than a cognitive process with relatively predictable stages. Earlier in the chapter, when we discussed how learning is generally a social process, several of our examples involved literacy learning, or precursors to literacy learning: one child coming to understand the meaning of "fork" by encountering forks at dinnertime, another child learning the names of colors using her crayons, and a mother reading the text in a *Pokémon* game to her son. In each case, literacy learning was associated with a particular social and cultural context in which certain "ways with words" are considered important and associated with valued everyday activities, or what scholars call "social practices." Typically, we gain the ability to read and write (as well as speak and listen) in socially and culturally appropriate ways through immersion in social practices and with the support of more experienced others who can teach, model, and otherwise support our learning. School is just one of many contexts for literacy learning, and "academic literacies" are associated with their own norms and social practices. Literacy learning is lifelong; adults may need to learn new literacy-related practices when they take on a new job, volunteer opportunity, or leisure activity, and as digital technologies support or require new forms of communication.

What it means to be literate varies across societies and history, social and cultural groups within societies, and particular contexts for any individual. Historically, due to the rise of digital technologies, we have experienced a recent and rapid transformation in tools, texts, and practices associated with literacy. Children's first reading experiences may involve an e-book or app on a tablet or phone, contrasting significantly with their parents' or even older siblings' early encounters with texts. The nature of reading and writing has also changed, as we have become accustomed to the increasing integration of written language, images, sound, and video, as well as the ability to move rapidly in a nonlinear way from, say, web page to document to chat and so forth. Debates over the effects of these changes on our minds and social relationships continue, but there's no question that what it means to be literate in society at large has been altered significantly.

Expectations and opportunities for literacy learning, as well as the value placed on particular kinds of literacy skills and practices, also vary across social and cultural groups within society. For example, in some cultures, reading a book alone is perceived as antisocial and a waste of time, while in other cultures it is valued as a form of personal development and learning. Even the role of literacy in seemingly mundane, everyday tasks can vary significantly. Does a grandmother cook by following a recipe or by using knowledge passed down orally by relatives? Does a dad tell his children to look up information when they ask a question about science, or answer it himself? Does an uncle read a passage from a holy or inspiring text, or is there a moment of silence at a holiday dinner? One way that different social groups vary is in the extent that their everyday literacy practices are consistent with the kinds of literacies valued in school (academic literacies). Middle-class and upper middle-class families with parents who have pursued higher education tend to use both oral and written language in ways that are consistent with and prepare their children for success with academic language. They may, for example, encourage children to develop interests in topics such as dinosaurs or history that require mastery of complex language and texts. They may ask questions that require higher-order thinking skills, mirroring the kinds of questions children are expected to answer in school. This does not make them better parents, but it does mean that their children may have an advantage in school.

Last, our individual affiliation with different social groups affects how we think about and participate in various social practices associated with literacy. For example, a teenage girl might write fan fiction and share it with an online audience of other writers she's never met; use Snapchat, Instagram, or other social media tools in particular ways to engage with her peer group; take notes and write science lab reports for her biology class at school; and spend time every evening playing video games with her little brother. In each situation, different forms of literacy are important for successful participation. To participate in the fan fiction community, she must learn the conventions of reading and writing fan fiction, including how to seek and give feedback in an online environment. To engage with her peers on social media, different forms of reading and writing—in particular the use of brief, abbreviated texts, often combined with images—are required, along with awareness of conventions regarding how and when to respond. To write a successful science lab report for school, she has to take notes, review them, and write an extended document that uses appropriate scientific terminology. Playing video games with her younger brother requires yet another set of literacy skills and knowledge, which might include interpreting text, numbers, and icons that are part of the game interface; reading in-game dialogue or instructions; and even reading online game reviews or comments on game forums. In each case, literacy goes far beyond decoding or comprehension of discrete texts, and requires an understanding of the social context that shapes the purpose and meaning of these texts.

Now let's look more closely at video games and literacy. The game scholar Constance Steinkuehler has described video gaming as a "constellation of literacy practices,"[10] a characterization that we used as the heading for this section. Let's start with more familiar literacy practices involving reading texts within the game itself. Although some genres of video games, such as puzzle games like *Angry Birds* or *Tetris*, may not involve extensive reading, in many video games reading is necessary to progress and succeed. Here's Maggie, a mother of three, describing how her daughter improved her reading skills while playing games on the Nintendo DS:

My middle child struggled with reading; still kind of does. She has ADD. So that Nintendo DS, the games she plays on it, you really have to read to understand what they want you to do to be able to do it. And occasionally, she'll bring it to me and say "I don't know what this word is" and I'll help her with the word or whatever. But I see her reading it and it's like, let's sit here and read for twenty minutes out of this book, it's like, "Oh, forget it." Are you kidding me? It's World War III in this house. "I'm not reading a book, what are you talking about?" And while she's playing the DS I'm happy because I know she's reading for at least ten minutes to go to the next screen. So, there's some benefit in the reading for it, for me, for her especially, because she does still—even being eleven years old at this point—she's still struggling with reading. So, it's helping, and I see it getting better for her with the reading. She says she loves to read now.

Maggie was one of the few parents in our research who recognized the role of reading in video game play. Maggie told us that she deliberately bought games that involve reading—not games that intentionally teach reading but games that require reading to understand how to play and to follow the game's story line (if it has one). Let's look at an example of such a game: the popular *The Legend of Zelda: Phantom Hourglass* for the Nintendo DS. Players take on the role of Link, a young boy who roams the world trying to save his friend Tetra from an evil ghost ship. (Unfortunately, the game reinforces the "boy saves girl" trope.) The player encounters text throughout the game in the form of instructions; descriptions of people, places, and items; dialogue; and narration. For instance, when faced with a problem, the player will often be given instructions such as, "When pulling the levers: First, second from left." Items are described as they are found, with pertinent information about their use: "You got a Courage Gem! It radiates courage, but it can't be used like this." Dialogue and narrative keep the story moving: "Looking for Linebeck? Sure, I know him! And that chair there knew him recently!"

The way that text is presented in games can be particularly useful for supporting children's vocabulary development and comprehension skills. Language is integrated with images and actions that help players understand the meaning of text, even if a particular word is unfamiliar. The purpose and value of reading is clear: to complete tasks, solve problems, and make progress in the game. In fact, reading is so seamlessly integrated with gameplay that children may not even realize that they are reading, particularly since we so often associate reading with books or other lengthy documents.

Gameplay can also prompt players to engage with other kinds of texts and literacy practices. For example, an Internet search for *The Legend of Zelda: Phantom Hourglass* yields myriad game reviews, walkthroughs, fan sites, and a series of graphic novels. In our research, we found that parents and children did not access such resources very often, but they represent potentially promising ways to connect gameplay to opportunities for exposure to new forms of texts and practices. While parents frequently place greater weight on reading books, reading game reviews and other expository texts exposes children to varied kinds of writing that resemble academic texts. And finally, games can be a starting point for fostering an interest in reading books. Parents might start with a book about or related to the games their children are playing, and gradually introduce other books that have overlapping themes but contain more academic language to support their children's literacy development. In the case of *Phantom Hourglass*, related books could be on topics such as ships, islands, and pirates.

Engaging children in reading, within or around gameplay, is only one way that video gaming can promote literacy development. Broadly speaking, any medium can be a resource for learning and literacy development, depending on the conditions in which one engages with that medium. Reading some books can be just as mindless and escapist as playing the most trivial game or watching a television show. A child who reads a book aloud with a parent, stopping to ask questions and talk about related experiences, will learn differently compared to a child reading alone or a child who is not allowed to ask questions while reading. Similarly, a child who watches a television show—whether it is *Sesame Street*, a documentary on animals, or *Family Guy*—with his parents and talks about what is happening, asks questions, and engages in discussions will learn something different from what a child who watches a television show alone or with parents without any meaningful conversation may learn. In fact, there is a robust literature that documents the important role verbal interactions between parents and children play around books and television in promoting children's literacy learning.[11,12,13] Unfortunately, little, if any, research has been conducted around video games and literacy learning in the context of families. However, we can extrapolate that a child who engages in conversation with a parent while playing games will learn differently compared to a child who plays alone or a child who plays with a parent who does not encourage conversation.

Video games can support children's literacy learning by creating shared literacy experiences between parents and children, similar to reading a book together. Let us demonstrate this point by sharing our observation of Luca (age thirteen) and his father, Gabe, playing *Civilization V* at a family gaming event we held at a school site. In *Civilization V*, the player chooses a civilization to play and the game starts with a long text passage that describes the civilization and establishes a context for the game. Gabe started off their gameplay by asking Luca to read the text out loud so that they understand what they need to do in the game. This is similar to a parent asking a child to read a book out loud—a strategy that is effective in helping children develop fluency in reading and comprehension skills. Luca began reading but gave up quickly. Gabe took over reading the text aloud while reminding his son to pay attention while he read. Soon, Gabe gave his son a chance to read again, but first asked: "Do you understand that, son?" Gabe checked for comprehension several times during the ninety minutes he played with Luca. Playing *Civilization V* relies heavily on reading instructions on pop-up screens about different aspects of the civilization. Players must choose from among different categories of information and read about the different features, abilities, and powers available in the game. Luca, with his father's encouragement, read the text on the screen, but midway through their gameplay he started to skip pages of dialogue. While at first these pages seemed inconsequential, it became evident that they provided important information about the order of actions in the game. After spending time trying to increase the population of his civilization, Luca figured out that he needed resources to feed his population in order to send his workers to battle. Gabe made a point about how essential reading is to succeeding at the game:

Okay, so, see, it's creating. It's all this stuff is, *mijo*, is having—you've got to read all this stuff. You've got to read it and find out if that—that's our problem is that we don't know nothing about it, you know what I mean? That's why we're having problems, dude. So if we read—we're—we're going to have to—I know you want to be, like, boom, boom, boom, and you want to know what to do, you know, but it doesn't work like that, son. You've never played this game before so we've got to read it—we've got to read everything.

Later, he said:

Okay. "Assigning citizens." See, all this—if you click on this stuff right here, son, it'll tell you what—whatever we're trying to do and it's going to tell us how to do it, you know what I mean?

In addition to pointing out the importance of reading to their gameplay, Gabe also modeled reading for his son. He and Luca started taking turns reading the text. At first, Gabe did more of the reading than Luca. After reading the text, Gabe explained what the text meant for their next

Figure 3.1
Luca and Gabe playing Civilization on the computer

action. He also engaged Luca in the process of making sense of the information by asking him for suggestions about their next strategy after reading. As they continued to play, Gabe gradually gave the responsibility of reading to Luca. He encouraged Luca by pointing out that they were able to progress through the game faster and experience some successes in the game because he was reading the text aloud (see figure 3.1).

We don't usually think of playing video games as a shared literacy experience, but here we have a father and his thirteen-year-old son reading and making sense of information together to accomplish a shared goal of successfully accomplishing the tasks in the game. Research suggests that parent-child talk during shared book reading promotes children's literacy development. During shared book reading, parents support their children's learning through providing explanations around unfamiliar words and story lines, connecting the story lines to real-world experiences, modeling reading, asking questions, and encouraging children to read.[14] Not every strategy will apply to all games, but parents can adapt them when appropriate while playing together with their children. Furthermore, not only does reading during gameplay support literacy learning but talking about video games can as well. The literature on parent-child talk around books recommends that parents engage in conversations around the story and illustrations outside of the shared reading experience.[15] Similarly, parents can ask questions about the games their children play and discuss the story line, graphics, and game mechanics to promote their children's literacy learning. In this way, video games can be considered a resource and part of the home literacy environment as opposed to a threat.

Finally, children's literacy learning can extend beyond conversations about games or the immediate gameplay experience. Children spontaneously use game characters, story lines, and actions in their imaginative play outside the game. For instance, Amelia Perez told us that she enjoyed playing *Minecraft* with her brother Matias on the computer, but found it just as much fun to physically enact stories they created about the game in their make-believe play. Some gamers, both young and adult, create artwork inspired by games, write fan fiction to elaborate game-related story lines, produce machinima (game-based videos) and walkthroughs, and modify the game itself, at times even creating entirely new games using a variety of game design platforms. These creative activities not only help children and youth develop technical and artistic skills but also support their literacy engagement. In our interviews with families, we rarely found families who engaged in such practices together, or even as individuals, reflecting the relatively small proportion of gamers overall who do so. We will revisit this observation and discuss ways families can engage with these practices in chapter 5.

Talk and Family Learning

Talk is a process and a product of learning. The role of talk in learning begins at birth as parents and other adults speak to or around infants. Young children's exposure to talk in the context of home and family is particularly important, not only to their language learning but also to their later success in school learning.[16] Through talk we learn to name things, make meaning of our experiences and observations, and share these insights with others. By its very nature, talk involves two or more people engaging in information sharing—collective and collaborative sense making with others. Of course, we also talk to ourselves without another person being there; however, even in the case of self-talk, we treat ourselves as a conversational partner and talk to ourselves as though we were talking to someone else. Our thoughts often take the form of words in our minds. So, there is a direct link between thinking and talk.

Earlier, we mentioned that children internalize the meanings constructed through social interactions, and through this process come to learn about the world and themselves. According to Lev Vygotsky, the internalization of external dialogues (talk) and actions is how language and thought become internal. As such, learning and development are fundamentally social and happen at two levels: (1) interpersonal (between people) and then (2) intrapersonal (within the person). Observations and analysis of talk reveal learning processes that later become products of learning once they are internalized and can be expressed externally by individuals.[17]

Since families are the first social group in which children interact with others and learn how to be a learner, parent-child interactions and talk have been studied as a context for teaching and learning for many decades. Researchers have studied naturally occurring parent-child interactions and talk as families engage in everyday activities such as reading books, cooking, driving in the car, and visiting a museum or a zoo. Studies also have been done in lab settings where parent-children conversations are observed during problem-solving tasks. Findings from both types of studies indicate how parents can support their children's learning during shared activities by providing explanations and calibrated support, modeling learning strategies, pointing children's attention to relevant information and resources, and connecting tasks to children's prior knowledge and real-world experiences.[18] The different ways in which parents support teaching and learning may affect how well children learn in other situations, particularly in school and, later on, in the workplace.

Of course, it is not just the child who learns during shared activities, especially when they are older. More recently, parents have been conceptualized as "learning partners" as opposed to "teachers" around shared activities.[19] Families develop shared understandings as they collaboratively engage in such shared activities and make sense of their experiences. This view shifts the focus of learning from the individual child to the family as a whole. Family learning includes parents, grandparents, siblings, and other family members, and is about discovering and exploring things together as a family. Family learning can take place at home or beyond; for example, museums and libraries are two popular locations where families spend time together in learning activities. With the rise of digital technologies, family learning can take place even when family members are apart from each other. As a unique learning group of mixed ages and backgrounds, families bring a complex set of shared experiences, beliefs, and values to their learning in these spaces. Family learning is often self-directed, voluntary, and guided by the needs and interests of the family members as learners.[20]

There are similarities and differences between visiting a museum, a zoo, or a library and playing video games in their opportunities for family learning. Like visits to various informal learning spaces, playing video games is self-directed, voluntary, and guided by the needs and interests of family members. The participatory and interactive nature of video games, however, offers a different sort of learning experience than what is typically available in a museum or library setting. In games, family learning involves taking an action, assessing consequences, and making a choice about what action to take to achieve an outcome or a goal. The game is a *system* of goals, rules, and resources, and winning a game requires the player to figure out how the system operates (for example, by discovering which actions lead to certain consequences). In other words, the game offers players a *designed problem space* with constraints within which players must work.[21] Video games strike a balance between a structured experience where the educational goal is predetermined and information is delivered directly to the audience, such as attending a lecture or watching a documentary, and an unstructured experience, such as visiting a museum or zoo, in which people explore their environment at will and gain knowledge as they go. Notably, museums and other informal learning organizations are beginning to incorporate games of all sorts to enhance the museum experience for visitors, recognizing that gameplay (appropriately designed) can deepen engagement and encourage more thoughtful interactions with exhibits, content, and other visitors.[22]

Games as a Context for Learning Conversations

Over our years of studying and facilitating family gameplay, we have heard the following comment quite frequently: "Yes, families have fun and feel connected while playing video games, but what are they really learning?" To answer this question, we need to start with the sociocultural view of learning we described earlier in this chapter and take a closer look at the interactions and conversations that take place while families play video games together. In their book *Learning Conversations in Museums*, Gaea Leinhardt, Kevin Crowley, and Karen Knutson describe conversations in the context of museums as both process and outcome of museum learning. They observe that people do not come to museums to talk but often end up talking, and in these varied conversations—what they call learning conversations—much learning can take place.[23] Similarly, people do not play video games to talk, but they often do talk while playing. This talk ranges from discussions of managing gameplay, to negotiating and resolving disagreements around different strategies, to connecting gameplay experience to other family experiences. These conversations support learning by creating opportunities for problem solving and collaboration, as well as cultivating patience and persistence.

Problem Solving

One set of abilities that cuts across different content areas and professional domains such as mathematics, science, and language arts is, broadly speaking, problem solving. Problems are, simply put, any situation in need of a solution to achieve a goal. We run into problems, from small to complex, in our everyday, academic, and professional lives all the time. Although problem-solving skills are highly valued in schools and workplaces, they are difficult to define. In part, this difficulty is due to differences in the nature of problems and their contexts. Two broad types of problems are commonly recognized. Well-defined problems have clear goals and readily identifiable paths to a solution. In contrast, ill-defined problems are those that do not have clear goals, solution paths, or expected solutions. A well-defined problem can be simple (tying a shoe) or complicated (building a chicken coop from a kit) but in all cases, the steps toward the solution can be readily determined, and if followed, will achieve the goal. Ill-defined problems are typically more complex; that is, there are more variables or parts of the problem that can't be readily anticipated or controlled.[24] Growing a healthy tomato plant is an ill-defined problem, since any set of instructions cannot account for all the variables—sunlight, soil quality, moisture, possibility of insect infestation—that might affect it. Ill-defined problems also vary in scale as well as complexity; solving the water use problem in California and Arizona is obviously a far more complex and overwhelming problem than keeping that tomato plant alive.

In general, problem solving requires both analytical skills and creative thinking. The kind of abilities that are necessary depends on the problem and the situation. In school, children are frequently given well-defined problems, those with one correct solution and often one "right" way of solving them. Real-world problems are more likely to be ill defined, or at least have more than one solution. Before one can identify possible solutions, one must define the problem itself. For example, if you are unhappy spending an hour in traffic on your way home from work every day, what's the underlying problem? Is it the sense that you are wasting time in general? That you are missing an hour with your family? Defining the problem one way or another will affect how you solve it—staying at work an hour later or listening to informational audiobooks might be appealing to the person who feels like she is wasting time, whereas the person who misses the opportunity to be with her family might want to consider telecommuting on alternate days.

In video games, players are confronted with many different kinds of problems, ranging from well defined to ill defined, and more or less complex. In many games, problems gradually become more difficult and solving them is challenging and takes longer. For example, in *World of Warcraft*, the solo quests are fairly well-defined problems with clear goals and methods for successfully completing the quests (e.g., "Obtain Five Gigantic Catfish. Deliver the fish to Robby Flay in Stormwind City"). However, players still need to solve problems such as navigating the virtual space and being able to use their resources and powers to defeat different enemies within the well-defined structure of the quest. In *Angry Birds*, each level is a problem that players need to solve to move on to the next problem (e.g., fling the red bird straight ahead at the wooden ball, making it roll down to take out the two pigs below). In other games, problems are neither presented in a linear fashion nor are they clearly defined. In the open world of sandbox games such as *SimCity* and *Minecraft*, players can set their own goals, and then identify and solve problems that arise as they pursue these goals. Rather than the game challenging the player through well-designed and sequenced problems, players challenge themselves and develop their problem-solving abilities along with gaining new knowledge about the game.

Families can engage in learning conversations that support problem solving around video games. Let's demonstrate the form that learning conversations can take by examining the interaction between Julie (age twelve) and her father as they make a twelve-by-twelve block pyramid, a design challenge we created for families in *Minecraft*:

Julie: So we do E (*brings up the inventory*), we get that cobblestone. How big do you want our pyramid? (*Knocks down trees to flatten an area and starts placing blocks, but there is not enough space to build a pyramid.*)

Father: You need to figure out how big to make it. A twelve-by-twelve block area is where you have to build it. So we need a bigger area.

Julie: Oh. (*Flies up to have a bird's-eye view of the world.*) Tell me when you find an area.

Father: What?

Julie: Well, it's mostly trees, so we're going to have to take some trees down. The deepest area is—would be right here.

Father: All right, how about this area? (*Points to a large area on the screen.*)

Julie landed on an area and started chopping down trees with the cobblestone in her character's hand. She realized that she didn't have the right tool to efficiently chop down the trees. So, she brought up the inventory and picked an iron axe.

Father: Yeah, destroy all that stuff. (*Julie starts chopping down trees.*) This is going to take a while. Let's find a different area.

Julie: OK. (*Starts flying again, spots a larger flat area near water, and lands.*)

Father: OK, cut out a twelve-by-twelve area first, all right?

Julie: (*Starts digging holes on the ground.*) One, two, three, four, five . . . twelve.

Father: Now turn.

Julie continued digging holes in the ground and counted to twelve three more times. She ended up with a twelve-by-twelve square.

Father: So just clear out everything in that area. (*Indicates the middle of the square.*)

Julie: (*Starts clearing out the middle of the square.*) Now, we've got a pyramid to build. Now we have, like, two other goals.

Father: All right, so how big is your person? How many blocks tall did you make your house?

Julie: It was two. (*A standard door in* Minecraft *is two blocks tall, and players quickly learn to craft doors to provide access to the structures they build.*)

Father: Four blocks?

Julie: Four stories is how big my house was.

Father: Right, but how many blocks per story? Each one of those should be considered a level.

Julie: (*Ignoring the question because she already gave the answer, she continues.*) We should make it hollow, too.

Father: Hollow?

Julie: So we can go inside.

Father: Sure.

Julie: (*Finishes clearing out the square and discovers that there are holes underneath some of the blocks she cleared.*) Okay, now we've got to fill some of [the holes] in.

Father: All right.

Julie: I'm filling in my holes. Clearly I have a lot of them. I've got a lot of holes. (*Fills all the holes.*) So now we start building?

Father: How much space do you want? We have a twelve-by-twelve area. So maybe ten-by-ten? (*Julie places blocks, starting from one corner and filling the entire twelve-by-twelve space.*) So, you have a little bit of open area around [the pyramid]. Do ten-by-ten, so it's a little bit smaller. (*Julie does what her father suggested.*) There you go.

Julie then built the second and third stories of the pyramid. When she reached the top (the fourth story), she ran into a problem. She first tried staying inside the pyramid to place the last block, but then she couldn't get out of the pyramid. She destroyed the blocks and placed a block while she was standing outside, but then she couldn't get inside the pyramid.

Julie: I need to put a door to get in. (*At this point, each story of the pyramid is one block tall and a door is two blocks tall.*)

Father: Hollow out around it.

Julie: (*Finishes hollowing out the pyramid.*) How do I get in?

Father: Destroy the blocks until you get in.

Julie destroyed one block, then ran into another block and still couldn't get inside. She walked back and entered the pyramid from the top to see how far she had dug into the ground.

Julie: Ah, I needed to destroy this one. (*Now the pyramid has an entrance. Julie closes the top of the pyramid. The pyramid gets dark inside, so she takes out some torches and puts them on the walls.*) Done.

Here, Julie and her father worked together to complete the task of building a pyramid within a twelve-by-twelve block area. This task can be considered a well-defined problem in that there was a clear goal. However, the path to accomplishing the task was not defined—similar to many real-world problems, as we noted earlier. Early in the episode, Julie's father observed the area where Julie had begun to knock down blocks and suggested that they find a larger area to successfully accomplish the task. When Julie found another area to build the pyramid, she needed to find the appropriate tool to chop down trees. But even with the right tool at hand, chopping down the trees would have taken a very long time. If her father had not been there to guide her, Julie might have spent most of her time chopping trees rather than building the pyramid. Julie's father modeled a process of anticipating the consequences of choices and changing direction by suggesting that Julie find a new area to build the pyramid. Once settled on an area, Julie's father discussed strategies for building the pyramid with her. Toward the end, Julie ran into small problems—putting up the last block without getting trapped inside the pyramid or locking herself out, for example—that she solved through trial and error. She came up with the solution of adding a door but encountered a problem again. Her father made a suggestion that helped Julie successfully finish the task.

While this is just one example, Julie and her father's interactions illustrate several features of what we feel are beneficial learning conversations focused on problem solving. Julie's father was an active participant, but Julie made all the moves in the game. He alternated between watching her make choices, asking questions to prompt her thinking, suggesting alternatives, and occasionally telling her what to do next. He encouraged her to explain her reasoning and reminds her of relevant past experiences. Both of them remained focused and intent on the task at hand, and Julie even added a final touch—torches—to make the pyramid more appealing and complete.

Collaboration

Broadly speaking, collaboration refers to situations in which more than one person works on a single task. For collaboration to result in completing the task successfully, those who are collaborating need to coordinate their actions, develop a shared understanding of the task, and effectively communicate with one another. Collaboration often involves a division of labor, with each person being responsible for one or more aspects of the task. People may bring different types of knowledge and expertise to the task. These differences need to be communicated, discussed, and acknowledged for the collaboration to yield an equitable partnership. The collaborators need to monitor and reconcile divergences in perspective to build a shared understanding of the task and what they need to do together and individually to succeed in a game or any other activity.

As we mentioned earlier, playing video games with others involves cooperation and collaboration, not just competition. Multiplayer video games like *World of Warcraft* and *Halo* support interactions between players in the virtual environment and through talk around the game. People in the same room can communicate face-to-face, while those who are playing elsewhere can use text and voice chat to coordinate actions. There is extensive research on collaboration to solve complex problems in multiplayer video games,[25] but little attention has been given to such collaboration among families playing video games. Furthermore, single-player video game experiences are rarely studied to understand how they might support collaboration and cooperation. This is a missed opportunity, because although many of the video games that children play are designed for a single player, they can become a shared gaming experience if we look at the many different ways that families can participate together. We share the following interaction between Marissa and her mother around *Minecraft* to illuminate how they give each other feedback, make connections, and teach one another as they try to accomplish a shared goal. In this episode, Marissa and her mother are attempting to corral chickens, cows, pigs, and sheep:

Marissa: So for food—animals like food a lot. So, let's say . . . (*Looking at meat options in the inventory*)

Mother: They're not going to eat beef. They're vegetarians.

Marissa: Yeah. No, they're not.

Mother: They're not carnivores.

Marissa: We need wheat. Where's wheat? (*Continues to look through meat options*)

Mother: The cows are going to eat chicken? I don't think so.

Marissa: OK, we need wheat.

Mother: I saw some here. (*Points to the screen*)

Marissa: They go crazy for carrots on sticks.

Mother: Animals love wheat—the smell of the wheat . . . how many animals do we need?

Marissa: One of each.

Mother: You've got the wheat in your hand and you don't have a fence yet. So why don't we . . . (*Marissa is still looking through the inventory.*) What are you doing?

Marissa: I'm trying . . . OK, so it's nighttime. I am going to put up a torch so we can see.

Mother: Can I build the fence?

Marissa: OK. (*Gives the controller to her mother, who starts building a fence.*) Yep. No, it doesn't have to . . . yep, then turn. Good job.

Mother: How do I put wheat in my hand?

Marissa: Let me get you through this. (*Takes over the controller, picks the wheat from the inventory, and gives the controller back to her mother.*) Now, open the gate. Right-click the gate. (*A pig is near the fence.*) Go by the pig.

Mother: (*Hits the pig with wheat in hand. Hearts come out of the pig.*) Oh, why did I hit him? Did I hurt him?

Marissa: No, he loves you.

Mother: How do I get him to follow me?

Marissa: (*Takes over the controller.*) OK, now watch this.

Marissa moved closer to the pig. The pig began to follow her. Another pig wandered by. Marissa corralled both pigs in the fenced area. She tried to leave the fenced area, but the pigs followed her, making it difficult for her to escape.

Mother: You need to close the gate. They're leaving. Quick, close the gate.

Marissa closed the gate and was able to escape to the other side of the fenced-in area. She and her mother moved on to finding cows. Marissa's mother took over the controller, found and corralled the nearby cows in the fenced area, and tried to leave the fenced area, but she was not fast enough.

Marissa: You are letting the pigs out. Close the gate.

Marissa's mother closed the gate. She was able to keep the pigs inside the fenced area, but the cows escaped and they continued to follow her. She gave the controller back to Marissa so she could try to get the cows back in the fenced area.

Marissa: We need to make the fence bigger.

Mother: Can't you just break [part of the fence] real quick and let the cows in, and then build the fence back up?

Marissa: I think I know what to do. I could just put fence in [around the cows].

Marissa started building an extension to the existing fence to trap the cows where they stood.

Mother: Then I'll break the other [fence separating the cows and the pigs] out.

Marissa built the second fence and then gave the controller to her mother so that she could remove the fence dividing the animals. They ended up having a larger fence with cows and pigs. Marissa and her mother then moved on to finding sheep and then chickens to complete the challenge.

As they began the task of herding animals, Marissa and her mother had to develop a shared understanding of what food various animals eat and how to interpret the ways that animals respond. Marissa was more knowledgeable about the game than her mother, while her mom was able to draw on her real-world experience to make suggestions. For example, Marissa's mother pointed out that cows are vegetarians, not carnivores (nice academic terms for Marissa to learn) when Marissa was looking for food to attract them. At other times, Marissa had to correct her mother's misunderstanding; for instance, when she thought that hearts rising from a pig were an indication that it was injured, or when Marissa tried to do things without explanation, such as look for a torch when it was getting dark. Thus, they both had knowledge to contribute.

In addition, Marissa and her mother shared responsibility for actions in the game by alternating use of the game controller. The one without the controller pointed out things that were relevant to the task but might momentarily be outside of the *attentional scene*[26] of the person using the controller. For instance, when Marissa tried to get out of a fenced area, her mother pointed out that she needed to close the gate to prevent the animals from leaving. When Marissa's mother took over the controller, Marissa provided the same kind of support to her mother by reminding her about the gate. This reciprocal support and coordination of actions helped Marissa and her mother work as partners to successfully accomplish the task as a team.

Patience and Persistence

One concern we have sometimes heard from parents is that, as a result of video gaming, their children will develop a need for instant gratification and have limited tolerance for tasks that require extended effort or concentration. Certainly many games are fast-moving, require quick reflexes, and reward players for what might seem to be mindless button-mashing. What might not be obvious from watching a skilled player, however, is the time and effort it can take to master challenging gameplay, including repeating parts of the game again and again until the player achieves success. Some games have quests comprising many tasks that can take hours to complete or require players to build complex armies or civilizations over time. Even so-called casual games, like *Angry Birds* or *Tetris*, can be easy to learn but hard to beat—it takes considerable practice for a player to successfully complete the more advanced levels of the game.

Such games can promote the development of patience and persistence, two qualities often cited as "soft skills" that are crucial to achievement in all realms of life, from finishing a lengthy term paper at school to building a successful business to (yes) raising happy and healthy children. Parents can use conversations during joint gameplay as well as conversations about games to help children cultivate such attributes and become more aware of their value. Let's use another child and parent building a pyramid in *Minecraft* as an example. In this case, the child, Oliver, is again the more experienced player, and his father is new to the game:

Father: What did you just push?

Oliver: OK, E is your inventory. This is where you check things. We are going to make a . . .

Father: Stone?

Oliver: Do you want stone or dirt?

Father: What does [the challenge] tell us to do?

Oliver: It says make it stone or dirt. Which one do you want to make?

Father: Which is better? Which one is sturdier?

Oliver: Either one.

Father: OK then, your choice.

Oliver: I like stone.

Once Oliver had procured all the materials from the inventory, he found an area to build the pyramid and then gave the controller to his dad.

Oliver: OK, right-click to place blocks. Left-click . . . (*His father destroys a block on the ground.*)

Father: How did I get in the hole?

Oliver: Do you want me to help you out here?

Father: Let me practice. I'll get it. You just gotta have a little patience with me, okay?

Oliver's father practiced destroying and placing blocks. He then began to build the first story of the pyramid.

Father: One, two, three, four, five, six . . . (*Places one block at a time.*) We are not going to have enough [space] for twelve, are we?

Oliver: So, when this happens . . . (*Takes over the controller.*)

Father: Are you going to get the existing land to do it? (*Oliver starts destroying the dirt blocks around where they are building to create space for the pyramid.*) Oh, you are making a space.

Oliver's father took over the controller to finish the base of the pyramid. He destroyed a couple more dirt blocks around the area. While he worked on building the first story of the pyramid, Oliver's father needed to continuously clean out the area.

Oliver: All right, we are finding a new space.

Father: Are we starting over?

Oliver: Yeah, it is going to take a while.

Father: Why?

Oliver: Trust me. Because that was going to take so long. We were going to have to destroy a few more things.

Oliver found a larger space to build the pyramid in a different part of the virtual world. He built the first story of the pyramid, then gave the controller to his father.

Father: OK, now we got to fill [the base] in, right?

Oliver: No. (*Takes over the controller.*)

Father: We don't? But we need a base.

Oliver: Yes, this is our base. (*Places two blocks on top of each other at the inside corner of the base, then destroys the block underneath; this way, the block can float in the air. This is the first block of the second story of the pyramid.*) Once you have this first block, you don't have to put blocks underneath. They will attach to one another as you build sideways. (*This strategy allows players to create a slanted shape, like a pyramid, as opposed to a vertical structure, like a house.*)

Oliver finished the second story of the pyramid and gave the controller back to his father.

Father: (*Practicing what he just learned.*) OK, now I want to do the next [story] right here.

Oliver: OK, place one block down and one block up and then destroy the one underneath. (*His father follows the directions.*) See. It's easy. Once you get the hang of it, it will be very easy for you.

Father: You have good patience with me. That's good.

Oliver's father finished the third and fourth stories all by himself. He ran into a couple of challenges—not being able to stand at the corner of the pyramid without falling off of the structure—but he persevered and completed the pyramid.

By playing with his father, who was less knowledgeable about and skillful at the game, Oliver was learning to be patient and work with someone who had a different level of expertise. His father demonstrated patience and persistence as he practiced the moves that Oliver taught him and did not give up, even though he was making mistakes and had to start over several times. Although he could have chosen simply to watch Oliver build, by assuming the role of learner, he took advantage of an opportunity to reinforce the value of patience and persistence through his own actions. In addition, he explicitly asked Oliver to be patient and then commended Oliver for his patience later on. Rather than experiencing frustration, Oliver told us that he really enjoyed teaching his father how to play the game and how to build. Oliver's father also enjoyed being in the role of a student—a role he rarely took on in other aspects of their family life. He set a positive tone by laughing with Oliver when they made mistakes and things didn't work out exactly the way they wanted. Oliver's father also said he learned that "it's okay to let go"; in other words, he, too, gained some insight into how to learn from and with his son.

Conclusion

In this chapter, we demonstrated the value of a sociocultural perspective for understanding family learning through video gaming. From this perspective, learning is more than acquiring facts or isolated skills, but instead involves meaningful interactions with the world and with other people, through which we can develop and test our understandings of each other and how the world works. Well-designed video games, even if they are not designed to be overtly educational, promote learning by engaging players in a process of experimentation, giving them feedback on their actions, and helping them to develop hypotheses about the rules of the game world. Players also develop dispositions toward learning and a sense of their strengths and limitations, or identities as learners through gameplay. Learning extends beyond the game itself, when players interact with other players to solve problems and discuss gameplay strategy, or use out-of-game resources such as walkthroughs or game guides.

More specifically, we described how gameplay can be viewed as a valuable opportunity for developing children's language skills and engaging them in meaningful literacy practices. Parents can engage with children in learning conversations, which can promote problem-solving abilities and collaboration as well as cultivate patience and persistence. While we discussed these potential learning outcomes separately, we stress that learning through gameplay—like learning in real life—is typically multidimensional, with many kinds of learning happening simultaneously.

We'd like to conclude this chapter with the idea of video gaming as *preparation for future learning*[27] and the potential role of families in this learning. The learning scientists John Bransford and Dan Schwartz argue that active experiences with a domain of knowledge or practice, even when they are not designed to be educational, can prepare students to be more successful in future formal learning situations. We can readily think of simple examples, such as how building with blocks can improve children's spatial skills and mathematical problem solving in school.[28] Bransford and Schwartz caution that not all experiences are helpful, however; learners may acquire knowledge that is too fragmented to be useful, or even develop misconceptions that can pose barriers to subsequent learning. To be effective, prior knowledge needs to complement, not contradict, formal learning goals, and students may need assistance in making connections between prior experience and formal educational content.

Video games can provide learners with experiences that present ideas or models about how the world works and may later be useful in school or other formal educational settings. From a preparation for future learning perspective, what players learn from games may go beyond more obvious skills and dispositions such as literacy, basic problem solving, or persistence. Because games are complex systems, players may develop an intuitive understanding of how systems operate, how intervening in one aspect of a system can lead to changes in another part, and so forth. They may also gain an understanding of more specific domains, such as physics from *Portal*, history from *Civilization*, or urban planning from *SimCity*.

There have not been many formal studies of how gameplay can serve as preparation for future learning of this sort. The existing studies suggest that simply playing games, even becoming an expert in a particular game, does not automatically provide a foundation for future academic learning. The particular features of a game play a role, such as whether it has clear goals that scaffold players' learning or whether players have other prior experiences that shape their understanding of the domain. There is agreement, though, that players' preparation for future learning can be enhanced when they are prompted to make connections between gameplay or elements of the game and more formal academic concepts or material.[29,30] This suggests an opportunity for parents and families in general who seek to take greater advantage of the learning potential of video gaming. Viewing games as preparation for future learning can prompt a change in how families engage with and talk about games. Simple questions about gameplay or game features can be a starting point for investigation and deeper learning: "Is a 'portal' such as those in *Portal 2* really possible?" "In *Mario Kart*, your weight affects your speed, acceleration, and vehicle handling. How does weight affect these factors in real-world movement?" "*Zoo Tycoon* is a simplified model of how to run a zoo and care for animals. What other things would we need to do to keep animals healthy in the real world? How would you change the game to make it more realistic?" Parents do not need to be experts in a domain to facilitate their children's learning in this way; in fact, learning together with your child can be just as or even more effective for modeling how to be a successful learner. In chapter 5, we return to family learning with an emphasis on how families can learn together. But next, in chapter 4, we address the topic of how video gaming can reinforce positive family relationships, values, norms, and identities.

4

Understanding Oneself, Each Other, and the World

What is it about "play" that makes it a powerful context for developing family identity and fostering social ties? In this chapter, we discuss how play supports families in expressing their feelings, sharing experiences, developing understanding, and making sense of the world around them. From philosophers to psychologists, many have explored and written about the nature, form, and value of play for human development, social interactions, identity formation, and cultural reproduction. The Greek philosopher Plato suggested that play is a leisurely activity, something that disrupts work and the seriousness of life.[1] This view continues to dominate the way we think about play in our society and is shared among parents, including those who participated in our research projects, who reported that house chores and busy schedules are the reasons why they do not play games with their children.[2] Parents perceive playing games as something that they do when they have time to spare from life's obligations, and not necessarily an integral aspect of life.

Johan Huizinga, in expanding the realm of play to include animals and adults, makes the following observations: (1) play is a voluntary activity in that people choose to play, and (2) play is not "ordinary" or "real" life because people know that they are "pretending" while playing.[3] Despite the affordances of play in escaping from the realities of ordinary life, Huizinga, unlike Plato, views play as "serious" because people's actions mean something beyond the play itself. Similarly, Gregory Bateson points out that while what happens in play is "unreal," it evokes emotions that one experiences in real life such that the person must remind himself, "This is play."[4]

Let us demonstrate this aspect of play with an example. From a design stance, chess is a game that is played between two opponents on opposite sides of a board with sixty-four squares, in an eight-by-eight grid. The squares alternate colors, usually black and white, to mark the pathway for each player. Each player has sixteen pieces: one king, one queen, two rooks, two bishops, two knights, and eight pawns. The goal of the game is to capture the opponent's king. The game requires strategic thinking in that players must evaluate the actions of their opponents and anticipate their possible future moves. The game has very little, if any, room for chance. While both adults and children have to devote similar mental energy toward winning the game, the game can have multiple meanings beyond its stated goals and rules in the context of different families.

For a seven-year-old girl who has a history of losing the game to her father, chess could represent her status as the less knowledgeable and less skilled member of the family. The child may be upset by losing the game because it means her current position as novice is reinforced, even though her father reminds her it is just a game. At the same time, winning the game could signify a change of her status from a novice to a more knowledgeable and skilled member of the family. By contrast, in a family with older children, playing chess could mean something totally different. For a thirteen-year-old boy and his father who are at the same skill level with respect to the game, playing chess can be considered not a rite of passage but a rehearsal for another game, soccer, in which the father coaches his son around tactics and strategies. For the boy, beating his father in chess evokes a sense of confidence about soccer and losing the game means he needs to better understand the tactics and strategies that are involved in soccer as well. Finally, for another family that values discussing politics or is interested in history, playing chess can be a ritual for making sense of current events and foreign policy. In this case, losing or winning the game is not so much about those who are involved in playing the game but about making sense of different nations, constituents, and historical events.

It is the unique quality of crossing boundaries between real life and fantasy, as well as leisure and work, that makes play a rich context for families to negotiate, endorse, and define individual and family identity (see figure 4.1). Plato believed that children explore their desires and future adult roles and acculturate into society through play.[5] Later, psychologists explored how play creates opportunities for children to learn adult ways of thinking and doing. For example, Jean Piaget suggested that play provides an opportunity for children to imitate reality.[6] According to Piaget, during the first stage of development (from birth to age two), children do not differentiate between reality and play. Through their sensorimotor skills, children develop schemas (ways of thinking about the world) by trial and error through play as they explore and learn about their environment. During later stages of development, play functions

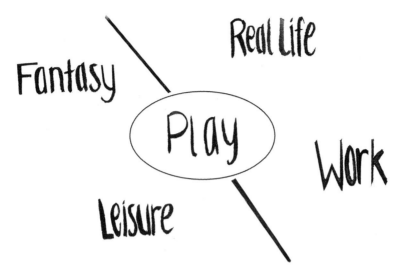

Figure 4.1
Play sitting in between reality and fantasy

not as "an effort to learn" but a "happy display of known actions." In later developmental stages, rather than repeating and practicing schemas that already exist in their minds, children become more sophisticated in their combination of schemas.[7] This leads to the development of symbolic thought and play wherein children can see a cardboard box beyond its physical properties and pretend that it is a car. Any parent who has watched their children engage in imaginative play would know that, while playing, children take on adult roles and reenact real-world situations that they have observed. It is the development of symbolic thought that enables children to represent the real world in the context of play. As children grow older, play becomes a manifestation of their inner world, thinking, and emotions.

Similarly, Vygotsky found play to be important for the development of symbolic thought and for children to internalize socially and culturally constructed meanings. According to Lev Vygotsky, children stretch themselves within the *zone of proximal development*—the distance between the actual developmental level of children, measured by what they can do independently; and their potential developmental level, measured by what they can do with support from more knowledgeable others (e.g., parents)—such that "a child's greatest achievements are possible, achievements that tomorrow will become their basic level of real action and morality."[8] He suggests that play is not a "novel situation" to which the child applies her existing knowledge but a "recollection of something that has actually happened." Said differently, play exists as a cultural practice within a society that children inherit from preceding generations and use as "a tool for grappling with reality and identity construction."[9] From this vantage point, play functions in society as a catalyst for generational continuity, social order, and social identity formation.

Erik Erikson, a psychologist who wrote extensively about identity, suggests that the "playfulness" of play provides a context for adults to step out of their social reality without fear or worry over the consequences of their actions.[10] For children, play functions as a coping mechanism for undesired or painful events caused by parent-child conflict. The field of counseling psychology has taken up the idea that play can bring relief to children and adults through escaping from reality and releasing emotions that are difficult to deal with in the real world. Since the 1980s, play therapy has been used to help children make sense of and communicate their thoughts, feelings, and life experiences.[11] According to Eliana Gil, play therapy allows children to express themselves through the use of symbols, compensate for problems in reality, find solutions to problems, and rehearse the myriad situations children might encounter through play.[12] By using storytelling, board and card games, toys, and make-believe play, therapists create a safe environment for children and facilitate learning about self and others. This approach has been extended to supporting families in resolving conflicts, understanding the perspectives of others, and building closer relationships between parents and children.

In this chapter, we move beyond a view of play as a context for intervention when families face a problem, with the sole purpose of improving the socioemotional well-being of children and families. Instead, we discuss how play offers opportunities for forming, reinforcing, and negotiating family values, norms, and identity in the daily lives of families. Specifically, we delve into how video games open conversations between parents and children as individuals and as a family unit. Drawing from our own research, we share how video games create opportunities for identity work around families' ethnic and cultural backgrounds. Furthermore, we examine how parents and children learn about each other and themselves through intergenerational play, and the meaning of these interactions in the context of family life. Finally, we conclude this chapter with examples of parents using video gaming as a context for discussing real-world issues with their children that may be difficult to wrestle with otherwise.

Playing Games as an Opportunity Space

Before we share some of the ways families engage in identity work around play, it is important to talk about the identities at stake when one plays video games. We started this chapter with a discussion of how play sits between the realms of reality and fantasy. Here, we extend this idea to include different identities that emerge and are negotiated as a result of the boundary-crossing nature of games.

According to James Gee, there are three identities at play when a person plays video games: virtual, real, and projective.[13] *Virtual identity* refers to one's identity as a virtual character in the virtual world of the game. This identity has no connection to the real world. The actions of the virtual character have meaning within the context of the game only. For example, a person can play *Super Mario Bros.* as the Mario character, which has certain characteristics and capabilities within the virtual world of the game such as defying gravity and jumping higher than a human possibly can. *Real identity* consists of the roles and identities we assume in our daily lives as a spouse, child, parent, friend, employee, and so forth. The identities we take on in our daily lives may vary and even can be contradictory; for example, the identity a woman assumes as the dutiful and subservient daughter of a demanding parent can conflict with her identity as a successful and assertive corporate executive in the workplace. Finally, *projective identity* is the blend of the real and virtual identities we experience when playing video games. This type of identity emerges as a result of the boundary-crossing nature of video games, and includes projecting one's values and desires onto the virtual character. Our real and virtual identities interact while we are playing video games, allowing for identity negotiation, formation, and reflection through the work of projective identity. As such, playing video games provides opportunities for thinking through what one values, desires, and cares about in the real world, and becomes a context for identity in the making.

The anthropologist Elinor Ochs and her colleagues describe dinnertime as an "opportunity space" in which family members construct roles, relationships, values, and worldviews through the stories they tell while spending time eating dinner together.[14] An opportunity space is a temporal, spatial, and social moment that provides the possibility of joint activity among family members. Spending time eating dinner together creates an opportunity to generate knowledge and social order as well as disorder through interactions with family members. This happens through the stories families share with one another and construct together at the dinner table. For instance, when parents and children share their experiences at school or work around the dinner table, they create shared understandings as they collectively make sense of what happened. Such moments can reveal differences of opinion and perspective between family members that need to be negotiated, confirm shared norms and values, or become an opportunity for parents to reinforce expectations for children.

We have found that something similar happens when parents and children talk about and engage in the joint activity of intergenerational play around video games. Video gaming becomes an opportunity space for families through the interplay among real, virtual, and projective identities. Families project, construct, and negotiate individual and family identities, values, norms, and desires as they have conversations about video games and interact with each other while playing video games together. The following comment from Katie, one of the parents who participated in our focus group study, about her son's decision not to use cheat codes on his Nintendo DS highlights this aspect of video gaming:

Also for the DS, whoever has DS, you can get this, like, cartridge that you plug into it and it downloads everything and you have ultimate endless whatever. And I know a lot of my son's friends who are at school has it. He didn't want it because he felt like the cheat codes were cheating—so he didn't want it. So he's like, "What's the point? Why would I play? You should be able to win without doing that." And I'm like, "*Right! You're right.*" So, and he does, and he has his strategy guides, he buys the strategy guides.

By making the choice not to use cheat codes (a method of manipulating game code to make the game easier or harder), Katie's son takes a moral stance on what counts as legitimate play. While using cheat codes is a socially acceptable practice among his peers and within the larger gaming community, he perceives this practice as cheating, and something that he would not do. Katie is pleased to hear her son's rationale and decision not to use cheat codes while playing. For Katie, her son's decision says something about the kind of person he is and the values that they both share. Parents like Katie were proud to see their children exhibiting behaviors aligned with family values, such as calling out people when they were using inappropriate language or bullying while playing multiplayer online games. Parents also used video games as a way to convey messages and life lessons while playing or watching their children play. Mark, another parent in our research, was surprised to find out that his son was slaughtering the animals in *Minecraft* with no purpose and purely for fun. He let his son know that animals should be killed only for food or making clothes in real life, and that he expected his son to apply this principle while playing as well.

Playing Out Ethnic and Cultural Identity

At any given time, we take on multiple roles and identities such as professor, woman, daughter, spouse, and so on. One aspect of our identity pertains to our understanding of and relationship to our cultural and ethnic background, which we develop through talk and interactions with others. Children are first socialized into cultural practices and ways of knowing the world in the home. Parents communicate messages to their children about their cultural heritage by engaging them in customs and traditions, talking about cultural history and events, and encouraging children to use their family's native language.[15] Positive ethnic and cultural identity promotes a sense of belonging and pride, and thus plays an important role in children's socioemotional development.[16] Furthermore, children who have a positive sense of cultural and ethnic identity have stronger family ties and cohesion.[17] A shared cultural background reinforces group membership, which people draw upon to understand their own sense of identity and place in society.[18]

One common way parents reinforce ethnic and cultural identity is through the use of cultural artifacts with their children. Traditionally, songs and stories were the primary means of sustaining customs, values, beliefs, and behaviors across generations. In modern times, books, radio, and television shows have been added to the artifacts used to reproduce social values and cultural traditions. More recently, video games have emerged as another cultural artifact that provides opportunities for making connections to one's cultural heritage. A good example is *Oregon Trail*, the first educational game designed for schoolchildren, which teaches players about the settlers who traveled westward in the nineteenth century. The goal of the game is for players to move from Missouri to Oregon and make decisions about food, supplies, and relationships along the way to survive the journey. This game, first published in 1974, reinforces American cultural values such as overcoming barriers, resilience, hard work, and patriotism. At the same time, the game also introduces cultural biases with respect to westward expansion and the concept of manifest destiny by portraying the relationship between the settlers and the Native Americans as amicable and excluding the experiences of African Americans and women on the trail.[19]

Of course, not all video games address cultural heritage, history, and values while introducing implicit or explicit biases against other cultures or social groups. Since *Oregon Trail*, there have been many video games designed around historical places and periods and the societies therein, allowing players to take on different roles as the protagonist in the story and experience culturally different ways of thinking and doing. One of these games is the turn-based strategy game series *Civilization*, first released in 1991, in which players represent the leader of a nation or ethnic group and must guide its growth over the course of thousands of years through diplomacy, advancing technology, strengthening the economy, and other means. Gabe and his son Luca (age thirteen), whom we discussed in chapter 3, played this game at one of our family gaming events. Below is the interaction we observed between them around choosing what civilization to play:

Gabe: Ooh, I want to be a . . . maybe a Viking. Go down more, son. Scroll, scroll . . .

Luca: No.

Gabe: . . . scroll, scroll.

Luca: Vikings have . . .

Gabe: Scroll, scroll, scroll, scroll.

Luca: Montezuma . . .

Gabe: Oh, the Aztecs.

Luca: The Aztecs? I like the Aztecs actually. Napoleon?

Gabe: No. I am short but not that short.

Luca: Short but not that short? (*Laughing*)

Gabe: I am not Napoleon. Ramses. Go down, son. Come on, kid.

Luca: Washington?

Gabe: George Washington. The Americans.

Luca: I'll be an American kid. All land military units.

Gabe: No, go down. Go, go, go . . . (*Nothing seems appealing.*). Let's go be the Aztecs, kid.

Luca and Gabe played first-person shooter video games such as *Black Ops 2* and *Modern Warfare 3* together regularly. They wanted to try *Civilization* because they had never played a turn-based strategy game before and wanted to explore this genre. The historical content of the game was also a feature that they really liked. Luca and Gabe negotiated different ways to project their collective identity in the game, and ultimately picked a civilization that reflected their Mexican heritage. While the game provided a couple of options, Luca was inclined to pick the Americans and project an aspect of his real-world identity onto the game by playing as an American kid. On the other hand, Gabe was excited to see the

Aztecs as an option in the beginning, and did not seem to be interested in other options as much as Luca was. Here, choosing a civilization to play became an opportunity for Gabe to connect with Luca around their Mexican heritage.

Not all video games provide opportunities for connections to one's ethnic and cultural background. Regardless of the content of a game, people can relate different aspects of the game to their cultural experiences and heritage. For instance, in our ethnographic study of Mexican American families, we found that playing the video game *FIFA Soccer* reinforced ethnic and cultural identity among parents and children, although the game is not intentionally designed to serve this purpose. Parents like Soledad Badillo (age thirty-four), a mother of three, viewed many of the video games her children played as not very educational with the exception of *FIFA Soccer*. Soledad, a stay-at-home mom who played in an amateur women's soccer league and practiced soccer once a week, loved to watch her boys play the video game when there were no soccer matches to watch on television. The family owned five television sets, one of which was located in the living room and had two game consoles hooked up to it. Most of the family's time in the living room was spent watching Mexican *telenovelas* (soap operas) and soccer matches together. At the time of our study, the entire family was immersed in watching the 2014 FIFA World Cup, which was taking place in Brazil.

Soccer is one of the most popular team sports worldwide, and it plays a pivotal role in Mexican culture.[20] Similar to how children in the United States start playing football and baseball at a young age, children in Mexico grow up playing soccer. The game is a source of national pride as Mexicans and other countries in Latin America have dominated the international soccer scene with famous soccer clubs and players and memorable soccer matches.[21] Mexico, which has never won but has always been among the favorites, has hosted the World Cup twice.[22] Mexicans identify themselves through their favorite teams, and their affinity for a team often stretches across generations. Soccer is associated with family time as watching soccer matches involves children, parents, grandparents, and relatives gathering around the television. The game also functions as a way for Mexican immigrants in the United States to organize and sustain social ties among themselves and connections to their home country and cultural heritage.[23]

Soledad believed that her children benefited greatly from playing *FIFA Soccer*. Her two sons Abel (age five) and Carlos (age six), who attended soccer practice once a week, played *FIFA Soccer* together while other family members, such as Soledad's husband and daughter Jocelyn (age eleven), watched them play the game. She described the game as "bonding time" both for the brothers and the entire family. She thought that the video game motivated her sons to play soccer, an activity that she and her husband valued deeply. During one of our home visits, Soledad mentioned that her children developed new skills and tactics from playing *FIFA Soccer*, and practiced the things that they learned in the game when they were outside. While she did not feel confident or comfortable with guiding her children around other games, Soledad watched her children play soccer in and outside of the game and supported her children's learning by facilitating the transition from gameplay to physical play.

Negotiating Individual and Family Identity

During adolescence, a growing sense of autonomy plays an important role in children's identity development.[24] Family relations undergo major transformations to accommodate the cognitive, behavioral, emotional, and social changes children go through during adolescence.[25] Adolescence is often marked by disagreements and conflict between parents and children, a dramatic decrease in time spent with family, and a lack of warmth and closeness.[26,27] Children also become more private and less likely to share experiences with their parents.[28] In our research, we found that intergenerational play around video games provides opportunities for the construction, negotiation, and enactment of family and individual identities in nonthreatening and playful ways between parents and adolescent children.

As we discussed in the previous chapter, parents and children learn together through taking the positions of "learner" and "teacher" and engaging in problem solving, strategic thinking, and collaboration. While many well-designed video games are conducive for supporting family learning, not all games engage adolescent children and their parents in identity play. Out of many video games we observed parents and children play, one game stood out as being more successful in creating opportunities for family conversations around the issues of identity than others. Interactions between parents and children around *The Sims*, the single-player simulation game in which players create and manage characters called "Sims" in a manner similar to real life, was by far the most revealing with respect to understanding how video games support identity construction and negotiation. In what follows, we share the experiences of three families who played the game at one of our family gaming events, and discuss how parents and children project their perceptions of each other and negotiate individual and family identities in the context of video games.

Samantha and Her Father

Samantha (age thirteen) attended our gaming event with her father, Bob. She had played *The Sims* previously with her friends and positioned herself as the "expert" during gameplay. Samantha's favorite aspect of the game was creating Sims. She wanted to be the first to create a character in the game so that her father could watch and learn from her. Samantha was meticulous in making sure her character looked as close to herself as possible, and took a fairly long time to create her character. Bob, who occasionally played *Angry Birds* on his phone, thought Samantha's attempt to create a character that looked identical to her was a waste of time. He wanted to "get on with the game" and perceived character creation as peripheral to their intergenerational play experience because it seemed to have no bearing on the actual gameplay. Yet Bob's demeanor quickly changed when Samantha moved from working on the physical attributes of her character, such as eye color, hair color, nose size, and lip shape, to representational attributes that had social meanings, such as clothing and makeup.

Samantha considered herself as a teenager in real life and chose to make her character a teenager in the game. She wanted her character to reflect who she wanted to be through her choice of clothing and makeup. Bob did not agree with Samantha's choice of having her character wear a bikini top with shorts. He protested when she put a low-cut T-shirt on her character. He also wanted Samantha to "go easy on the makeup." The negotiation between Samantha and Bob around clothing and makeup was playful throughout their interaction, with lots of laughter and teasing. Samantha's father knew the game was not real life, but he reacted to Samantha's choices of clothing and makeup as if they were real. His reaction did not create a conflict between the father and the daughter, however, nor did it have a negative impact on their interaction. What would have happened if Samantha wore a bikini top with shorts and makeup to meet her friends in real life? Samantha and Bob would probably have argued about what was "age appropriate." Instead, while playing *The Sims*, they negotiated their understanding through the symbolic meanings of their characters in the game. In this sense, playing video games created a safe environment for Bob to express his feelings and thoughts and for Samantha to test her father, learn about his perspective, and negotiate what was "appropriate."

Samantha cared about how her father represented himself in the game as much as he cared about how she represented herself in the game. When it was his turn, Bob wanted to create a character that had little resemblance to himself and did not want to spend the time to make his character look like him. Samantha protested her father's lack of interest in making his character "beautiful." The following interaction, while it took place around a game, captures how Samantha saw her father in real life:

Samantha: No, Dad, you're an adult. You're not an elder. Oh my gosh, Dad. You're not an elder! (*Both Samantha and her father laugh.*) You're not an elder yet. You look all gross and saggy. [My character] is beautiful. Dad, you are not fat. And you're not super thin either. Put a lot of muscle on you. That . . . that really makes you look weird! Dad, turn down the muscles. Dad . . . just . . . (*Laughs while her father makes his character really big.*) Dad, you're not that fat! Down, there you go. Keep it there.

Bob: OK, are you good?

Samantha: Now, you gotta turn down the muscle a little bit. It makes your legs look all weird. Okay, there we go. You look beautiful.

Members of a social group are interrelated in that one member's actions reflect back on the entire group, and vice versa. As a social group, families function similarly in that parents perceive the way their children conduct themselves as a reflection of their parenting and family values. At the same time, children care about how their parents carry and present themselves to the outside world, as they see their parents as a reflection of who they are in the world. Both Samantha and Bob shared how they wanted each other to be represented in the world while playing the game. The comments that they made about each other's characters revealed how they viewed each other in real life.

Mia and Her Mother

It was Mia's (age thirteen) and her mother's first time playing *The Sims*. Mia played games like *Diamond Dash* and *Mario Kart* with her brother at home. Her mother, Lourdes, however, did not play any type of game and saw our gaming event as an opportunity to learn more about games. Mia wanted to play *The Sims* because she heard about the game from her friends but never had a chance to play it. She positioned herself from the beginning as the "driver" of the gameplay. She took over the keyboard and mouse and controlled them the entire time. When the person sitting next to them asked what they were doing, Mia responded by saying they were playing *The Sims*. Her mother laughed and said, "Pretending to play because [children] don't let you. She needs to show me how to play." Although she was disappointed about not being able to experiment with the controls herself, Lourdes was engaged with playing the game with her daughter throughout the event.

Unlike Samantha and her father, Mia took advantage of the opportunity to experiment with different representations of herself. For example, she picked green eyes for her character, causing her mother to protest, "You don't have green eyes." When Mia picked out a jacket for her character, Lourdes protested again, revealing her perceptions of gender-appropriate attire by saying, "Those are for boys." Lourdes was eager for Mia to finish creating her character in the game. She kept asking Mia, "Is it time to do mine?" When Mia began to create her mother's character, Mia tried hard to make sure the character looked like her mother. At the same time, she took the opportunity to engage in gentle and affectionate teasing, also known as prosocial teasing:[29]

Mia: I love doing this now. Is that how you do your hair?

Lourdes: Like that.

Mia: Like that? It looks pretty. Aw, that's so cool.

Lourdes: Leave it like that. What is that, a tattoo?

Mia: Yup, OK, OK, wrong character.

Lourdes: No! (*Laughs*)

Mia: Oh, come on! (*Laughs*)

Lourdes: Come on, no no no! I don't have tattoos. Take off the tattoo. Let me see what kind of pants I want.

While teasing is often associated with harassment and bullying, it can take on beneficial forms in hierarchical and intimate relations such as those between parents and children. Prosocial teasing allows family members to enhance their bonds through indirect expression of affection, shared laughter, and the message that the act of teasing communicates.[30] Family members learn about, negotiate, and assume social identities through teasing that is playful and positive. Prosocial teasing promotes a sense of closeness and affinity between parents and children.[31] Mia could have manipulated any physical feature of her mother's character, but she chose to put a tattoo—something that has cultural and generational meanings—on a character that was supposed to represent her mother. By so doing, Mia gently parodied traditions, established social norms, and the generational gap between herself and her mother.

This type of identity play was common among families playing *The Sims*. Parents and children would intentionally manipulate a physical aspect of the character that represented different developmental stages and social meanings attached to them. For instance, another mother created her eleven-year-old daughter's character as a child, but then enlarged its breasts to tease her daughter about growing up. Prosocial teasing almost always elicited protest from the person who was being teased and was followed by laughter from both the teaser and the teased. Mia and her mother were no exception. When we asked them what they liked about playing together and what their favorite part of the experience was, Mia wrote: "I enjoyed hearing her laugh. She enjoyed [*sic*] because I laughed a lot. I would play with my mom again because I want to be able to hear her laugh and have a good time. She would do it again because she wants to spend time with me. We learned how to work together and communicate with each other."

Tomas and His Mother

Tomas (age twelve), the only child in his family, played first-person shooter video games like *Halo* with his father and card games with his mother at home. His mother, Theresa, worked as a program coordinator at the school where our gaming event was held. His father worked as a plumber forty or more hours per week. Theresa played *Candy Crush* and *Tetris* on her phone during her spare time, and did not play video games with Tomas at home. At the same time, she enjoyed playing card, board, and puzzle games, as well as simulation-strategy games. Theresa's interest in playing simulation-strategy games drew her to *The Sims*. Tomas had some experience with playing *The Sims*, so when his mother suggested that they play the game together, he agreed.

Tomas and Theresa decided to create each other's characters in the game. Tomas wanted to go first and his mother happily agreed because she saw this as an opportunity for her to learn how the keyboard and game interface worked. Tomas quickly put together a character that physically resembled his mother, without any objection from her—that is, until he started choosing the skills and psychological attributes of his mother's character:

Tomas: (*Chooses "absent minded" from the drop-down menu.*) That is *you*.
Theresa: Whatever.

Tomas: Absent minded. How is that not you? You don't love to throw parties!

Theresa: I'm clumsy.

Tomas: Yes, you are. You are easily impressed.

Theresa: Yes, you too.

Choosing the attributes of his mother's character allowed Tomas to express his perceptions of his mother as a person. Theresa took advantage of what was shared by her son to transform the moment of Tomas positioning her as "an absent-minded person" to positioning them as "we are easily impressed people." By so doing, Theresa reinforced the familial bond that they shared while subverting Tomas' claim about the kind of person she was. When it was Theresa's turn to create and pick attributes for Tomas's character, she started by choosing "absent minded," continuing their conversation about being the same type of person:

Theresa: (*Chooses "absent minded" from the drop-down menu*) Absent minded.

Tomas: I am not absent minded!

Theresa: Yes, you are.

Tomas: Not as bad as you are!

Theresa: You are just like me, so . . .

Tomas: Well then, give me clumsy.

Theresa: You are exactly like me . . . couch potato . . .

Tomas: I am not a couch potato!

Tomas negotiated his own individual and family identity by protesting and then acknowledging that he is absent minded like his mother, while at the same time positioning himself as being different by reminding his mother that he is not as bad as she is. Later in his interactions with his mother around the game, Tomas used character attributes as a way to express who he was in the world beyond the context of his family. Children participate in multiple communities in home, school, and after-school settings at any given time in their everyday lives.[32] Although parents may know which activities children engage in across different communities, they may not be aware of the different identities children take on within communities outside of home. Here's an example of how Tomas saw himself in the context of school:

Tomas: Flirty. Flirty. Look at me at school.

Theresa: Flirty? Really? Okay, whatever. Okay, done.

Tomas: Wait, change . . .

Theresa: What? Physical?

Tomas: Athletic.

Theresa: No, you're not.

Tomas: I am very athletic. Social.

Tomas probably would have not shared the identities he took on within his school community with his mother in his everyday life. However, while playing *The Sims* with her, Tomas shared things about himself as part of the natural flow of gameplay. While the moments of negotiation around individual and family identity may seem on the cusp of being oppositional or even contentious, they were productive in revealing perceptions, views, and understandings of family members. As with many other families, the intergenerational play experience was positive for Theresa and Tomas. Theresa wrote on the exit survey: "We had fun. We created each other and built a dream house! I liked decorating [the house] and deciding what it would look like. I would play this game with Tomas at home because we talked and spent time together. The most favorite part of playing the game was probably thinking and sharing together." And Tomas said: "It was really fun playing with my mom. We had to make our home, create each other and I very well enjoyed it. My favorite part was creating her character as I saw her, and it was the same with her creating me."

Building a House Together

In her renowned book, *Critical Play*, Mary Flanagan describes *The Sims* as a "doll house" that represents the external realities of a capitalist worldview, consumer culture, suburban lifestyle, and domestic sphere that is historically associated with women, and thus is a vehicle for reproducing traditional family roles and social realities.[33] While the game certainly is built upon and reinforces economic, political, and ideological models, parents and children subvert these models when they play the game together. Across the three cases we shared above, the process of building a house together meant that parents and children took on different expert identities: children as experts of the controls and game mechanics, and parents as experts of domestic life. Both identities were legitimate and coexisted for parents and children around the task of building a house together. Negotiations over differences in opinion about how to go about building a house took place in the service of accomplishing the shared goal of building a house for "us."

As they positioned themselves and were positioned by their parents as the experts on game mechanics, the children learned new skills that they could contribute to building a house for their family. For instance, Tomas learned a cheat code called "motherlode" that allowed players to obtain unlimited amounts of money (called "Simoleons" in the game) so that he and his mother could design their "dream house." This was important to Tomas, who later wrote about his play experience with his mother: "I learned about all of her dreams in a house and how she would do it if she had the money and how I want my house." Mia, meanwhile, learned to use the sledgehammer tool so that she and her mother could rearrange the walls of their house.

Despite differences in their socioeconomic and cultural backgrounds, all parents positioned themselves and were positioned by their children as the experts of domestic life. When it was time to build a home, parents encouraged their children to consider the cost of purchasing a lot for their house, building the structure of the house, and populating it with objects (e.g., beds, couch, table, television). Children, perhaps buying into the capitalist worldview and consumer culture represented in the game, initially wanted to purchase houses that were closer to the beach and more expensive. Parents expressed budgetary concerns through making jokes about how they were going to pay the mortgage and reminding their children that they need to reserve enough money for actually building the house and covering other costs of living. In all three cases, families eventually opted for a cheaper house.

Parents also provided guidance on how to lay out the rooms in the house. For instance, they suggested putting the kitchen, living room, and dining room closer to each other while moving the bedrooms to the back of the house. Likely to have more experience with choosing and moving into houses in real life, parents focused on the efficiency of the overall home design rather than the size of each room, something that children privileged over design. Children also designed houses without hallways, making it difficult for characters to move around. Parents kept reminding their children that they needed to leave space for hallways in their design. Overall, families projected their own identities and ways of thinking onto the virtual world while reinforcing their own values, rather than simply buying into the values reflected in the game. Playing *The Sims* became not so much about mindlessly buying into a capitalist worldview but rather an opportunity for sharing ideas about how to live in the real world.

Making Sense of the World through Gaming

Parents—mothers in particular—across the different studies we conducted reported the content of games their children play as one of the barriers to intergenerational play. Other barriers included their clumsiness with the controller and a lack of time to play games. Parents found the content of most games their children played unappealing and did not see the relevance of game story lines to their personal and family lives. Even though parents expressed an interest in playing video games with their children, they struggled to get past the content of the games and quickly stopped playing after a few trials. Here's how Sarah described why she did not play video games at home with her son, Justin:

With other games, like, they play a game where they build empires or blow stuff up . . . I have no interest in that. To be drawn into that and sit next to them . . . I will be bored really easily. And if I wanted to play, for him to sit down with me would be boring for him because my choices and interests are different.

Many parents faced the challenge of finding video games that were mutually enjoyable and challenging for them and their children. Furthermore, they expressed a preference for playing video games that addressed the real-world issues they cared about. Console games such as *Wii Sports*, *Just Dance*, and *Family Game Night* that are traditionally marketed as "family friendly" did not satisfy this desire. As one parent pointed out, such games were great for spending fun time together as a family but did not prompt family members to engage with one another or have meaningful conversations.

Parents are not alone in wanting to play video games for reasons beyond being entertained. In the last decade or so, there has been a growing interest in designing and playing "serious games."[34] This genre of digital games aims to primarily engage, educate, and inform players around real-world issues rather than entertain them. That is not to say that serious games are not entertaining or that games have never had a serious purpose. For instance, the impetus for the design of the widely popular board game *Monopoly* was to demonstrate the lucrative business of renting for landowners and its negative impact on those who rent properties. While the idea of serious games is not new, it has recently been adopted more widely within the gaming community and across different sectors such as education, business, military, journalism, and health as an alternative to mainstream entertainment gaming that is dominated by large software developers such as Electronic Arts, Nintendo, Sony, Activision, and Ubisoft. Serious games address a wide range of social, economic, and political issues to catalyze change in the world for better educational and social outcomes.

Many parents are unaware of serious games available across different platforms because their children tend not to play them. It is also hard for parents to find these games because there is no organized sector of serious games or game designers who focus specifically on games designed for families to play together. For parents to find serious games that address real-world issues, they need to locate the right online resources, read a lot of game reviews, and find games that address a social, economic, or political problem. Even if they find a game that they want to play with their children, they may not have access to the right platform. When parents do play a serious game with their children, however, it can be a powerful opportunity to collaboratively make sense of real-world issues.

The Family Quest project was inspired by the need for a collection of games that intentionally engage families in meaningful play and collaboration in a virtual world. As part of this project, parents and children (ages nine to thirteen) played role-playing games that immerse players in scenarios relevant to their lives. For instance, in one game, parents and children assumed the role of the friend of a nonplayer character, Susie, who is conflicted about her experiences with Linser, another student at the same school. Susie solicits the help of the players in determining whether Linser, who has been teasing and making comments about Susie to their mutual friends, is bullying her. Parents and children playing as Susie's friend must talk to different people in the school to gather information about the situation and decide if it is indeed bullying. The game offers possible actions that parents and children can take based on their decision, and provides feedback so parents and children experience the consequences or impact of their action on Susie and Linser.

This game, despite its simplistic mechanics, created what Edward Castronova calls a "synthetic world," where virtual and real-world experiences cross over and blend.[35] Extending Huizinga's term "magic circle," which refers to the "separate world" games create around those who play them, Castronova argues that there is a transactional relationship between the game and the real world. For instance, Olivia (age twelve) played the game with her mother and decided that Linser was bullying Susie. She concluded that causing someone emotional harm is a form of bullying. On the other hand, her younger brother, Cameron (age ten), who played the game with his father, decided that Linser was not bullying because there was no evidence of physical harm. Following their gameplay, a "teachable moment" occurred while Cameron and his father were driving back home. Cameron

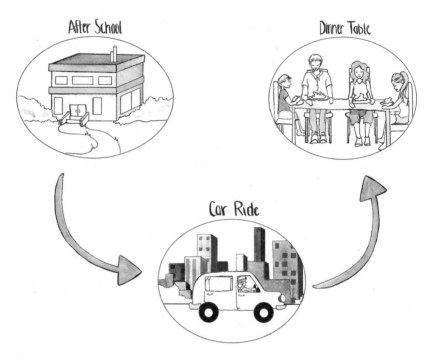

Figure 4.2
Learning around games across contexts

got upset when his father teased him about something during the car ride, to which his father responded, "Am I bullying you?" According to his father, Cameron had a "light bulb" experience when he found himself in a situation similar to Susie's and understood how a person can hurt someone with words. When the pair went home, the whole family engaged in a discussion at the dinner table in which Cameron and Olivia each shared the decisions they made in the game and described how and why bullying can be both physical and verbal. According to Cameron's mother, this was a transformative experience for Cameron because he developed an appreciation of how teasing can sometimes be bullying without being confronted with this concept in the real world, where he might have become defensive had he been the one doing the teasing. Here, the gameplay experience spilled over into the real world and stretched across the context of the after-school gameplay session, the car ride, and the home (see figure 4.2).

Situated within the boundaries of real and virtual, the game also created a magic circle within which children shared their real-world experiences of bullying at their own school. In the beginning of the game, parents and children were prompted by Susie to share their own experiences to help her make sense of her own situation. This was a learning experience for many parents who reported that ordinarily their children were reluctant to talk about bullying but did not mind sharing as part of the game. Here's an excerpt from a parent who described the experience:

The bullying [game] opened up something. I didn't even know how he was getting bullied at school . . . it's not huge, but what his comment was . . . well, we each wrote our experiences, mine in school and his, and there was something I didn't even know. So, I learned something. I mean, I kind of knew about it, but it was the first time he said anything. He actually didn't want me to know about it. But I shared mine and so you [Victor] share yours.

While playing the game, children shared their experiences as a means to move forward in the game. They were neither asked directly by their parents about their experiences with bullying at school nor were they confronted with a bullying situation themselves in the game—it was Susie who was potentially being bullied by Linser. There was a distance between the situation and the children's personal experiences in the sense that the children were immersed in a fictional context. Within this fictional context (inside the magic circle), sharing one's real-world bullying experiences took on a different meaning than in the real world. Linda, Victor's mother, described the difference between talking about bullying with Victor in the real world and around the game as follows:

So, if I were at home and said, "Hey, have you been bullied before?" he probably would say "no" because he wouldn't want to talk about it. Having the game up and having us think about it got him to at least confirm that he's been bullied before. Unfortunately, he wouldn't talk more about it. It's typical about him but it was good because . . . it was a better thing to get him to talk about it. [The game] opens up a dialogue that might not open because it is awkward or there is not an opportunity. Normally, you try to talk about it but when it comes up in a game, it's organic . . . Well, when it comes up in our family, it is organic, too. But it is uncomfortable, like, let's say if he gets bullied by another kid. He comes home and he is in a bad mood. It may not be the best time to talk about it . . . you know . . . because he is all upset and he is not in a learning place. But, when he is playing the game, he is in a learning place and he is going to take in that knowledge. He might not when he is right in the middle of the situation.

The magic circle, which involves a sense of escape from the real world, can be transformative for those who play games—including families. The fictional world helps us to distance ourselves from the real world while at the same time allowing us to make sense of our own experiences and question our understanding of who we are in the real world. Video gaming is a powerful means for families to engage in identity experimentation, negotiation, construction, and conversations around real-world issues that are difficult to discuss in the real world. This is because games are not only interactive, meaning through an interface the players take actions and the technology responds to these actions, but also transactive.

What we mean by transactive is that, when playing video games together, parents and children interact not only with the game but also with each other. Their interaction involves not just the particulars of game design components, such as where to move the avatar in the space, where to click, or how to advance in the game, but also making meaning of real-world issues and understandings. The temporal space families occupy through play is neither real nor unreal. Families bring their outside experiences organically into their game experience while their experiences in the game help families to develop individual and shared understandings, values, and norms related to the real world.

Bidirectional Socialization

For many years, researchers conceptualized parent-child interaction with media, such as television and books, as a socialization process through which families create shared understandings and provide a frame of reference for children to make sense of and interpret other situations, problems, activities, and communities outside of a family context.[36] This conceptualization assumes a unidirectional relationship between parents and children; that is, parents socialize their children into thinking, believing, and behaving in certain ways. Parents transmit their own values, attitudes, and behaviors to their children. They also model and construct what is acceptable for their children and ensure continuity across generations. The idiom "the apple doesn't fall far from the tree" perhaps best captures this view of socialization.

However, more recently, drawing upon the sociocultural theory of learning (discussed in chapter 3), researchers have introduced terms such as *social coviewing* and *participatory learning* to highlight the bidirectional nature of socialization around media.[37] Research on socialization more broadly has recognized that both parents and children are social agents in making sense of information and experiences in the world. Children do not mindlessly absorb their parents' values, behaviors, or beliefs but actively construct their own understandings. Furthermore, they do not just accept but also resist values, norms, beliefs, and behaviors that are implicitly or explicitly communicated or imposed by their parents, community members, and society more broadly. Therefore, intergenerational continuity actually involves change and resistance. As much as parents influence their children, children influence their parents in making sense of the world. Parents and children are active agents that change over time. They generate new understandings individually and together as a collective unit through different experiences.

Out of many different media that families use, the bidirectional socialization between parents and children is perhaps most evident around video games. As we saw in chapter 2, parents who have a history of playing video games introduce the activity to their young children. Although children share the interest of their parents, they also create their own preferences, practices, routines, and rituals around that interest. At the same time, as we discussed in this chapter, children who are more skilled with video games socialize their parents by helping them develop an understanding of what to do and how to behave in the game. Fundamentally, parents and children socialize each other while playing video games as they simultaneously take on different expert-novice roles and connect their gameplay with real-world experiences.

Conclusion

Shared activities such as eating dinner, visiting museums, and reading together as a family play a key role in supporting positive family relations because they create opportunities for connection, communication, and learning. Families build closer relations and intimacy when they spend time together around shared activities. Furthermore, family members exchange ideas and perspectives with one another as they try to make sense of the information in their environment. The time spent together around shared activities later becomes memories that families refer back to when facing new events, experiences, and situations. For instance, families can engage in an impromptu conversation about what friendship means while reading the book *Charlotte's Web* together. This can be an experience that family members remember when trying to make sense of a conflict with a friend later on. Families create a shared understanding, history, and social identity through the activities they do together. Individual family members also develop their own sense of identity as they negotiate different beliefs, norms, and values with one another. Similar to other unplugged family activities, intergenerational play around video games also provides a rich context for constructing and negotiating individual as well as family identities.

Sitting in between reality and fantasy, video games create situations that are similar to the real world yet distant enough to allow people to safely talk about their feelings and share their thoughts, perspectives, and understandings. In this sense, video games create a safe space where people can emotionally distance themselves from real-world experiences but consider these experiences from a different vantage point. This aspect of video games is quite powerful for families, especially during a time when children go through cognitive, social, and emotional changes as they transition into adolescence. Children, like adults, can easily feel attacked, uncomfortable, or even insecure when confronted by their parents about difficult situations. Furthermore, as one parent pointed out, children are not always in an emotional state that allows them to be receptive to other perspectives, let alone their parents' perspective, when facing problems, challenges, or conflicts. However, when families play through challenges in a game context, the situation takes place in a fictional world. They make sense of the fictional situation not just through their real-world identities or through the roles they play in the virtual world but through the blend of their real and virtual identities (projective identity).

Unlike other experiences, such as reading a book or visiting a museum, video games provide feedback to families about their actions due to the interactive nature of video games as a medium. This feedback allows families to reflect on their actions and the meaning of those actions both in and outside of the game. Families need to make decisions while playing video games. These decisions have consequences in the fictional world in the sense that the game will unfold differently depending on the decisions made. At the same time, these decisions have meanings outside of the fictional world as they signify who family members are individually and as a collective in the real world. As we saw with *The Sims*, an action as simple as putting shorts, a tattoo, or a hairstyle on a virtual character creates an opportunity space for families to negotiate norms, values, and different ways of being in the world. Similarly, when families decide to buy a cheaper property or live away from the beach in the virtual city of Sunset Valley, they are making strategic decisions in the game about how to spend their money (a limited resource) and identity claims about who they are as people; that is, "We are the kind of people who spend their money wisely."

Last, we introduced the concept of bidirectional socialization to emphasize the active role that children as well as adults can assume in this process of negotiating individual and collective identities. Intergenerational video game play can provide opportunities for children and parents to share the roles of novice and expert and learn together about who they are and who they want to be as individuals and as families. In the next chapter, we take a closer look at the nature of family learning in the context of video game play.

5

Developing a Learning Culture through Gaming

My bottom line was that parents should recognize the need to build new kinds of relationships with their children and should see the computer as a vehicle for building, rather than as an obstacle to, family cohesion. Parents should spend less time worrying about what the kids are doing or are not doing with computers and more time trying to find common interests or projects to do together.

These are the words of Seymour Papert in his book *The Connected Family: Bringing the Digital Generation Gap*, published in 1996.[1] As a visionary, prominent scholar, and prolific writer, Papert has had a great influence on our thinking about children, computing, and learning. He is primarily known for his design and study of the LOGO programming language for children and for his learning theory, *constructionism*. Expanding Jean Piaget's constructivist theory of learning, which suggests children learn through building internal mental models (or representations) of their experiences in the world, Papert argues that children also build these models through making public artifacts or tangible objects, ranging from sand castles to video games.[2] He introduces programming as a tool for children to develop mathematical thinking in the process of creating meaningful products that are visible to others.

What is less known about Papert are the ideas he introduced in *The Connected Family* about the relationship between families and technology, ideas that were ahead of their time. In this chapter, we revisit his work because we believe his ideas are relevant to the discussion of families and video games, and yet to be realized in our society. Specifically, we discuss the concept of a *family learning culture* and how it applies to understanding the role of video games in family life. We describe how the traditional expert-novice relationship between parents and children has dramatically changed over the last decade, with children taking on the role of expert when it comes to technology. We propose that, for children, successful participation in the twenty-first century starts with intergenerational play experiences at home around technology, and video gaming in particular can be a promising context for parents and children to work as collaborative partners and develop skills that can transfer to other contexts (such as the workplace). Finally, we discuss four different forms of family engagement with video games that we believe support the formation and cultivation of a family learning culture at home.

Family Learning Culture

Traditionally, parents are positioned as "guides" when it comes to children's use of technology and are viewed as playing a key role in cultivating children's interests and learning around technology. However, Papert suggests that children's enthusiasm for and interest in computers can be a basis not only for children's learning but also for a family learning culture, shifting the focus of technology's potential from the individual child to the family as a unit. He defines family learning culture as "a family's way of thinking about learning—its beliefs, preferred activities and traditions associated with learning."[3] A family learning culture is based on mutual respect and family members' understanding of shared ideas and norms as well as divergences and disagreements.

"The relationship between the computer and the family learning culture is a two-way street," says Papert.[4] The family learning culture influences how computers are used at home, and computer use has an impact on the family learning culture. The different ways families approach computers can amplify or undermine learning for all family members. Papert argues that parents already use strategies to support and help a family learning culture grow around movies and books. These strategies include consuming and talking about these media together with their children, as well as expressing appreciation for and criticizing them. He observes that it has been more challenging for parents to implement this breadth of strategies around computers, and there has been more resistance and critique from parents around computers than acceptance and participation. In the more than twenty years since Papert's book was published, parental attitudes toward computers have become more accepting, but his advice about incorporating new technologies into a family learning culture remains relevant.

Papert sees breaking away from traditional conceptions of parental roles as a key aspect of forming and maintaining a family learning culture. He states: "One thing I've been saying over and over again is that parents should learn from their kids. Of course kids should learn from parents. I say this less often because everyone knows that. But the point is that it goes both ways."[5] Indeed, parents' roles as "teachers" and "experts" have been a primary area of research in psychology, learning sciences, and education. We know that parents support their children's learning in a wide variety of ways. They provide emotional support to their children around difficult tasks in the form of encouragement and praise, which greatly contributes to children's sense of competence and confidence.[6] They use prompts, questions, and hints to guide their children's thinking around problem-solving tasks to help them become independent problem solvers and self-guided learners.[7] Parents model ways of thinking and doing through providing explanations, setting goals, and monitoring progress around shared activities.[8] They also support their children's learning through brokering learning experiences for their children.[9] Involving their children in school and after-school activities and acquiring material resources that they believe will enhance their children's learning, such as books and computers, are only a few examples of the support parents provide to their children. Research suggests that parental engagement and support during the early years and beyond contributes greatly to children's academic success in school and their positive socioemotional development.[10] Through a variety of strategies, parents help children develop knowledge, dispositions, and habits that are foundational to children's future learning and participation in society.

Parents play a crucial role as their children's first teachers. However, defining family interactions and their relation to learning solely through this lens is limiting in the twenty-first century. Such conceptualizations ignore the dynamic and evolving nature of family relations over time, as well as the societal and material conditions that shape and influence these relations. What do we mean by this? We often forget that parents do not stop learning once they have children; they continue to grow, learn, and evolve as individuals, and parenting in particular provides many opportunities for learning. When taking on the role of teacher, parents also learn about themselves and their children during their interactions. In addition, children develop more complex cognitive skills as they grow older that allow them to participate more competently in adult tasks such as cooking, competitive sports, and so forth. For example, a child who is interested in cooking might first participate in this task by watching his mother cook. By the time he is seven years old, he starts helping his mother cook by taking on simpler aspects of the task under her guidance, such as measuring ingredients. And when he is thirteen, he is able to cook a meal for the entire family by himself, at which point the parent and the child may participate in cooking as colearners. The child might discover a new recipe or cooking technique that he in turn can share with his mother, adding to her repertoire of cooking knowledge and skills.

Furthermore, children develop interests and expertise at an early age in domains that are different from those of their parents. For instance, a child who is interested in dinosaurs at the age of four may develop her expertise through playing with dinosaur toys, visiting museums with her parents, having books about dinosaurs read to her, and watching television shows about dinosaurs. As she grows older her sustained interest in dinosaurs motivates her to read books about dinosaurs on her own, research dinosaurs online, and do school projects about dinosaurs. By the time she is nine years old, she is more knowledgeable about the topic of dinosaurs than her parents are; they have supported their daughter's interest throughout the years but are not necessarily invested in developing their own expertise about dinosaurs. When scientists announce the discovery of a new type of dinosaur, the daughter may be the one who explains the significance of this discovery to her parents.

In addition to these developmental and domain-related trends that make the expert-novice roles between parents and children more fluid than we would normally think, the social and material conditions of families' lives also challenge the construction of parents as more knowledgeable than others in the family. In many immigrant households in the United States in which parents speak a language other than English, children support their parents in navigating the difficulties of living in a new country.[11] Children tend to acquire language proficiency in English and adopt American cultural norms much more quickly than their parents do. They often mediate their parents' experiences through interpretation and translation. For instance, children translate documents from school for their parents, help them navigate legal and medical issues, and provide care for their younger siblings.[12]

Likewise, Papert notes that the entry of computers and game consoles into family homes may disrupt traditional parental roles if children become more adept and dexterous than their parents at using technology. These technologies have different affordances than television, namely interactivity and connectivity, and they influence expert-novice relationships between parents and children in different ways. Our assumptions about children's cognitive abilities are also challenged by children's creative ways of using these technologies. Just because children are more adept does not mean that they have nothing to learn from their parents while using these technologies. In fact, the widespread availability of computers and game consoles presents exciting new opportunities for family connection, communication, and learning that come about with the changing and dynamic nature of parent-child relations that have the potential to benefit all family members in the twenty-first century.

The Twenty-First-Century Landscape

Developing a family learning culture is increasingly important to the success and well-being of children and adults in the twenty-first century. The current workforce landscape looks drastically different from what it looked like twenty years ago. Today, employers are looking to hire people with "soft skills," which include interpersonal and communication skills, as well as personal traits such as adaptability and self-motivation.[13] They rank the ability to learn new things, critical thinking, and problem solving as top competencies in their employees. By the same token, the ability to effectively collaborate with others is increasingly becoming a necessary skill for success in the workplace. In a digital, networked, and constantly changing world, expertise is distributed across time, places, people, and tools.[14] The ability to exchange ideas, knowledge, and resources with others is fundamental to utilizing our collective intelligence for innovation and solving the complex problems our society faces.[15]

A diverse workplace includes employees from several generations—baby boomers, Generation X-ers, and Millennials—each bringing drastically different experiences with technology to the job. Many have written and commented on the changing dynamics in the workplace as Millennials entered the workforce.[16] The different expectations, values, and styles each generation brings to the workplace can be an asset as well as a challenge when employees struggle to effectively communicate and collaborate. The rigid corporate hierarchies created by baby boomers are breaking down, and in some workplaces they no longer exist.[17] In today's workplace, a thirty-year-old managing a forty-five-year-old employee is not uncommon. Furthermore, in today's multigenerational workforce, the Millennials have an advantage over previous generations with respect to the high demand for workers with technology skills. Beyond generational differences in approaches to work, the workplace has changed in the last two decades as a result of globalization, advancement in technology, and the emergence of new organizational models created to drive innovation and sustain the competitive edge of the United States.[18]

While the adults who are currently in the workforce are learning to adapt to these changes, schools are trying to find ways to support children in developing the skills to successfully participate in the twenty-first-century workforce. Schools emphasize problem solving, critical thinking, collaboration, and strategic thinking—collectively referred to as "twenty-first-century skills" in education—as much as, if not more than, content learning.[19] The skills that adults need to exercise in the workplace are the same skills that children are expected to develop in schools. According to Douglas Thomas and John Seely Brown, the twenty-first century is about learning to embrace change and figuring out how to get most out of it.[20] They suggest that both adults and children can use play as a strategy for dealing with change and adapting to the new demands of the world. The constantly changing world has also resulted in a new culture of learning that Thomas and Brown describe as embedded in everyday social interactions in communities, intertwined with the identities people develop, driven by shared interests and passions, and propelled by digital media technologies.

We believe play is an important aspect of cultivating a family learning culture. While there are many forms of play involving digital media, video games are an especially powerful medium that families can leverage to develop skills that are valued in the twenty-first century. The successful participation of adults and children in the new learning culture starts with the creation of a family learning culture around digital media at home. As we have discussed in previous chapters, families exchange ideas, collaborate, solve problems, negotiate identities, share interests, and learn from each other through intergenerational play around video games. All of these skills that families build around video games resemble what parents would do at work and children would do in schools. Social interactions around video games among family members at home can be a vehicle for both parents and children to deal with change and develop skills that are important in the twenty-first century.

Families as Communities of Practice

Although as a society we have begun to reimagine the workplace, schools, and learning as a result of the rapid changes we are experiencing in the twenty-first century, we have yet to do the same with respect to how we think about families in the digital age. One obstacle we foresee in developing a family learning culture that is aligned with the demands of today's society is the traditional notion of parent-child relations, in which expertise is attributed to and conceptualized as the domain of parents. As Papert pointed out two decades ago, parents have just as much to learn from their children as children have to learn from their parents. This could not be truer in this day and age, when children are the ones keeping up with constantly changing technology and using it to learn, connect, and collaborate with others. We believe a better conceptualization of the expert-novice relations between parents and children in the twenty-first century is through the lens of *communities of practice* (CoP).

In their book *Situated Learning*, Jean Lave and Étienne Wenger propose that learning is a process of moving from being a newcomer to an old-timer in a community of practice.[21] They describe a community of practice as "a set of relations among persons, activity, and world, over time and in relation with other tangential and overlapping communities of practice," suggesting that we belong to multiple communities at home, school, and work at any given time.[22] Our membership and participation may vary across different communities of practice. For instance, we might be a new-comer in one community and a central member in another. Communities of practice share three qualities: (1) members of the community engage in a joint enterprise, meaning the relationships between the members of a community are organized around shared activities in which they participate; (2) members share a social (or group) identity as members belonging to a community; and (3) there is a shared repertoire of communal resources, including routines, rituals, artifacts, vocabulary, and styles that members have developed over time. Overall, members of a community of practice share ways of doing, thinking, and approaching things in the world.

The CoP framework has been used in schools, corporations, and non-profits to facilitate collaboration, learning, and organizational change.[23] People in many different work settings collaborate with one another to achieve a set of shared goals. However, what separates the formal team or group work that takes place in many organizations from a community of practice is that while team members disperse and move on to other problems once a task or a project is completed, a community of practice is sustained over time around a shared interest, enterprise, or passion. Another difference is that people who belong to a community of practice are self-selected, while those who work in teams typically are assigned or obligated to work in a group as a job requirement. The focus in a community of practice is on learning together, advancing individual and group capabilities, and improving a practice or domain, not merely completing a task.[24] For instance, language arts teachers who are required by the school principal or district to participate in monthly professional development workshops do not comprise a community of practice. However, language arts teachers who get together three times a week during lunch to exchange ideas, resources, and best practices and reflect on how to improve their teaching make a community of practice.

Scholars also use the CoP framework to understand player interactions in multiplayer online games and virtual worlds, such as *World of Warcraft*.[25],[26] Players are often introduced to the game—either by watching someone else play or through an invitation to play with someone they know—as a "legitimate peripheral participant," to use Lave and Wenger's term. Often, an experienced player in the virtual world takes the beginner player under their wing, which may take the form of showing the player around, taking over difficult tasks, and modeling actions in the virtual world. We saw this happen with Carol Morgan, the single mother of two interviewed in chapter 2. She started playing *WoW* with her friends and colleagues who introduced her to the game, and later she taught her son, Alex, how to play, helping him develop expertise by structuring his participation in the game.

As players spend more time in the game, they slowly learn how to manage resources (money, gear, spells, etc.) and better perform their role when collaborating with other players to accomplish a shared goal. For instance, when a beginner plays as a healer, they might struggle to figure out when and how to heal other players during a battle, but over time become more effective in their role as the healer and better coordinate with others during battles. The process of evolving from a legitimate peripheral participant into a full participant in the community involves players developing their identities, understandings, and competencies as members of the community.[27]

A marker of learning is a player's ability to assume more central roles in the community. As players develop expertise, they become mentors for others who are newcomers to the community. They also take on leadership roles such as becoming leader of a guild (a group of players that play together), engaging in combat against other players (as opposed to fighting against nonplayer characters programmed by the game), and organizing raids (groups of players working together to defeat a powerful enemy). These roles require not only the ability to play competently but also the ability to monitor and provide guidance to others for the group to succeed as a collective—qualities of an expert player or a full participant in the community. These are some of the practices followed and roles assumed by Alex Morgan when playing as his level 100 character in *WoW*.

Families "with their own practices, routines, rituals, artifacts, symbols, conventions, stories, and histories" are one of the most important communities of practice in which children participate.[28] Family members as a community share a social identity that gives them a sense of belonging and pride in being a participant in the group. Fundamentally, it is love and caring toward one another that unites family members and supports a group identity that the individual members draw their own identities from. Relationships between family members are organized around shared activities, routines, and rituals such as eating, doing household chores, watching television, shopping, vacationing, and playing video games. During these shared everyday activities, family members interact with one another and learn together.

The interactions among family members around video games in the Perez household demonstrate how families are communities of practice. Members of the Perez family participated in all kinds of shared activities around video games: they watched each other play video games, played video games together, talked about games, and searched online for information about different games. Felipe was a central participant in the community because of his knowledge and expertise as well as the roles and responsibilities he assumed in the community around video games. Amelia, the youngest child of the family, was a legitimate peripheral participant in the community. Her knowledge and skills were those of a novice gamer compared to her father and her brothers. In the Perez family, expertise around video games was passed from one generation to the next, with Felipe Perez, the father, modeling ways of thinking and learning around video games to his eldest son, Daniel, who then modeled it for his siblings. For example, Daniel introduced the game *Wizard 101* and *Minecraft* to Matias, and they frequently played these games together until Daniel moved on to playing more complex games with his father. Amelia then began playing these games with Matias, who had more expertise with these games than she did.

A difference between families and other communities of practice is that while membership is informal and self-selected in other communities, children's participation in the family is not voluntary. Although they can choose how and when to participate when they become adults, children are born into the family community. Another potential point of divergence is that typically communities of practice are organized around one primary joint endeavor or domain. Schools are communities of practice organized around the shared endeavor of supporting the education of children. A field of study can also be conceptualized as a community of practice in which people are organized around the endeavor of generating knowledge in a domain, such as medicine, philosophy, engineering, or the humanities. *World of Warcraft* players comprise a community of practice when their gameplay is organized around shared language, practices, tools, and histories. In each of these three cases, a new member goes through an enculturation process wherein they adopt the community's ways of thinking, doing, and being while contributing to knowledge generation around the domain.

Parents are also old-timers in the civic community of practice that we call "society." They work, vote, pay taxes, and engage in other activities expected of members of society. Children are newcomers; when they are born, they know nothing about how to behave, approach, or think. They develop skills, competencies, beliefs, values, practices, and identities as they move from being a legitimate peripheral participant to a full participant in society with the support of their parents. This is how Barbara Rogoff describes children's cognitive development and learning in her seminal work *Apprenticeship in Thinking*.[29] She refers to the process as "guided participation," in which children develop new skills and competencies through their participation in socially valued activities with parents and other more knowledgeable and experienced peers. As children develop independence and autonomy over time, they need less assistance from others to successfully participate in society. This is consistent with the traditional view of parent-child expert-novice relationships in which parents are more knowledgeable than others in the relationship and are the primary agents of socializing children into different practices and teaching them how to behave in the world.

However, families interact and participate in shared activities around multiple domains or joint endeavors in which family members (adults, children, or both) move from being peripheral participants to full participants. While adults are full participants compared to children when we consider the broader society as a community of practice, they may be peripheral participants in other domains. As we have demonstrated throughout this book, parents, children, or both can be experts in the domain of video games. In addition, we mentioned previously that each of us can participate in multiple and at times overlapping communities of practice, and we may take on different roles in each community. Thus, Alex, through his participation in a wider *World of Warcraft* community of practice, surpassed his mother Carol in his expertise and identification with that community. Alex still needed support and guidance from Carol to navigate the demands of daily life, but when playing *WoW*, he was a full participant on his own.

In summary, we believe that thinking about families as communities of practice offers a more nuanced and complex way of understanding how learning occurs in family life, including around video games. Our framework takes into account the notion that families are dynamic systems that change over time, not just mechanisms for funneling sociocultural knowledge, beliefs, dispositions, and values to children. Conceptualizing families as communities of practice helps us to better understand the multigenerational aspect of learning, working, collaborating, networking, and connecting in the twenty-first century.

Gaming as a Family Routine and Ritual

Routines and rituals play an important role in engaging members of a community of practice in joint activities that are meaningful to the community and reinforce collective identity. Like other communities of practice, family activities also include routines and rituals. According to Barbara Fiese and her colleagues, rituals organize family activities and help families find structure and meaning as a collective unit.[30] The terms "routine" and "ritual" are often used interchangeably; however, there is a difference between the two. Both routines and rituals occur naturally in the flow of family life. Routines refer to repeated mundane activities that families do without much thinking, related to instrumental aspects of human communication. Rituals, like routines, are also repeated activities, but they have symbolic meanings for families that promote a sense of belonging and tradition as well as a group identity. They are often continued across generations, and a lack of continuity in such rituals threatens family cohesion and closeness. Routines have pragmatic value in the sense of getting something done, while rituals have sentimental value in family life.

To clarify the use of the two terms, Fiese and her colleagues discuss how mealtime can be both a routine and a ritual. A mealtime routine involves such actions as picking up ingredients from the grocery store or designating someone to set the table. These actions may be repeated several times a week without much thought and meaning beyond the goal of preparing family dinners. A mealtime ritual, however, involves family conversations about different topics and particular styles of interactions during mealtime. For instance, a mealtime ritual might involve parents starting conversation at the dinner table on weeknights by sharing their own experiences at work that day. This is a ritual that parents initiate to model family norms and the style of interactions around the dinner table. It is important to note that any routine can become a ritual once a repeated activity has a special meaning for the family as a group.

As with mealtimes, playing video games can also be a routine or a ritual within the family. A game routine involves families playing video games together a couple of times per week to kill time between activities. For instance, they might turn on their Xbox for thirty minutes before dinner, or pick up their phones while waiting at the doctor's office. Family members do not put much thought into their gameplay, and the activity does not have a special meaning for them. It has a practical purpose of keeping family members busy. Conversely, a game ritual involves symbolic meanings and identities that families construct, reconstruct, and deconstruct collectively around video games. The cases we shared in chapter 2 are good examples of how gaming can be a ritual in the context of families.

In the Livingstone and Morgan households, playing video games organized family life. These families connected with other family members, specifically siblings and cousins who lived far away, by scheduling a time to play together during weekends. Family members carved out time and space from other activities and obligations to get together and play video games. Playing video games together with family members brought about positive feelings and promoted a sense of closeness. What made playing video games a ritual in these two families, as well as in the Perez and Contreras families, is that the activity was carried out across generations—parents played video games when they were growing up and continued playing video games with their own children as adults. Gaming had the symbolic meaning of "this is what we do and value as a family." Family members shared a collective as well as an individual identity of "gamer" around video games. These families had vivid memories of social interactions that took place while playing video games, and what those interactions meant for the relationship between family members and their shared history.

The Gastelum family demonstrated clearly how a family routine around video games can become a ritual. The family gaming routine in the Gastelum household involved Hector coming home from work, giving his cell phone to his sons, and watching them play for thirty to sixty minutes before dinner a couple of times a week. However, this routine became a ritual because of the emotions it evoked among family members and the meaning it carried for those involved. Both Hector and his sons looked forward to the repeated activity of playing video games because it meant that they spent time together as father and sons. Furthermore, playing video games was not perceived as "killing time" before dinner, but a way for Hector to connect with his children.

Transforming a gaming routine to a ritual can play an important role in cultivating a family learning culture. A gaming routine, whether it is a routine for the individual child or the family, establishes the regularity of playing video games in the context of family life. As a routine, playing video games becomes a natural part of family life, like eating dinner, going to the movies, watching sports, and other activities family members do alone and together. Playing video games is already a routine in many families in the United States. National surveys suggest that almost all children play video games, and companies such as Nintendo, Sony, and Microsoft are targeting families to market their video gaming devices and developing "family-friendly" games to engage the whole family in playing video games. Many parental monitoring practices around video games support a gaming routine for children. For instance, parents reinforce rules, examples being that children can only play video games after they complete their homework and before dinner, or that their time spent gaming is limited on a daily or weekly basis.[31] However, these practices alone do not support the formation of a family learning culture. The act of playing video games needs to move beyond a family routine and become a family ritual—a meaningful part of family life that enriches family experiences.

Forms of Engagement to Support Family Learning Culture

Families can transform a gaming routine into a ritual by being more mindful and intentional about how they engage with and around video games together. First and foremost, parents must broaden their perspective on video games to realize the opportunities for family learning, connection, and communication around video games. They need to not only be aware of and take measures to address safety issues regarding video games but also actively participate in gaming alongside their children. In this section, we identify four different forms of family engagement with video games that we believe support the formation and cultivation of a family learning culture at home. These different forms of family engagement influence how video games are taken up in the context of home, and in return the kind of impact video games have on the family learning culture. We briefly summarize each type of engagement, and then move on to a more detailed discussion of specific examples and strategies to support each type.

The first form of family engagement is watching children play video games. From "skeptics" to "gamers," many parents watch their children play video games. Furthermore, watching someone else play video games (someone who is more knowledgeable about and skilled at the game) is one of the first things people do as novices to learn how to play a new game. We will discuss how watching can be an entry point to constructing meaningful joint gaming experiences for families, and the types of questions that parents can ask so as to engage in discussions with their children that are mutually beneficial to both parties.

The second form of family engagement is actually playing video games together as a family. Many parents with whom we spoke reported difficulty with using the controllers and getting their children teach them how to play games. Others faced challenges in starting conversations with their children while playing games. Later, we provide a list of strategies with which families can experiment when they play video games together. These strategies focus on increasing collaboration among family members during gameplay.

The third form of family engagement involves aligning family gaming practices at home with the online practices of the wider gaming community. Participating in the online gaming community broadens all family members' opportunities for learning as they engage in a different set of activities outside of the games that enhance their learning. It also connects families with other people who share their interests and can be resources for them.

Last, we discuss creating video games together as a family as a form of engagement around video games, and how this practice plants the seed for other kinds of learning that may seem out of reach for families (e.g., coding) and helps families connect with people in their local communities through making.

Watching Children Play Video Games

We tend to think about "watching" as a passive activity that requires minimal mental effort unless a person is watching an expert do something to learn from them. For instance, watching television is considered to be inconsequential or even harmful because we assume that the person is not actively engaged, whereas watching someone else tie their shoes when you are learning how to tie yours is considered beneficial because you need to pay attention to the procedure and actively process what you are observing to execute the steps and tie your own shoes. What makes watching more or less active is the intention of the viewer. Watching television can be beneficial depending on the viewer's motives. If the motive is to learn something about a topic, then watching television is as valuable as watching someone tie their shoes.

The same is true for parents watching their children play video games. They can either watch their children mindlessly (or because they are worried about the game content and the time spent gaming) or with an intention to facilitate their children's learning as well as learn from them. This form of engagement—which is referred to as "coviewing" around television, and involves parents having conversations with their children while watching television shows with them—can lay the foundation for a learning culture to flourish. As we discussed in chapter 3, learning is not simply the acquisition of knowledge but a process of meaning making by which people negotiate and construct their understanding of the world and various situations, events, experiences, identities, and relations. Talk is important for learning because people express their own thinking through verbal interactions while internalizing what is being negotiated and constructed with others. The types of questions one asks and the connections one makes between ideas and experiences affect what can be learned.

An example would help demonstrate the importance of talk to family learning culture in general. Imagine two different families watching the television show *Full House*, a sitcom about a widowed father raising three daughters with help from his brother-in-law and a friend. Let's say in the episode that the teenage daughter, D. J., is trying to lose weight by starving herself to get ready for a pool party. In one family, the parents and children watch the show together and make a few comments, such as "That was a great episode" or "It must be difficult to try to lose weight in a short time," but do not really engage in conversation. After the show, the family moves on to doing other things around the house. In the other family, the parent starts a conversation by asking: "What do you think about D. J.'s approach to losing weight?" or "Have you ever felt pressure from your friends about your weight?" The family spends another ten minutes after the episode reflecting on the situation, and moves on to talking about what a healthy diet and exercise regimen might look like. This sparks a question about the nutritional value of different types of food, so the family turns on the computer to search online for which fruits and vegetables are the most fibrous and have the least amount of sugar. In which of the two scenarios is family learning taking place? The second one, of course. The questions parents ask prompt children to analyze the situation and connect it to their own experiences, and the rich content of the family conversation creates an interest in learning new things.

The same happens around video games when parents watch their children with an eye toward opportunities for learning and connection. For example, video games are particularly suited for learning and having conversations about systems thinking. Systems thinking is the ability to see the "big picture" and understand the complex ways that the elements of a system interact to create the whole. It is increasingly recognized as important skill in the workplace and the classroom, as well as for civic participation as we discover that the complex issues the world faces can only be solved through a systems thinking lens. While systems thinking is an important skill, it is difficult to master. This is because systems thinking requires nonlinear thinking, the ability to handle complex concepts, and an understanding of the relationships between components of a system and how they generate system outcomes.[32]

One way for parents to learn more about games and help their children develop higher-order thinking skills is to view games as systems. Almost all games involve components that interact in different ways to create a whole; that is, the game itself. These components include the player(s), the goal(s), the rule(s), and the game mechanics. The complexity of games varies, but the core characteristics of a game look similar across different games. One simple experiment families can do to start thinking of games as systems is to pick a game that they usually play, change the goal or rule(s) of the game, try to play the game with the new goal or rule(s), and see what happens. What families will quickly discover is that when they change one component of a game, the entire game will change and consequently produce different outcomes. Or perhaps they will have a broken or out-of-balance system in which the game will no longer be playable unless they change other components of the game and experiment with how to create a playable game with different goals and rules.

Questions to Ask Children

In this section, we identify a set of questions that parents can use to learn about the games their children are playing and help their children reflect on their gaming experience and understanding of the game as a system. Because many games, video games or not, share common features, the questions can be used with a wide range of games with minor adjustment. We organized the questions so that families start with "what" questions to develop an understanding of each component of the game, and gradually move onto "how" questions that help them reflect on the interactions between different components and how these interactions produce game outcomes. Not all questions will be relevant to every game. Think of these questions as conversation starters.

WHAT
The goal of this set of questions is to identify the components of the game.

- What is the goal of the game?
- What character do you play in the game?

- What role do you take on in the game?
- What is the storyline in the game?
- What other characters are in the game?
- What are the rules of the game?

WHERE & WHEN

The goal of this set of questions is to understand the context of the game.

- Where do you go for . . . ? (Choose an item or an action of the player; e.g., magic spells, fishing)
- Where is the . . . ? (Choose a character or a place in the game; e.g., enemy, castle)
- When do you . . . ? (Choose an action of the player in the game; e.g., jump, die, shoot, pick)
- When does the . . . (Choose a character or an item in the game) do . . . ? (Choose a behavior of the character or the item)

WHY & HOW

The goal of this set of questions is to understand the interactions between different components in the game.

- Why did you . . . ? (Choose a player action; e.g., collect, stop, continue)
- Why do you like . . . ? (Choose a player action, item, or character in the game)
- How do you . . . ? (Choose a player action or an activity in the game)
- How does . . . (Choose a player action, item, or character in the game) interact with . . . ? (Choose a player action, item, or character in the game)
- How does the game change when you . . . ? (Choose a player or a character action)
- When do you win the game?
- When do you lose the game?

Playing Games with Children

This form of family engagement around video games is the cornerstone of this book. As we have discussed, intergenerational play around video games can promote positive family interactions and experiences. Earlier in this chapter, we discussed how intergenerational play is a family routine and ritual that supports the family as a community of practice. In the previous section, we described watching children play video games as a good starting point for parents to become involved in their children's gaming and to plant the seeds for a family learning culture by asking questions that help parents and children understand video games as systems. That said, simply watching children play video games is not enough to cultivate a family learning culture. Watching someone else do something is still a spectator sport rather than a participatory act. A truly shared experience is created when both parties are involved in the same activity as "doers." Therefore, it is important for parents to join their children in playing video games. Additionally, parents will be better positioned to monitor their children's gaming while participating in intergenerational play. Shared experiences around video games support communication, connection, and learning between parents and children as they create a context for family conversations around a wide variety of topics. Furthermore, intergenerational play around video games supports a family learning culture by providing opportunities for families to engage in collaborative problem solving. In the next section, we discuss what families can do while engaging in intergenerational play around single- and multiplayer games to create collaborative learning experiences around video games.

Single-Player Games

When people think about collaboration around video games, they often think about multiplayer games in which two or more people can play together. However, any game can support collaboration between family members if the experience is structured accordingly. Since collaboration takes the form of meaningful interactions and conversations around video games, the social arrangement around video games (i.e., interactions between people) is more relevant to collaboration than the material arrangement (i.e., the interaction of individual players with the game through a controller). In fact, families that participated in the Family Quest and Families@Play projects collaborated around single-player games just as much as, if not more than, multiplayer games. One successful strategy that emerged from our observations of families playing single-player games in their homes and in other settings outside of the home is *turn-taking*.

As we mentioned in chapter 1, parents who consider themselves as nongamers still played casual games such as *Candy Crush*, *Solitaire*, and *Tetris* on their cell phones. While these games are single-player games, they can be an entry point for intergenerational play around video games. Similarly, the single-player games that children like to play on their own or a parent's cell phone, such as *Flappy Bird* or *Subway Surfers*, can also establish a collaborative family gaming environment. One common feature that these games share is a short play cycle in which players engage in rounds of trial and failure. These games also have simple gameplay mechanics and controls, making it easier for people to learn how to play the game. Players can therefore step into and out of the game with minimal effort. Together, these features make it easy for family members to take turns playing these games. For instance, the members of the Cruz family, whom we met as part of our ethnographic study, often sat down at their kitchen table and played *Flappy Bird* as a family before dinner, with each member taking their turn to play the game and passing the phone to the next person when they failed. Whether parents start with a game that they enjoy playing and invite their children to take a turn, or a game their children enjoy playing and ask to take a turn, single-player games can support collaboration between parents and children while engaging them in intergenerational play.

Multiplayer Games

By their design, multiplayer games involve the participation of two or more people in the same game space. Games like *Just Dance*, *World of Warcraft*, *Halo*, *Eve*, *Lego Star Wars*, and *League of Legends* were some of the multiplayer games families reported playing together. Not all multiplayer games afford the same level of social and verbal interaction between family members. For instance, in *Just Dance*, up to four people can dance together at the same time; however, each player is responsible for performing their own dance moves correctly and does not need to talk with other players. In the two-player version of *Portal 2*, problem solving is collaborative, but in-game communication channels are limited to basic pointing gestures directing the other person to the next location. In massively multiplayer online games like *World of Warcraft* and *League of Legends*, teamwork requires coordination of actions and different skill sets to slay enemies through verbal and written communication. So, just because there are other players involved in a game does not mean that family members will engage in collaboration, verbal interactions, or meaningful conversations. Furthermore, families bring their own interaction patterns and dynamics to multiplayer games, and thus take advantage of the affordances for collaboration and social interactions of these games to different degrees. Conflict, as opposed to collaboration and coordination, can arise quickly when parents and children disagree while deciding on which task to complete or become frustrated with each other's performance in the game.

Families can optimize multiplayer games for collaboration, social interactions, and learning through *division of labor*; that is, families can assign different parts of the gameplay to different family members and switch roles and responsibilities while playing. This includes having a family discussion about what each person enjoys doing in the game and the parts they like or feel comfortable and confident playing. It also involves a balanced approach as to who takes the role of leader, guide, or teacher while playing. Parents need to be sensitive to the power dynamics associated with being a guide versus being a follower. We observed that conflict between parents and children while playing video games can occur when one family member claims the role of expert and guides the other person, but never steps out of that role. For instance, children who knew how to play *Minecraft* always wanted to guide their parents who were less knowledgeable about the game, even though the parents expressed an interest in exploring the game themselves after learning about basic game mechanics. We also observed the opposite. Some parents wanted to guide their children the entire time they were playing, even when their children expressed an interest in sharing leadership responsibility. Monitoring who is developing what kind of expertise and switching roles across different tasks helps family members to share power and control over gameplay and thus promotes collaborative interactions and conversations around multiplayer games.

Aligning Game and Family Communities

When people think about video games, they often think about the gameplay and the social interactions between people within and around the game, and nothing more. However, video gaming includes players engaging in other practices around video games that are as valuable for learning and social interaction as playing the games themselves. These practices include, but are not limited to, contributing to online forums, modifying game code, and creating videos of gameplay. Together, these practices support what Henry Jenkins and his colleagues call a "participatory culture" through which people develop valuable skills and exercise a new form of engaged citizenship by producing media content (not just consuming it) and learning from, as well as contributing to, the collective knowledge of a broader community.[33] The participants in a gaming community play the game as well as engage in the aforementioned practices around the game.

As we discussed earlier, families can be viewed as communities of practice wherein playing video games can become a routine and a ritual.

Families can connect their gaming practices at home with the larger gaming community by participating in activities that members of the larger gaming community partake in outside of the game. By so doing, families continue to cultivate a family learning culture as these activities present new opportunities for learning and developing skills together. A common activity among members of the gaming community is to contribute content to online game forums and websites. Through posting comments and responses to others, members of the gaming community use these online spaces to share information and experiences with the community, exchange ideas with others who play the game, and make new connections. Nowadays, almost all video games have some kind of online space for players to connect with one another and contribute content. Families can share their gaming experiences on these forums and use online content as a resource to advance in the game.

Another common activity among members of the gaming community is to watch and create videos about games, typically on YouTube. The videos include content ranging from recordings of gameplay, often featuring player commentary, to reviews that analyze the strengths and weaknesses of a game. There are many reasons why people watch these videos. Newcomers might watch videos to learn about a game before they begin to play. For those who are already playing the game, walkthrough videos can help them with a challenging part of the game. These walkthroughs also teach others about different ways of playing the game or different aspects of the game. Game reviews inform community members about shortcomings or highlights of the game. Families can search for videos of the games they like to play, watch them together, and reflect on the information provided in the video. They can also post comments to provide feedback for the creator of the video. Finally, families can create videos about their own gaming experiences or their thoughts on a particular game and share them with other members of the gaming community. Through the process of creating their own videos, families can explore how to use movie-editing software and learn how to post a video on video-sharing sites.

The last activity we will discuss here is using cheat codes to modify games. Players have the ability to change some aspects of certain games, such as their character's health or appearance, using cheat codes—commands that trigger a change in the game. Almost all video games have cheat codes that players can use to modify the game. In chapter 4, Tomas used a cheat code while playing *The Sims* with his mother to get more Simoleons—the in-game currency—so that he could purchase items in the game. Finding and implementing cheat codes can be a starting point for family conversations about computer programming and the technical skills involved in making video games.

Creating Games Together

In addition to watching their children play video games, playing games together as a family, and engaging in online practices that connect the family gaming to the larger gaming community, parents can also make video games together with their children. When people hear the phrase "designing video games," they often think about programming and coding. This makes designing video games seem like an impossible task for them as individuals, let alone as a family. Designing video games, like other things in everyday life, starts with an idea. If people can come up with ideas about what to cook for dinner, where to go for a summer vacation, or how to fix a creaky door, they can also come up with an idea for a game. If they brainstorm and collaborate with others (e.g., their family members) to come up with the idea, that is even better. Although video games that are currently available may make it seem like people can only design shooting games, puzzle games, simulation games, adventure games, educational games, location-based games, or exercise games, there are genres of video games that we have yet to discover and topics that we have yet to design video games around. A game can be about anything. People just need to look around for inspiration.

In the beginning of this book, we discussed humankind's long history of playing games. Games have been around for as long as humans have. Like any other human endeavor, games evolved over time as technology improved. Not all of the games people have enjoyed playing throughout history were designed by professional game designers; many games grew out of ordinary people's daily activities and play. Designing games is as ancient an enterprise as playing them.

Why have people been designing games for tens of thousands of years? Designing games, much like drawing a picture or telling a story, is a form of creative expression, a way of preserving culture, and a leisure activity. People represent their understanding of the world through images (in the case of drawings and paintings), words (in the case of stories and books), and a combination of images, words, and performance (in the case of film and games). Like paintings, books, and movies, games are also used as a medium for storytelling. However, games stand out as a participatory medium in which the audience experiences and is actively engaged with the unfolding of the story. People use different media as they become available to capture and share their own family experiences. For instance, people draw pictures to represent their family experiences, write stories that document their experiences, take photos of where they were and what they were doing at a particular time, or make movies about their family. In addition to looking at their surroundings to find inspiration for game design, people can also represent their family experiences through designing video games about them.

Two things come to mind when we think about "designing," "creating," or "making" in the everyday lives of families: doing arts and crafts activities, and cooking meals together. These fairly common activities play an important role in supporting family bonding and learning through the process of collaboratively creating a tangible product. They also offer an outlet for families to express themselves creatively. Playing and making are activities that are beneficial for children and families as they provide different kinds of opportunities for social interactions, learning, and connection. Throughout this book, we have demonstrated how playing video games is similar to other play activities families do together and illustrated some of their unique affordances for family learning, connection, and communication. We believe making games has overlapping qualities with other making activities that families do together. When families design video games, they also collaboratively create a tangible product; that is, the game. They can also share this product with others just like they would if they made dinner or painted a picture together.

For a long time, researchers and commentators used the term "digital divide" to describe those who have access to information and communication technologies and those who do not. This is often discussed in one of two ways: first, from an international perspective, as a gap between developed and developing countries with respect to the level of technology acquisition of their citizens; second, from a national perspective, as a gap between groups of people from different socioeconomic backgrounds within a country with respect to its level of technology acquisition. Citizens of developing countries and people from low socioeconomic backgrounds are disadvantaged by not having access to technology in a world where technology not only is infiltrated into everyday life and work, but also propels change and innovation.

More recently, US researchers have discussed the "participation gap," the gap in skills and abilities to use information and communication technologies that perpetuate inequalities between people from more or less advantaged backgrounds.[34] S. Craig Watkins argues that, while the digital gap with respect to acquiring technological devices is closing between people from different socioeconomic and ethnic backgrounds, the practices people engage in around these technologies still look different.[35] The issue around technology is not necessarily about having access to a technology but what people are able to do with it. Socioeconomic, racial, and ethnic divides exist with respect to who consumes versus who creates content using technology. From this vantage point, designing video games in addition to playing them can set children and families on a trajectory of learning and developing skills that are important for successfully participating in the twenty-first century. Next, we share some ideas about how to get started with designing video games as a family.

Brainstorm Game Ideas and Components
The first step in the game design process is to come up with an idea for your game. The best way to come up with an idea is to generate lots of ideas and choose the one that seems the most fun, the most feasible, or that your family would most like to pursue. This process can be accomplished by holding a family brainstorming session. The brainstorming session can take place anywhere in the house—the kitchen, the living room, even at the dinner table. If possible, we recommend having sticky notes and pens or pencils around so family members can write down their ideas. One productive way to structure the brainstorming session is to have time limits. You would be surprised by how many ideas people can generate in as little as five minutes.

A simple way for parents to kick off a brainstorming session is to say, "Let's come up with as many ideas for a game as we can in five minutes!" and set a timer. Each family member should have a stack of sticky notes that they can use to write down their individual ideas. Once the five minutes is over, each person can share their ideas with the rest of their family. Or, family members can collectively generate as many ideas as possible within the five-minute time limit. If producing as many ideas as possible is too broad for family members to get their creative juices flowing, another productive way to structure the activity is to pick a topic such as cooking, sports, friendship, or family around which to generate as many ideas as possible.

Once the five-minute (or however much time was allocated for brainstorming ideas) session is up, family members need to take some time to sort the suggestions and choose one to develop into a game. Similar ideas can be clustered together and ranked based on family members' preferences, or each family member can first pick the idea that they like the most, then debate as a family and select one idea that everyone has agreed upon. If a brainstorming session at home is uninspiring, you can always change the scenery and brainstorm while shopping in the mall, eating out, or even visiting the zoo. You can use your phone to write down or voice record your ideas. If none of these brainstorming strategies work for your family, you could take the plot of your or your children's favorite book or TV show and design a video game around that. After a while, your family may become so attuned to game design that they may find inspiration for games during everyday conversations or activities, allowing you to skip the brainstorming session altogether.

The second step in the game design process is to identify the components of your game. This initially includes the goal, the rules, and the game mechanics. Later, you can develop the aesthetics of the game (how it looks and feels). The questions we introduced earlier in this chapter for parents to use while watching children play games should be helpful in this stage of the game design process as well. Families can utilize the structure we laid out for the brainstorming session to determine the goal, the rules, and the mechanics of their game. If you want to make a game with multiple levels, you also need to think about what you will change about each level to make it more challenging than the previous one. The goal is to come up with the skeleton of a game, not necessarily design a complete game at this stage. Writing down the ideas you have or drawing some scenes of the game on a piece of paper should be sufficient at this stage. If you were a professional game designer, you would document your ideas on a "game design document," which identifies all the components of a game and how they interact at this stage.

Identify a Game Design Tool

While we position identifying a game design tool as the second phase in the game design process, families can explore tools before they brainstorm ideas for their game. Since different game design tools support designing different genres of games, experimenting with varied tools can help you define the kind of game your family wants to design. There are many design tools available for people of all ages and experience levels. Some tools are specifically targeted toward children, and many tools position parents as champions of their children's game design rather than codesigners. Such framing misleads many adults, including parents, who are new to game design. They perceive these game design tools as inappropriate for adults. However, when these game design tools are framed as "for kids," it only means that they provide a good entry point for novices to game design.

We recommend that families start with game design tools that do not require programming and coding, and then gradually move onto tools that are more advanced and even teach these skills. A common misconception among adults who are unfamiliar with designing video games is that video game design starts with or even requires programming and coding skills. This, however, is untrue. As with any other design project, video game design begins by first designing the system, and then engineering it by using a programming language. Programming is used to build games, not design them. A programmer does not necessarily know how to design video games. In fact, many game designers work with programmers, artists, and producers to build the games that they designed. While learning to code may be a beneficial outcome of family engagement in game design (and many educational programs have used game design to motivate children to learn programming), the process of game design itself can be a useful introduction to "thinking like a designer" and learning concepts that are applicable to a variety of design situations.[36]

Next, we review some of the tools that are available for designing and creating video games. This is not an exhaustive list, but it will give you a sense of where to start and what games you can design as a family without any knowledge of programming languages. Each of these tools has a website where you can access the tool and additional resources.

Gamestar Mechanic (https://gamestarmechanic.com/)   This is an online game design platform that uses a drag-and-drop interface to create top-down and platformer games. Families can start using this tool by completing "quests" that introduce various game design elements, playing games created by other users, or diving right into creating their own original games. The Gamestar Mechanic design tool is available free of charge, although other options can be purchased for a fee. This tool is best used for creating action-adventure games, similar to classic Nintendo role-playing and platformer games.

Twine (https://twinery.org/)   This is a free online software tool that can be used in-browser or downloaded for Windows, OS X, and Linux operating systems. If your family enjoys stories, this text-based tool is right for you. With Twine, families can create role-playing games reminiscent of the classic *Dungeon & Dragons* that provide interactive story experiences.

Scratch (https://scratch.mit.edu/)   Unlike tools that are specifically developed for creating games, Scratch is a free online programming environment that allows users to design interactive art, media, stories, and games. The term "programming environment" should not scare families away from using this tool. The environment aims to engage users with basic elements of programming using blocks of commands written in plain

English, with an easy-to-use drag and drop interface. This tool works best for designing puzzle games.

GameSalad (http://gamesalad.com/)   Similar to Scratch, GameSalad is a drag-and-drop coding platform that introduces programming fundamentals. However, GameSalad is dedicated to game creation and offers many resources for beginners and more advanced game developers. If you want to add a level of polish, take advantage of the large library of preprogrammed characters and behaviors, or even publish your game on one of the app stores, GameSalad may be the right tool for your family. It is appropriate for creating a broad range of games, including puzzles, platformers, 2.5-D adventure games, and more. Much like Scratch and Gamestar Mechanic, GameSalad also offers a community publishing site where you can explore and learn from fellow developers.

Unity3D (https://unity3d.com/)   If you want the capabilities of a professional game development platform and are interested in jumping into the depths of programming and art production, Unity3D is the tool for your family! It is a free engine with a deep feature set, but is accessible to users at every level of expertise and is a favorite tool of many independent game developers. It supports programming in Javascript and C#, and publishing to Web, mobile, and desktop platforms. It is appropriate for building any type of game, ranging from virtual card games to first-person adventures to virtual reality experiences. There are many tutorials, books, and online guides that can help you build your dream game.

Prototype and User Test Your Game
Throughout this book, we describe video games as systems with multiple components that interact in complex ways to create a fun and playable game. Designing a system, whether it is a video game, a school, or a social networking site, is not an easy task. Building all the components and expecting the entire system to run like clockwork is unreasonable, unrealistic, and inefficient. Rather than spending a lot of time and energy on building and risking the failure of an entire system, designers first develop a prototype of what they want to build and engage in an iterative process of testing and revising until they have something that works. A prototype is a sample or a model of a product that can be tested and improved upon in the process of working toward building a finished product. While the word prototype is associated with software development and sounds technical, we often engage in prototyping in our daily lives.

For instance, when someone is developing a new recipe for blueberry muffins, they usually experiment with different ingredients to produce a small sample for others to try, then refine the recipe before baking a whole tray of blueberry muffins to share with others. Similarly, if you have ever tried crocheting or sewing, you know that prototyping is embedded in the process. You first crochet a sample granny square and iterate until you master the pattern before you crochet a dozen granny squares for a blanket. When sewing a dress, people often construct, test, and tweak the pattern of the dress using inexpensive muslin before they sew the dress using the desired fabric. Even learning a sport involves prototyping. For instance, when learning how to surf, people start closer to the shore with small waves while they practice, iterate, and finally master their technique before riding bigger waves.

Once designers have built a prototype, they test it with people who represent the desired users of their product. This phase is called *user testing*. User testing allows designers to solicit feedback and improve upon the design of the product. Designers go through multiple rounds of testing and revisions of their prototypes. Like other designers, video game designers first build a prototype of their game and test it with players to ensure that the game is playable and fun. Given that many game design tools are designed for a single user, it might seem hard for families to design a prototype and test their game collaboratively. One way families can overcome this limitation is to switch between the roles of designer and tester during the prototyping and user-testing phase.

Here's how it works: First, decide who will design the prototype of the game. We recommend letting children take on the role of designer. Once the child finishes designing the first version of the game, the parent can test this version and make small improvements before passing the game back to the child. The child then takes the role of a user, playing through the second version of the game and making adjustments based on their own user testing. This process can continue until both child and parent are happy with their game. If switching the roles of designer and tester does not work for your family, you can always stick to one role during this process. Once family members are happy with their prototype, they can test their game with other family members, friends, and coworkers.

Share Your Game with Others

Once families receive feedback and improve their games, they can share their finished games with a larger group of people. Some of the game design tools we reviewed earlier, such as Gamestar Mechanic and Scratch, have their own online communities within which families can publish and share their games. Another way for families to share their games is through entering them in a video game challenge or competition such as the National STEM Video Game Challenge (http://stemchallenge.org/). Families can also submit a proposal to showcase their games at Maker Faires (http://makerfaire.com/). These conventions, held annually in different cities across the United States, gather people to share all kinds of projects that involve making, designing, and creativity. Families can also find and join a group devoted to playing games on the Meetup social networking site (http://www.meetup.com/) and share their games at one of the meetings. Of course, families can always organize a game night at home and invite extended family and friends to play games, including the ones that they have designed, or bring their games to a gathering with friends and family.

Conclusion

Over the past decade, our everyday life and work experiences have been transformed by the rapid development and adoption of digital media technologies. We have come to understand the world as a dynamic system marked by constant change. The ability and willingness to learn new things has become not only a desired skill in the workplace but also a necessity for survival. Given this trend, developing a family learning culture is paramount to the success and well-being of adults and children in the twenty-first century. The boundaries that used to define the teaching and learning roles played by adults and children are quickly disappearing. The rate at which new technologies are released and the growing demand for new technology-adjacent skills compels everyone to become lifelong learners. Collaboration and problem-solving skills are becoming increasingly more important in confronting the social, environmental, and economic challenges our society faces today.

We started this chapter with an argument for reimagining the collective nature of families to understand the possibilities for family learning, connection, and communication in the twenty-first century. We conceptualized families as communities of practice and suggested intergenerational play around video games as a family routine and ritual that supports the growth of a family learning culture in which family members develop skills that are valued in the current landscape. For instance, video games create opportunities for collaboration and problem solving among family members. Although these opportunities can occur naturally, families can deliberately choose activities that develop such skills during the time they spend playing video games together. In addition to collaboration and problem solving, families can practice such skills as modeling and prototyping when they play and create games together. These skills are not only important for children but also useful for adults in the workplace and everyday life. Through different forms of family engagement, such as watching children play video games, playing games as a family, engaging in gaming practices, and creating games together, families can cultivate a family learning culture around video games and transform video games from a point of conflict to a context for learning for everyone in the family.

6

Designing for Intergenerational Play

There continues to be a generally negative portrayal of video games in the media. Specifically, in the context of families, beyond a few video games that are marketed for the Nintendo Wii and the Xbox Kinect (e.g., *Mario Kart, Just Dance,* and *Family Game Night*) as family friendly, video games are still considered as a source of conflict rather than a context for togetherness. Many researchers have focused on the divisive role video games play in the everyday lives of parents and children. Parents, while trying to protect their families from the presumed perils of video gaming, are often at odds with their children, who want to spend time playing video games—and even worse, playing video games that have violent or otherwise inappropriate content. Throughout this book, we demonstrated that while tensions may emerge between parents and children around video games, the potential of video games to connect family members as well as support their learning and communication is far greater than their ability to evoke disagreements between family members. Still, we believe it is insufficient to simply share experiences of families who have already realized the positive potential of video games in their own homes. There is a need for systemic efforts to help families understand how to use this medium to facilitate productive family interactions and positive family outcomes. Educators and game designers can play a key role in creating opportunities for family learning, connection, and communication around video games. In this last chapter, we discuss how they can intentionally design family experiences and video games for intergenerational play to support family connection, communication, and learning.

Specifically, we draw upon our experiences in iteratively designing, implementing, and improving the design of family gaming events, workshops, and programs and share the lessons we have learned in encouraging parents to experience productive intergenerational play experiences around video games for themselves. Educational settings such as schools, museums, and libraries can offer resources and activities that enable families to learn about and engage productively with intergenerational play experiences around video games. Many parents who came to the events we held in both formal and informal educational settings commented that they learned more about their children's video gaming from these workshops than they did at home. Household chores can make it difficult for families to carve out time to play together at home. Furthermore, children become frustrated or impatient with their parents when trying to teach them how to play video games. The uninterrupted time spent together playing video games outside of the home in a session dedicated to gameplay is a neutral space where family members can explore together and learn about games and each other while having a good time. Our events have consistently attracted significantly more mothers and their sons than other parent-child configurations. Many mothers who came to our events did not play video games with their children at home but wanted to learn about the games their children played. Fathers were more likely to play video games with their children at home but came to our events to explore new games and extend their intergenerational play experience outside of the home. In the first part of this chapter, we discuss educators' role in supporting families' interactions around video games and what they can do to unleash the power of video games for families with diverse needs and backgrounds. We dedicate the second part of the chapter to the implications of our work for game designers.

Connecting School, Home, and Community through Games

Video games can support learning in varied forms across the different contexts of children's lives, including school, after-school programs, and home. For example, children can play *Minecraft*—a sandbox game in which players mine for resources and craft tools in an open environment to build different artifacts—as part of a lesson at school, in the computer lab at an after-school site, and at home. Many educators use video games to teach children academic (e.g., math, science, etc.) and nonacademic content (e.g., civics, bullying, etc.) as well as transferable skills such as problem solving, creativity, and systems thinking that are important for children to succeed in a world that is driven by technology and innovation. While educators are taking advantage of the affordances of video games for teaching and learning, many parents continue to be skeptical about video games as a medium and unsure of how to best support their children's learning around video games at home, let alone participate in gaming alongside with their children.

In this book, we shared the experiences of a small number of families for whom intergenerational play around video games, whether on a console, handheld device, or computer, was both a routine and a ritual. We learned many lessons about what video games can offer to families from interviewing parents and children about the value and meaning of their experiences and observing their interactions while playing games at home. We also shared the kinds of learning and identity work that families engage in when they are invited to spend uninterrupted time playing video games together in an educational setting—even if they do not necessarily play video games together at home. Regardless of their experiences with playing video games, all parents need support, guidance, and resources from educators to optimize the power of video games to support their children's learning and family cohesion.

Research suggests that parents and educators should engage collaboratively with children in shared activities to support their learning across the contexts of home, school, and other learning environments.[1,2] For the potential of video games for learning to be realized, it is important for adults to participate in video gaming with children by playing games, talking about games with their children, and using gameplay as a stepping stone for exploring other learning opportunities. Educators often face two challenges in their efforts to integrate video games into schools, libraries, museums, and other educational settings. The first challenge is to get parents' approval for educators to use video games as a means of supporting children's learning in their institutions. Once educators have parents on board, they face the challenge of connecting children's learning with and around video games at their institution to home. The disconnect between home, school, and community is a real problem because it undermines the development of children's interest and learning. To unleash the power of video games in preparing children to participate in the twenty-first–century workforce, we need parents, schools, and the community to work together.

Video game play and design may be particularly promising for supporting science, technology, engineering, and math (STEM) education. Over the last decade, improving STEM education has become a national priority, in part due to projections of an exponential increase in employment opportunities in STEM fields, and the gender, socioeconomic, and racial inequities between those who do and don't pursue STEM careers. In a world where technology drives innovation, these trends are concerning, and many have argued that the US economy is losing its competitive edge by falling behind in generating a qualified workforce to fill the jobs of the future.[3]

Video games have received national and local attention from educators, policymakers, and leaders in the information technology industry. Both playing and designing video games have been studied as a motivational context for getting children interested in STEM careers. Video games are being used in two ways: (1) to teach children STEM content through play, and (2) to teach children to code through making games. There are many educational programs that use video games as a tool to recruit and keep children and youth interested in STEM. However, while these efforts are important to raise awareness and expose children to STEM careers, the majority of such efforts have not been grounded in the perspective that has come to inform efforts to improve literacy education. That is, the educational goals we are trying to achieve cannot be addressed solely by focusing on individual learning; rather, these efforts need to involve families and communities. With respect to literacy, a number of educators, policymakers, and researchers have shifted their focus from children to families and communities, recognizing that literacy learning is embedded in social and cultural practices and starts in the home.

Some educators and researchers have begun to enact this shift in STEM education, emphasizing the need to appreciate and build on families' existing values, knowledge, and culture rather than simply trying to impose new practices.[4] Educational programs that use video games as a means to support children's STEM learning can be part of this effort to develop more socially and culturally situated approaches to STEM education, in and outside of school. Ideally, parents should be involved in children's STEM learning not just to provide social support but as coparticipants and colearners, so that STEM-related skills such as scientific problem solving, systems thinking, and even coding are connected to shared family and cultural practices. Efforts to address the lack of diversity, equality, and participation in STEM fields also can be hampered by a disconnect between children's formal and informal learning experiences. Educators can address this gap by creating opportunities for parents to be involved in educational programs alongside their children.

Supporting Intergenerational Play around Video Games

Supporting intergenerational play around video games in educational settings serves multiple purposes. First, in an increasingly digital world, parents are looking for resources from educators to harness the tools needed to support their children's learning and protect them from harm. Through family gaming events and programs, educators can share resources around video games, including websites that parents can use to learn more about video games and search for the ratings of games their children play, strategies that they can use to monitor their children's gaming, and topics for family conversation around different games.

Second, students' academic achievement is enhanced when schools work in partnership with parents; however, schools traditionally struggle to involve parents as participants in their learning communities. Inviting parents and children to come to school to play and explore a game as a family while spending uninterrupted time together and interacting with teacher facilitators can break down the barriers between home and school. Family gaming events can provide access to technology for families who may not have access at home, make parents more comfortable with asking questions about video games, and create opportunities for conversations with teachers about what parents can do at home with their children. Such activities also allow families to interact with other families, build new social connections, and promote a sense of community.

Third, expanding children's learning beyond the classroom by connecting it to other aspects of their lives enriches children's understanding of what they learned. Educators can structure family gaming events to create meaningful and collaborative learning contexts for families as a means of supporting children's connected learning experiences. Interactions between parents and children around playing video games can be opportunities for children to problem solve and reflect on a topic. These interactions can inform parents about their children's thought processes, give them ideas about how to interact with their children around video games at home, and inspire them to pursue other opportunities to support their children's learning beyond family gaming programs.

There are many ways to organize family programs to support intergenerational play around video games. One example is a family game night, to which educators can invite families once a year, semester, or month to play video games together for an hour or two. Another program could be sustained over a long period of time wherein interested families meet weekly for longer periods of time to explore games together. Educators can ask families to bring game consoles if they own them, or use computers and handheld devices already available to them. Regardless of program format, educators should consider the following when facilitating family connection, communication, and learning around video games.

Focusing on Social Interactions around Video Games

One of the first things educators need to think about is choosing the game(s) for families to play together. Video games that allow two or more people to play at the same time through separate avatars, controllers, or devices are often considered to be "social" and ideal for the whole family to play together. Yet the high levels of interactivity between the game and each individual player can potentially divide players' attention and reduce the social interactions between them. We observed this phenomenon during the Family Quest and Families@Play events. Families spoke more when they were playing the single-player version of the virtual Family Quest gaming environment than they did while playing the multiplayer version of the game. Similarly, families who played *Portal 2*, a two-player cooperative game in which players solve puzzles, interacted less with one another than those who played single-player games such as *The Sims* and *Minecraft*. Of course, not all multiplayer games undermine social interactions. As we discovered in chapter 2, families play multiplayer games at home for extended periods of time and engage in joint exploration and in-depth conversations. Rather, our point is that multiplayer games are not the de facto genre for intergenerational play around video games. When selecting video games for family events or programs, educators should focus not so much on selecting games that allow for parent-child interaction in the game, but consider opportunities for social interactions between parents and children around the game where they learn with, from, and about each other while playing. Educators always ask themselves, "What would I like for students/children to learn?" when designing experiences for youth. Similarly, educators should ask themselves, "What kinds of conversations do I want families to have?" when selecting and designing experiences around video games for families in their educational settings.

Connecting Video Games to Real-World Experiences
A quick search on Common Sense Media using the key word "family video games" brings up such video games as *Family Party*, *WiiSport*, and *Dance Central*. These games are designated as games that can be enjoyed by all family members. While these games have a high "fun factor," their potential to foster family conversations beyond the game is limited due to their content and simplistic game mechanics. Mothers who participated in the Family Quest project identified these games as vehicles for family socialization but did not necessarily find them meaningful or impactful for family learning. As we discussed in chapter 4, during the first implementation of the Family Quest program, the game that involved a real-world topic, bullying, prompted a family conversation that went beyond the four walls of the after-school club. Similarly, during Families@Play events, *The Sims 3* consistently stood out as the one game that elicited

family talk that crossed over from the virtual world into real life. As we shared in chapter 4, parents and children created Sims that reflected their physical attributes, personality traits, hobbies, and aspirations. This created an opportunity for parents and children to talk about and negotiate preexisting conceptions of themselves and of each other. When it was time to purchase a house for their Sims, parents brought their experiences in real life to bear on the task of making a decision in the game and modeled ways of thinking for their children. The real-world connections of the bullying game and *The Sims3* were entry points into gaming for parents who did not play video games. They participated in playing the game with their children as equal partners because they had a unique perspective to offer. The real-world connection and expertise parents could bring to gameplay was less obvious around *Minecraft*. Beyond herding animals and chopping trees, parents struggled to figure out how to meaningfully participate in playing the game with children who brought prior knowledge and experience from playing the game with peers. As we will discuss in a later section, for games like *Minecraft*, in which connections to the real world are missing or less obvious, educators can craft experiences around video games that engage families in an inquiry process to help them discover the connections for themselves.

Structuring the Intergenerational Play Activity
Educators know that providing access to technology devices to children is not enough to support their learning and development. Educators need to carefully consider which, when, and how technology devices will be used to achieve desired learning outcomes for children. Similarly, providing access to video games in educational settings to families is not sufficient. An hour of fun playing games will not have a meaningful impact on learning if the whole experience is not intentionally designed to accomplish educational goals for families. Educators must structure intergenerational play events to create opportunities for collaborative learning experiences around video games for families. Not all families will engage in collaborative problem solving and take advantage of the opportunities offered by video games for family learning and connection. Parents and children bring their histories, values, norms, preferences, and knowledge of games to the intergenerational play activity.

As they would do in a classroom setting with children, educators need to structure the intergenerational play activity to accommodate different experiences, styles, and dispositions families bring to the experience. For instance, during our first few Families@Play events, we observed that children who had previous experience with the games tended to control the keyboard and the mouse. Some parents, especially those who were already uncomfortable with using the controllers, often let their children take over the computer and quickly assumed the role of spectator during our event. At the same time, parents who wanted to take turns playing the game ran into conflicts with their children. To ensure that both parties actively participated, we asked parents and children to switch places every so often to give everyone the opportunity for a hands-on experience with the controllers. Later in this chapter, we share similar strategies that educators can use to structure intergenerational play activities and to cultivate the skills valued in the twenty-first–century workplace that these strategies help parents and children develop.

Challenge-based Learning

In the process of exploring and finding ways to support intergenerational play around video games in educational settings, we were inspired by the concept of challenge-based learning (CBL), a pedagogical approach used in K–12 settings to address the disconnect between students' learning in and outside of school.[5] It draws on problem-based learning (PBL), which educators use to engage children in scientific inquiry. Both CBL and PBL focus on students solving real-world problems that are authentic and meaningful. These real-world problems drive students' learning as they engage in a process of guided discovery to solve these problems. These strategies are also geared toward making learning relevant to students' lives. Both approaches aim to engage students in critical thinking and reflection throughout the learning process.

Although CBL and PBL have many commonalities, they differ with respect to how they instantiate these goals and values. First, PBL projects and activities are often implemented in educational settings within a shorter time frame, such as a single class period or a couple of weeks, while CBL requires a longer time commitment, such as a semester, a year, or more. Second, in PBL students often are given a real-world problem, while in CBL students can decide which problems they want to solve in their communities. Students identify a big idea, such as overpopulation or cultural conflict, and then explore an essential question in CBL. In PBL, problems are posed with the expectation that students will discover a solution. Every student is expected to arrive at the same solution although their process might look different. By contrast, in CBL students addressing the same problem arrive at different solutions. Each student might work on a different aspect of the problem. Finally, in CBL students are encouraged to not only find solutions but also implement them. They share their findings not only with peers in their schools but also with the larger community to garner feedback about the impact of their findings. Students cycle through a design thinking process wherein they define the problem, brainstorm ideas for a solution (also known as ideation), generate a model of their solution (i.e., create a prototype), and test their solutions with people in their community.

Educators can use CBL not only to support children's learning in their institutions but also to involve families as a whole through family gaming events and programs. One way to facilitate collaborative learning, productive interactions, and rich conversations between parents and children is through creating *design challenges* around video games. As we discussed earlier, not all games have obvious connections to families' everyday experiences; thus it can be difficult for parents to find ways to successfully participate in intergenerational play with their children. Furthermore, some games might be too open-ended (e.g., sandbox games that do not have clear goals) or have a steep learning curve that causes parents and children to struggle to successfully progress through the game within the time constraints of a family gaming event. Educators can create design challenges around real-world problems that parents and children can explore and find a way to solve, and later reflect on their findings together within the context of the game. Below, we provide guidelines for how to create design challenges around commercial, off-the-shelf video games. Educators can use these guidelines to support intergenerational play around video games in their own institutions and also use them to create experiences around video games for students alone.

Developing Design Challenges

Design challenges around video games can introduce productive constraints on the play experience, and therefore can facilitate learning among and collaboration between parents and children. Educators can create design challenges of varied scopes, from one- or two-hour challenges to weeks-long challenges. They can also create and organize design challenges based on their difficulty level; for instance, families can start with an easy challenge and move on to something a bit more difficult after gaining some experience. Furthermore, educators can create multiple design challenges around a topic, allowing families to deepen their understanding of targeted concepts and learning. These challenges can be used in family gaming events or given to children as "homework" to complete with their parents. Educators can even ask children to take a picture or video recording showing how they approached the challenge with their parents, post their photo or video on the classroom website, and write a reflection about the experience. Through an iterative process of designing, testing, and revising, we identified five components of a well-structured design challenge: (1) a goal, (2) a narrative, (3) rules, (4) tips and resources, and (5) reflection. We walk you through each of these components with an example below.

Setting a Goal

A design challenge needs to have a topic and a clear goal that families can work toward. The goal should grab the attention of the families and be easily understood. For instance, the topic of one design challenge we created around *Minecraft* was "Use Water in the Most Efficient Way in Your Farm to Grow Crops." The task was to "build and test three different farming layouts to grow wheat, and find out which one of your designs is the most efficient way to use water."

Creating a Narrative

Embedding the design goal within a narrative can immerse families in the experience and connect the goal of the design challenge to an authentic real-world experience relevant to families. The narrative should be short, playful, and give a sense of storytelling. The narrative of the farming layout challenge was:

One day, your family decides to move to a small farm out in the country. Everyone is excited because you are going to be growing your own food together. However, when you get to the farm, you realize that there is a problem: the field on the farm isn't very big and water supply is scarce.

It is important to introduce the challenge at the end of the narrative. The narrative should position the parents and children as a team to set the expectation that completing the design challenge involves collaboration.

Identifying Rules

Design challenges need rules to effectively support exploration and discovery. Rules provide productive constraints for the emergence of creativity, which is important for finding solutions. In the farming design challenge, one rule was that families had to design three layouts that looked different from one another. A second rule was that each layout could only be built within a six-by-six-block area including water and soil. By keeping the surface area equal, families were able to compare and contrast their layouts for efficiency of water use.

Providing Tips and Resources

Families bring different levels of expertise and knowledge about the game and the targeted concepts; therefore, it is important to provide them with just enough information to start exploring solutions. In the farming challenge, we identified the items families would need to complete the challenge (grass block, seed, hoe, and water bucket) and where they would find them in the game. We also provided guidance on game mechanics. For instance, as in real-world farming, players cannot place seeds directly onto a grass block in *Minecraft*. We prompted families to think about preparing the soil for planting seeds in the real world. These tips and resources were especially helpful for first-time players of *Minecraft* who were unfamiliar with the game interface and mechanics. Another way for educators to provide tips and resources for a design challenge is to provide links to websites or videos that can orient families to the game and prompt them to begin brainstorming solutions.

Reflecting on the Solution(s)

Reflection is an important part of the learning process in design challenges. We provided questions to spark reflection on the back of the design challenge cards. We wanted families to first work on the challenge and then flip over the card once they had completed the challenge to review the reflection questions. The goal of reflection questions is threefold: (a) to elicit conversations between family members about the process of completing the challenge, (b) to help families make connections between the game and the real world, and (c) to encourage families to further explore the topic. We used the following reflection questions in the farming challenge:

1. How did you determine which layout was the most effective? Why?

2. How is your solution similar to or different from what farmers actually do?

3. How would you optimize water use at your home around various tasks (e.g., gardening, doing laundry, washing the dishes)?

Differences across Educational Settings

Designing meaningful intergenerational play experiences with and around video games that are mutually enjoyable and challenging for parents and children is not an easy task. The physical and social arrangements in different educational settings add another layer of complexity to accomplishing this task successfully. Although schools, museums, and libraries share the same goal of supporting learning among children and their families, each educational setting offers different sets of opportunities and constraints when it comes to designing experiences with and around video games for families. That said, all of these educational settings are spaces to engage families in intergenerational play around video games and help them develop and grow a learning culture that lays the foundation for the successful participation in the twenty-first century.

Unlike museums and libraries, where families drop into and out of the space, schools have access to and relationships and history with families. It is easier for schools to communicate with families about the activities and programs they offer and ensure attendance and sustained participation. Both school and library environments are conducive to running single ninety-minute to two-hour events or weekly meetings for families to come together. A minimum of ninety minutes of play allows families to spend about thirty to forty-five minutes learning about basic game mechanics and controls, and spend an hour actually playing the game as a team. This setup works for both single- and multiplayer games. Educators can use a computer lab or bring computer carts to an empty room to run their activities and programs. Parents and children do not need to have their own computers; in fact, sharing a computer is more productive for learning how to work together.

Although libraries may run into issues with attendance, it is more feasible to design programs that extend over several months at libraries. Because libraries stay open for longer hours than schools do, a program that runs in the evenings during the work week may work better for families. We had the most success in schools when we held ninety-minute to two-hour events one evening per month and three-hour Saturday events. These events can be organized around and coordinated with other school activities targeting families, such as parent-teacher meetings, open houses, charity events, and homecoming. Alternatively, a parental engagement component can be added to existing after-school activities in schools. For instance, parents can be invited a couple of times throughout the semester to children's game design clubs.

Compared to schools and libraries, the time families spend at different exhibits or galleries in museums is limited. Families can spend as little as three to five minutes at one exhibit. This introduces a significant constraint on the type of game experience that can be designed and the kinds of learning the designed experience can support among families. Playing digital and nondigital games takes time because players need to learn the different components of each game. Additionally, players become more skilled and develop deeper understanding the more they play the game. We found that the best way to support intergenerational play in museums is to arrange one or two computers in a kiosk or booth where families can engage in short design challenges that allow them to further explore the theme of specific exhibits. Sandbox games like *Minecraft* and simulation games are particularly well suited for engaging families in meaningful interactions and learning in short periods of time in museums, as they allow for building and modeling structures and systems. The basic building tools can be mastered relatively quickly, or participants can be provided with premade structures that can be modified to illustrate a concept or idea.

Recommendations for Game Designers

We started this book by pointing out that families have a long history with games. Many families play board and card games to spend time together, have fun and connect. Games that require two or more players such as chess, checkers, *Settlers of Catan*, and *Monopoly* have been most popular among families. Although these multiplayer games are not intentionally designed for families, they engage all family members and sustain their interest over time. Compared to card and board games, playing video games is less common among families. Popular multiplayer games, especially role-playing games like *Call of Duty*, *World of Warcraft*, and *Halo*, are not appealing to many families due to their violent content. When families play video games together, they tend to play puzzle, action-adventure, sports, and trivia games that have neutral (or safe) content and low barriers for entry due to their simple game mechanics. At the same time, the game industry chooses which games to develop and how to market them. The aforementioned game genres are often marketed as "family friendly," with advertisements for these games featuring family members playing together and having fun, while advertisements for multiplayer role-playing games tend to target "hard core gamers" by using masculine imagery to attract men in their twenties and thirties.

The current conceptualization of "family-friendly" video games among game designers is narrowly defined. An online search of family-friendly video games brings up video games that share the following attributes: multiplayer game experiences, minimal content, and simple game mechanics. From a business perspective this approach makes complete sense. To make a product (such as video games) broadly appealing and marketable, one needs to design the product for the average consumer rather than considering the nuances of the varied needs of individual consumers. However, there is no single user profile that represents all types of families. To increase the participation of families in video gaming for the purposes of supporting family learning, connection, and communication and growing the game industry, we need to go beyond this simple business rule of thumb for making money.

As we stated in the beginning of the book, there is a sharp distinction between educational and entertaining video games both in the industry and in the ways many game designers and parents think about video games. More recently, educational video games have been located under the broader umbrella term or genre of "serious games," which aim to engage players with skills, knowledge, and understandings that transcend the game. Serious games often teach something directly to players or are intentionally designed for players to achieve a set of learning outcomes. On the one hand, compared to video games designed for entertainment purposes, serious video games have limited financial returns. They are harder to design well because of the challenges associated with trying to marry learning outcomes to enjoyable gameplay. On the other hand, designing video games solely for entertainment does not take advantage of their potential to contribute to a wider range of societal goals.

Like many other industries, the game industry might adopt a double bottom line approach to business and strive to achieve both financial and social gains. We believe that families are a great demographic for the game industry to target in exploring this new approach to business. An investment in exploring new ways of designing for families, reenvisioning family-friendly games, and creating intergenerational play experiences that support collaboration, learning, and communication can be both financially lucrative and socially impactful. We share here the design con siderations that emerged from our own work and others' to inspire game designers to pursue such a vision.

Establishing Personal Relevance

One observation that emerged across the different studies we conducted is that the personal relevance of the game is what initially motivates parents to play video games with their children. Personal relevance takes on two different forms. As we highlighted in chapter 2, parents who played video games while growing up or as adults engage their children with the video games they enjoy playing as a means of connecting around a shared interest. In the case of the Livingstones, for instance, *Halo* was a personally relevant game for the parents because of their own histories with the game. In other words, parents' own interest in and experience, sustained engagement, and relationship with a video game is what makes that video game personally relevant. The success of *Mario Bros.* arguably lies in this form of personal relevance; many parents played *Mario Bros.* while growing up and now play the game with their children.

The second form of personal relevance is tied to the connection of a video game to real-world issues. In the Families@Play and Family Quest projects, parents enjoyed the games that they played with their children when the game allowed them to talk about their own experiences and to see the relevance of game content to real-world issues. Given that many parents report disliking the content of video games as one of the primary reasons for not playing video games with their children, it is important for game designers to consider how they are establishing personal relevance when designing video games for families. One possible direction for game design is to create games around topics that are difficult for parents to discuss with their children, particularly adolescent children. Using media to raise awareness around important social issues, especially for teens, has gained popularity over the last two decades. Designing video games for families not only builds on such efforts but also can recruit parents as partners in confronting concerns such as bullying, depression, peer pressure, and other problems that affect our youth.

Finally, the third form of personal relevance is the connection of a video game to families' cultural identities and experiences. As we discussed in chapter 4, the parents we interviewed enjoyed video games such as *FIFA* and *Civilization* not because these games were overtly designed for people with Mexican heritage but because parents and children brought their own cultural heritage to the game experience and made connections to their heritage as a family. When they are personally relevant in this way, video games become a context for bringing generations together and help families maintain their cultural heritage over time. Many immigrant communities perceive technology, including video games, as a force that drives a wedge between the new and old generations. Game designers can address the desire for cultural continuity by considering how game content and mechanics offer opportunities for families to recruit and share their cultural heritage across generations.

Considering Developmental Appropriateness

Games designed for families tend to ignore the capabilities and needs of children in different developmental stages. While simple game mechanics can sustain the interest of young children for long periods of time, they may be too easy to master and therefore boring for older children.

Furthermore, parents enjoy playing video games with their younger and older children for different reasons. Parents may enjoy teaching their younger children and appreciate learning from older children while playing video games. Video games intended to support intergenerational play among families with younger versus older children need to be designed differently.

A good example is *Once upon a Monster*, an Xbox 360 game designed for younger children and their parents, who can play along with their children by taking on a different character than their children. As Cookie Monster and Elmo, parents and children go through different chapters of a storybook, using the controllers to collaboratively play a series of minigames in each chapter. This game is appropriate for younger children but not for older children who have more advanced cognitive skills and have already learned foundational skills such as identifying numbers and the alphabet.

Video games that young adolescents and their parents will enjoy playing need to be designed differently. Given their more advanced cognitive capacities, adolescents can complete more challenging tasks while still needing support from their parents. Furthermore, some online role-playing video games may be too open ended and others might be too simplistic to engage both parents and adolescent children. For example, a parent who is new to video games can enjoy a game with simple game mechanics whereas a child who is more experienced with video games might find the same game boring. A good video game for intergenerational play creates opportunities for parents and children to bring different sets of skills to solve interesting problems together.

One way to create interesting problems in games involves utilizing dilemmas—ill-structured problems that are similar to those people encounter in their everyday lives.[6] These problems have multiple potential solutions and require the integration of different conceptual, physical, and social resources to reach a solution. These problems also present opportunities for sharing opinions and beliefs with others, as well as what Daniel Schwartz and John Bransford call "sensitivity to differentiated information," as participants in collaborative problem solving need to pay attention to multiple pieces of evidence during consensus building.[7]

Facilitating Division of Labor

In MMORPGs, division of labor among players occurs as they take on characters that have different strengths and weaknesses and collaborate around shared tasks by assuming roles that match their current abilities.

In other words, each player contributes a particular form of expertise to the successful completion of the task. Collaboration is often dependent on such a division of labor both in video games and in the real world. *Once upon a Monster*, for example, facilitates this kind of division of labor. In one instance, Elmo gets onto the shoulders of Cookie Monster when they travel to their next destination. One player as Cookie Monster walks to the destination while the other player as Elmo ducks to avoid hitting tree branches. As we have demonstrated throughout the chapters of this book, parents and children engage in this type of collaboration when they play MMORPGs; however, there are few video games like *Once upon a Monster* that are designed intentionally for families to collaborate in these ways.

How are game designers currently engaging parents with their children's gaming? A common practice in the game industry is to design features that alleviate parents' concerns about the potential exposure of their children to negative or inappropriate behaviors and content. Many video games that target young children (e.g., *Club Penguin* and *Wizard 101*) ask for a parent's e-mail address to set up a username and password. To enhance (and display) the educational value of their video games, some game companies collect children's gameplay data and send e-mails to parents so they can track their children's learning trajectory within the game. Others provide parents with recommendations for learning activities that build on children's interests and learning around the game. Although these are useful ways to inform parents about their children's gameplay, these forms of engagement are not participatory in the sense that parents are not coengaging in playing video games with their children.

There are multiple ways that game designers can support collaborative intergenerational play experiences that are not as expensive as designing a multiplayer experience for families. As we have discussed in this book, parents and children take turns while playing single-player video games. A simple prompt to change places in a single-player experience can be an effective way to support parents' participation in intergenerational play. Furthermore, any single-player game can include guidelines or suggestions for how parents and children can play the game together by alternating the responsibilities of "driver" and "navigator" as they progress through the game.

Prioritizing Critical and Consequential Conversations

Video games are an interactive medium by design in that they respond to users' actions. In the field of game design, this unique aspect of video games is privileged over the traditional understanding of interactivity associated with books and movies. Interactivity in the context of books and movies takes one of two forms: (1) individuals thinking differently about a concept or a topic, and (2) interactions among people regarding the medium as well as the ideas introduced through the medium. For example, one engages with ideas of friendship while reading the book *Charlotte's Web* and can discuss this idea with others as well as talk about the book as a literary accomplishment. One can also think about interactivity in this case as the connection between the author and the audience or users. In video games that are marketed toward families, such as Nintendo's *Wii Sports*, the exchange between the players and the system mirrors real life and is seamless. While this results in a more enjoyable and engaging game experience for all family members, the *perceived interactivity* of the game[8]— that is, the game's ability to transform relations between those who play the game as well as between people and content—may be low.

As we mentioned in chapter 3, people do not play video games with the intention of talking, but they often do anyway. The quality of conversations is what makes playing video games an important activity in the context of families. Research suggests that meaningful learning—the kind of learning that results in the learner being able to use information to solve problems outside of the context in which that information is being learned[9]—requires children to move beyond conceptual engagement (understanding the content to be learned) and procedural engagement (learning about what to do).[10] Similarly, for families to see beyond the entertainment value of video gaming and invest their time in intergenerational play, the game needs to offer opportunities for families to engage in critical and consequential conversations among themselves around the game. Games that engage families in procedural conversations, such as managing controllers and gameplay, can only go so far in sustaining families' interest in intergenerational play.

We argue that perceived interactivity realized through critical and consequential conversations among families is more influential than designed interactivity of the game. Game designers usually focus more on designed interactivity and how to improve it through new technologies than perceived interactivity. There needs to be a shift in focus from a *technical* understanding of interactivity (i.e., the relationship between the person and the game system) to a *social* understanding of interactivity as the basis for designing video games that support family learning, communication, and connection. To design for interactivity in the social sense, game designers need to start their development process by identifying the kinds of conversations they want to promote among family members and moving back and forth between technical and social aspects of interaction design.

Conclusion

Throughout this book, we demonstrated how families learn and connect in powerful ways around video gaming. The family gaming experiences we shared in this book range from multiplayer experiences around game consoles to single-player experiences around mobile devices and computers. Intergenerational play around video games occurs naturally in the context of families' homes, but games can be designed to promote this kind of play as well. Although video gaming is a routine and a ritual in many families, we have yet to unearth the true potential of video games to support learning, connection, and communication among families. An evolution in the design of video games and the experiences we craft around them will play a key role in transforming video gaming from a trivial leisure activity to one that is transformative for families. The task of designing better video gaming experiences for families lies in the hands of educators and game designers.

The following quote by Steve Jobs rings true in the context of designing games and game-based experiences for families: "It's really hard to design products by focus groups. A lot of times, people don't know what they want until you show it to them."[11] When asked, many parents are concerned about their children's video gaming and may have difficulty imagining how video gaming could be productive both for their children and the family. They need to step into a meaningful designed experience with and around video games to realize what the medium could do for them and their children. On the one hand, the design of many commercial games that are popular among children are not overtly educational enough to persuade parents that they are worthwhile. On the other hand, so-called "family-friendly" video games are designed to be entertaining in often simplistic ways, and lack the potential for sustained engagement and impact on family learning.

As we discussed in this final chapter, educators and game designers can create opportunities for families to learn, connect, and communicate. Family events and programs that invite families to spend time together while exploring video games in formal and informal educational settings can serve multiple purposes. They can extend children's learning in the classroom to the home, help parents learn about video games, and support parental engagement with the educational institution. Similarly, video games that are intentionally designed to support intergenerational play can be a vehicle for connecting generations and learning across the real and fictional world of games. Design starts by empathizing with the user to create human experiences that transform people's relationships with each other and the world. In this book, we put families at the center of our inquiry to understand their experiences around video games and inspire better designs that support their well-being, connection, and learning.

Appendix A: Overview of Projects

Family Quest (2007–2011)
- **Investigator:** Sinem Siyahhan
- **Participants:** Thirty-two families with diverse backgrounds
- **Description:** A design-based research project aiming to iteratively develop and test educational video games that support intergenerational play between parents and children. Families played immersive role-playing games at various sites as part of a family after-school program. Observations of parent-child interactions during gameplay were video recorded. Surveys and interviews with parents and children were used to capture their gameplay experiences and interest in video gaming and playing together.

Focus Group Study (2012)
- **Investigators:** Elisabeth Gee and Sinem Siyahhan
- **Participants:** Thirteen predominantly Caucasian parents
- **Description:** Interviews with a group of parents at two different schools to understand their experiences, observations, beliefs, and values around video gaming. Interviews were audio recorded.

Families@Play (2013–2015)
- **Investigators:** Sinem Siyahhan and Elisabeth Gee
- **Participants:** Forty-four families with diverse backgrounds
- **Description:** A design-based research project aiming to optimize family learning around commercial video games through designing experiences around them. Parents and children (ages nine to thirteen) completed design challenges while playing games such as *Minecraft*, *The Sims*, and *Civilization* during ninety-minute family gaming events held at seven different sites. Observations of parent-child

interactions during gameplay were video recorded. Parents and children were surveyed and interviewed.

Games@Museums (2014)

- **Investigators:** Sinem Siyahhan
- **Participants:** Fifty-seven families with diverse backgrounds
- **Description:** A pre- and post-design study aiming to understand family learning around video games in the context of museums. Parents and children (ages nine to thirteen) played through a twelve-minute design challenge around *Minecraft* as part of a technology exhibit in a museum. Parents and children filled out a survey before and after gameplay. Observations of family interactions during the challenge were video recorded.

Joint Media Engagement, Play, Literacy, and Learning (2013–2015)

- **Investigators:** Elisabeth Gee and Sinem Siyahhan
- **Participants:** Sixteen Mexican American families
- **Description:** An ethnographic study of the use of digital media technologies within families' homes. Home visits took place every two months over a six-month period. The study involved interviews and surveys with parents and children about the content and the context of their digital media use. Observations of family interactions around digital and nondigital games were video recorded. Parents kept a photo diary between home visits.

Appendix B: List of Games

In this appendix, we provide brief descriptions of video games that were mentioned in the book. This is not intended to be a list of "recommended" games for families but rather a resource for readers who may be unfamiliar with these games and would like to know more about them. Video games and game platforms change rapidly, and some of these games may no longer be available or have been replaced by newer versions. For each game, we provide basic information such as the game's genre (single-player, first-person shooter, puzzle, role-playing game, etc.), platform, goals, and mechanics. We also note the Entertainment Software Rating Board (ESRB) rating for each game. For games that do not have an ESRB rating, we share the recommendation of Common Sense Media (http://www.commonsensemedia.org).

Angry Birds

This 2-D puzzle game features multicolored birds trying to save their eggs from evil green pigs. The goal of the players is to launch a limited number of birds from a slingshot to collapse the structures inhabited by the evil pigs. The birds fly and fall through the air guided by an in-game physics engine, and points are awarded for the player's efficiency in destroying enemy structures. The levels of the game become increasingly challenging. Since its release in 2009 for the Apple iPhone, the game has inspired numerous sequels and spinoffs in video games and various other media. The game can be played on mobile phones, handheld gaming devices, and game consoles. The current ESRB rating is E for everyone.

Animal Jam

Produced in collaboration with the National Geographic Society, *Animal Jam* is a multiplayer online environment and social networking site featuring a variety of games and other in-world activities. Players take on the role of virtual animals that can be outfitted and controlled in the virtual environment, which is made up of different biomes based on natural habitats. Players can interact with one another and even chat with varying levels of restriction. Players can watch videos in the virtual environment and earn in-game currency to purchase collectible items. The game can be played on computers with Internet access. Common Sense Media identifies this game as being appropriate for children ages ten and up.

Borderlands

This is a series of first-person shooter games in which players battle through a hostile landscape on an alien planet. The games are known as role-playing shooters because gameplay includes a character-building element, and players must strategize and choose skills for their characters as they level up. Players take on the role of a treasure hunter who is trying to find a mysterious treasure trove known as the vault. Players choose one of four characters to play, each with unique skills and abilities. The game can be played on computers and game consoles. The current ESRB rating is M for mature (ages seventeen and up).

Call of Duty

A first-person shooter franchise in which players take on the role of a soldier in combat and work with a team of allies to accomplish a variety of cooperative or competitive tasks to destroy the enemy. The game can be played in single- or multiplayer mode. Drawing heavily from military history as well as contemporary military technologies, the series has inspired a notable amount of technical discussions among fan communities around in-game specifics as well as how the game's design does or does not reflect the realities of combat situations. The game can be played on computers and game consoles. The current ESRB rating is M.

Candy Crush

A puzzle game in which players are presented with a game board covered with pieces of candy, and must match three candies of the same color either vertically or horizontally. When the candies are matched, they "clear" from the board and the player scores points. Players need to score a certain number of points in a certain amount of time to win a level. The game can be played on the publisher's website, through Facebook, and as a mobile app. *Candy Crush* is considered a "freemium" game (a game that is free to download and play, but allows players to purchase various bonus items). Common Sense Media identifies this game as being appropriate for children ages thirteen and up.

Civilization

A turn-based strategy game series where players take on the role of a historical leader of a civilization, such as Cleopatra, Alexander the Great, or Abraham Lincoln, and guide their civilization from ancient history to modern times (and beyond). The player does not have an avatar, and instead interacts with the game by researching technologies, building cities and expanding territory, conducting diplomatic relations with other civilizations, and moving units around the map. Originally released in 1991 for PC, the game can now be played on game consoles and some mobile devices as well. It is a single-player game, but some versions also have a competitive multiplayer option. The current ESRB rating is E.

Diamond Dash

A high-speed puzzle game in which players match three similarly colored blocks to earn points and clear the gameplay area. Players have sixty seconds per match to clear as many blocks as possible using the "match three" mechanic, with increased scores unlocking powers that can make block-clearing more efficient. The game can be played on the publisher's website, through Facebook, and as a mobile app. Like *Candy Crush*, *Diamond Dash* is a freemium game that allows in-app purchases. Common Sense Media identifies this game as being appropriate for ages thirteen and up.

Disney Infinity

An action-adventure sandbox game that uses collectible figurines that players can purchase, which are then synchronized with characters inside the game. Once they have unlocked an in-game character by synchronizing it with a figurine, players can take that character on adventures inside the virtual world. Players can play solo or with a friend through Play Set mode (the "campaign" or "story" mode), which features characters from specific Disney franchises interacting with one another (e.g., a *Pirates of the Caribbean* Play Set). Toy Box mode allows players to create a virtual "sandbox" to play in, and supports multiple players to join in games together. Some reviewers have compared the Toy Box mode to playing *Minecraft* with a

Disney twist, as it allows a similar degree of freedom and creativity and encourages players to be world-builders themselves. The game can be played on computers and game consoles. The current ESRB rating is E.

Eve

This game, also referred to as *Eve Online*, is a massively multiplayer online role-playing game (MMORPG) that requires a monthly subscription. The game invites players into an online world where they can engage in a variety of in-game activities, including mining, piracy, exploration, and combat with one another or computer-controlled opponents. There are over 7,800 star systems that can be explored by players. Choosing one of four playable races, players take to space in futuristic ships to explore a shared online universe. In addition to widely attended in-game events, such as wars between player factions, the game also features tournaments and even a volunteer program, which helps answer questions and accomplish a variety of other maintenance tasks to enhance the gameplay experience for other players. The game can be played on computers with an Internet connection. Common Sense Media identifies this game as being appropriate for ages fourteen and up.

EverQuest

A 3-D fantasy-themed MMORPG first released in 1997. It is recognized as the second commercially viable MMORPG and the first to use a 3-D game engine. Players take on the role of a variety of specialized heroes in such classes as strong-willed warriors, stealthy rogues, and powerful wizards, and join other players to battle monsters, seek treasure, and improve their characters' skills in an immersive world. More than twenty subsequent expansions to the game have been released since the game's debut, each raising the "level cap" (the maximum level player characters can reach by gaining experience points) and adding new quests and adventures. The game can be played on computers that have Internet access. The current ESRB rating is T for teen.

Farmville

In this simulation game, players place buildings and crops on their farm. The crops have a set period in which they grow, and once they are fully grown players can click on them to harvest them. As a result, players often check the game multiple times per day to harvest crops and plant new ones. The game is played through Facebook or via mobile app. The social component of the game is important, as players who are Facebook friends can visit each other's farms. They can also send invitations to Facebook friends who do not play the game. Although it is a single-player game, interacting socially on Facebook in-game gives players bonuses, such as coins to buy new buildings and upgrade existing ones. The goal of the game is to make money to improve the farm. Common Sense Media identifies this game as being appropriate for ages thirteen and up.

FIFA Soccer

This soccer simulation game is based on soccer tournaments held by FIFA, the Fédération Internationale de Football Association (International Federation of Association Football). The player can take on the role of both the manager and the players of different soccer teams that are members of the association. During a match, players can switch between controlling each of the soccer players on their team in real time as the ball is passed around the field. Initially featuring local competitive play, recent versions of the game have been expanded to include online cooperative and competitive gameplay. The game can be played on game consoles and mobile devices. The current ESRB rating is E.

Flappy Bird

A side-scrolling game designed for mobile devices, released in 2013. In this game, players control a flying bird by tapping the screen repeatedly. The goal of the game is to steer the bird and avoid hitting obstacles in the form of green tubes. The game requires a great deal of dexterity to successfully guide the bird through the obstacles. There are no levels; the player earns one point for each set of tubes they successfully pass through. The game was removed from the Apple Store and Google Play by the developer in 2014. However, remakes of the game are still available for those who enjoyed playing the original game. This game has neither an ESRB rating nor a review on Common Sense Media.

Grand Theft Auto

An action-adventure video game series first released in 1997. The games are generally set in fictional urban environments, often based on real-world locales. The games' various protagonists typically find themselves in dire circumstances and, deciding that their only chance for survival or success lies outside the law, attempt to rise through the ranks of the criminal underworld. Part of the allure of the game, however, is in the open-ended ways that missions can be accomplished—through stealth, conversational finesse, direct confrontation, or other means. The most recent release in the series also included a widely adopted online multiplayer mode for players to join cooperative or competitive gameplay. The game can be played on computers, game consoles, and mobile devices. The current ESRB rating is M.

Halo

This first-person shooter game series center on an interstellar war for the fate of humanity. Players take on the role of Master Chief John-117, one of a group of supersoldiers deployed to combat a theocratic alien race called the Covenant. Aside from the single-player, story-based campaign, players can also connect with one another online or in-person to play cooperative or competitive matches. High-tech gadgetry and vehicle-based combat are seamlessly integrated into the game, leading to a variable and highly acclaimed gaming experience for players. Hailed as the most successful game of its genre developed for the Xbox, *Halo* has inspired a host of sequels and spin-off media, including novels, comics, collectible figures, and even games of other genres. The game can be played on Xbox game consoles. The current ESRB rating is T.

Happy Action Theater

An augmented reality game for Xbox that uses the Kinect motion sensor to show the player on-screen. It was originally designed with small children in mind, and offers eighteen different short games that allow players to interact with virtual environments—for example, playing with balloons, interacting with fish, or dancing. These are not goal-oriented games; rather, they were designed for the ways that children tend to interact with games, in that they often ignore stated rules or find new ways to play. It can be played solo or with multiple players. The current ESRB rating is E.

Just Dance

A series of rhythm games released for game consoles in which players must dance to music to score points. Players follow the motions of a dancer on-screen, and they are tracked with a Wii remote (the controller for Nintendo's Wii and Wii U systems) or with a camera (in the case of the Xbox and PlayStation versions of the game). It is a multiplayer game for up to four players, and while it can be played alone it is generally considered a party game to be played with friends or family members. The goal of the game is to score more points than other players. The games feature licensed popular music, and in each installment of the game the soundtrack is updated to reflect current pop songs and as well as classic dance songs. There are also versions featuring specific music; for example, there is a Michael Jackson version, a hip-hop version, and so on. The current ESRB rating is E.

League of Legends

Belonging to a genre of games known as massively multiplayer online battle arenas (MOBA), *League of Legends* players direct a character known as a champion. Each champion has its own skills, strengths, and weaknesses. Players choose or are placed on teams, and the game consists of two teams battling each other. The goal of the game is to destroy the other team's base, while at the same time defending one's own base. The game is very popular in the world of electronic sports (eSports), in which players compete for cash prizes (up to millions of US dollars) and spectators watch gameplay, often streamed online or televised. Throughout the course of a match, characters gain levels and unlock powers; these improvements do not carry over into other matches, however. The game is free to play with optional purchases, and is available for download on home computers. The current ESRB rating is T.

The Legend of Zelda

First released in 1986, *The Legend of Zelda* is one of Nintendo's most popular action-adventure franchises, with more than twenty versions of the game existing across various platforms, including the Nintendo DS and Wii. The *Zelda* games combine puzzles, exploration, combat, and role-playing in a fantasy setting. The goal of the many versions of the game is for Link, the central protagonist of the series, to rescue Princess Zelda. In each installment of the game, Link encounters different obstacles in achieving this goal. The ESRB ratings vary across the series, but the game is usually rated either E or E10+.

Lego Star Wars

A Lego-themed action-adventure game based on the Lego *Star Wars* line of toys, first released in 2005. The first game in the Lego video game series, *Lego Star Wars* adapts the story line of the *Star Wars* prequel trilogy

(Episodes I, II, and III) and was developed for multiple game consoles, computers, and handheld devices. One or two players can play through the game's various scenarios, each based on various parts of the *Star Wars* prequel movies. Each character has a certain set of abilities that can be used to solve the game's various puzzles; players can interact with other friendly characters to unlock their abilities and use them to play through the game. While the main objective of the game is to complete all scenarios in the story sequence, players can earn additional currency, called "studs," to unlock new characters and features to use in free-play mode. The current ESRB rating is E10+ for everyone ten years old and up.

Mario Bros.

The first in a series of platforming games that put Nintendo on the map, this game was originally released for coin-operated arcade consoles in 1983. In the spirit of the original game, which involved players jumping across platforms to defeat enemies, successors such as the *Super Mario Bros.* series added side-scrolling functionality, which allowed players to progress across longer levels and navigate new obstacles. In most recent versions of the games, the concept has expanded into the 3-D world, with the titular Mario character now able to flip, climb, punch, or slide through obstacles, all in the pursuit of defeating the Koopa King Bowser and saving the Mushroom Kingdom from certain doom. The series has been critically acclaimed as "canonical" to the history of video games and its influence can be seen across all sorts of games, communities, and game-related media. *Mario* games have been created for every Nintendo console; the most recent installments can be played on Nintendo DS and Wii. The series' current ESRB rating is E.

Mario Kart

A go-kart–racing game series featuring characters and environments from the *Mario* franchise. Across all games in the series, players take control of one of a roster of heroes or villains, including Mario's more agile brother Luigi, the resourceful Princess Peach, or the heavy-hitting King Bowser himself. During each race, players compete with other racers to earn the fastest time on a variety of obstacle-filled courses. The single-player mode allows for single- or multirace "campaigns," while the multiplayer mode adds an extra "battle" mode in which players attempt to pop balloons on the karts of their opponents by throwing turtle shells, dropping banana peels, or using environmental hazards.

Last kart standing wins. The game is available only on Nintendo game consoles. The current ESRB rating is E.

Minecraft

This open sandbox game allows players to build anything they can imagine in a virtual environment that looks like a forest. Through an avatar, players mine for raw materials (e.g., wood) and craft tools with the raw materials to be able to create structures that range from simple to complex (e.g., a house). The virtual environment has day and night cycles. The game can be played in Survival and Creative mode. In Survival mode, players need to protect themselves from zombies called "Creepers" while they mine raw materials and craft tools to grow their inventory. In Creative mode, players have all the items and tools they need in their inventory. They can also build without the fear of zombies attacking them at night. The game can also be played as a single- or multiplayer experience. The game can be downloaded on personal computers, game consoles, and handheld devices. The game has no rules or specific goal to achieve; players merely need to know the recipes and materials needed to craft tools. The current ESRB rating is E10+.

Once upon a Monster

Released for the Xbox 360 in 2011, this game features existing *Sesame Street* characters Cookie Monster and Elmo and a new character, Marco. The game is presented as a storybook with several chapters that are broken into a series of minigames. These games require the Kinect peripheral and can be played with one or two players. The current ESRB rating is E.

Oregon Trail

Released in 1974, this point-and-click computer game was originally designed to teach schoolchildren about the harsh journey of nineteenth-century pioneers along the Oregon Trail. Players take on the role of a caravan leader and must hunt, trade, cross rivers, and make various decisions along the trail to ensure that as many of the caravan's residents as possible survive the journey. Gameplay is simple, with players pointing and clicking with a mouse to engage in various in-game activities. The player earns a score based on the number of family members and possessions that survive the journey, multiplied by each trip's "starting difficulty," which is determined by the initial profession selected by the player. The game's popularity and success inspired a multitude of sequels, spin-offs, and spoofs, and was recently inducted into the World Video Game Hall of Fame for its popularity among gamers growing up in the 1990s and 2000s. The game was recently adapted for the Nintendo DS and Wii. The current ESRB rating is E10+.

Pokémon Go

Released in 2016, this location-based augmented reality game is played on mobile devices, including iPhones and Android phones. Players walk around with their phones to find and catch virtual monsters known as Pokémon. These monsters are from the popular *Pokémon* series of games released for Nintendo handheld devices. The creatures in *Pokémon Go* are found in real-world locations, such as parks, malls, and other public places. They are superimposed over the real-life settings using the phone's camera, and players can capture Pokémon by throwing a Poké Ball at the creatures on their screens. Players then use these creatures to battle with other players for territory at "gyms." These gyms are situated at locations of interest in the real world, such as landmarks, statues, or buildings Common Sense Media identifies this game as being appropriate for ages thirteen and up.

Portal 2

Originally released in 2011, this 3-D puzzle platform game is a sequel to *Portal* for PlayStation, Xbox, and computer platforms. Played from a first-person perspective, this game challenges players to navigate environments using a "portal gun" to teleport from one position to an area that might be impossible to reach without it. *Portal 2* builds on the original game's features with tractor beams, speed-increasing gels, and bridges made of light. The game can be played in single-player or two-player cooperative split-screen modes, with each player being given a portal gun to work together solving puzzles. The current ESRB rating is E10+.

Roblox

In this MMORPG, players build their own virtual worlds and games. There is no way to win the game; rather, players explore the virtual worlds created by others using a customized avatar. Players can craft items, find resources, and engage in combat. A key part of the game is using *Roblox Studio*, a separate application, to build games and worlds for other players to enjoy. This is accomplished using a scripting language known as

Lua. Players can be paid with in-game currency for developing games, and this currency can even be cashed out into US dollars. As of 2013, players under the age of thirteen are permitted to create content and post it for others. Players in this age range are protected in chats with other players by a list of acceptable words. *Roblox* can be played on computers and game consoles, as well as iOS. The current ESRB rating is E10+.

Scribblenauts

A single-player puzzle action game in which players solve problems using written words. The player controls an avatar that traverses 2-D levels featuring several obstacles. Players must come up with creative solutions to these problems by writing a noun, which then appears in the game world. For example, the player may need to cross a river. The player could write "boat," which would make a boat appear to take the player across the river, or "bridge," which would yield a bridge that the player could walk across. Alternatively, "Pegasus" would also be a workable solution, as the player could ride this creature and fly over the river. The player advances to the next level by collecting stars. The puzzles grow more complex as gameplay continues. The game was originally released for the Nintendo DS, but versions have since been released for Nintendo's 3DS and Wii U, PC, and iOS. The current ESRB rating is E10+.

SimCity

A popular single-player city-building game series, with versions released for computers, game consoles, and handheld devices. The player has no avatar but instead takes on the role of a mayor, managing all aspects of a city. These include zoning, placing infrastructure, signing ordinances, and levying taxes. The player can see what effect specific actions have on the city overall. For example, decreasing industrial taxes will bring in less revenue, but will ultimately attract more industry and jobs to the city. While there are no specific goals in the main game, there are scenarios the player can select which offer specific challenges, such as dealing with a series of emergencies from the outset or reviving a town which has lost most of its jobs. The current ESRB rating is E10+ but some versions are rated E.

The Sims 3

This single-player life simulation game is the third in the popular series *The Sims*. In these games, players create and control virtual people ("Sims") and guide them through the tasks of everyday life. These tasks include going to work, making food, learning skills, socializing with friends, and taking care of family members. The player does not have an avatar; rather he or she directs the Sims to perform actions. These characters have some degree of autonomy and will perform actions on their own if not given directions by the player. An important aspect of the game is building, as players can design and build houses, including the overall structure of the house, the placement of furniture and decorations, the color of walls and floors, and the outdoor area of the home. While players must earn money in the game to build houses, it is a common practice for players to use cheat codes to acquire unlimited money with which to build houses and buy objects. The game can be played on personal computers, game consoles, and handheld devices. The current ESRB rating is T.

Spore

In this single-user simulation game released for PC and Mac, the player guides the evolution of a species from a single-celled organism to a sentient creature with a civilization to a space-faring species that explores other worlds. Each of the five stages of the game (cell, creature, tribal, civilization, and space) features completely different gameplay. For example, the creature stage involves taking direct control of a creature as it tries to survive. Players must hunt, avoid predators, and seek a mate to create the next generation. The goal of each stage is to survive and progress to the next stage. Once the player reaches the space stage, the game becomes more of a sandbox game about exploration. The current ESRB rating is E10+.

Street Fighter

Released in 1987 as a single-player arcade game, this series is often credited as setting many of the conventions of one-on-one fighting games over the years. Players choose one of the characters from different countries around the world and enter into martial arts matches with a nonplayer character (NPC) designed by the game system who is also a fighter. Each character has a unique fighting style and move set, and players must learn the button combinations that correspond to these special moves to master each character. When a fighter's health bar is depleted, the round ends, and after a set number of rounds, the match is over and one player is declared the winner. The game also features a campaign mode, in which players must win matches against several fighters from the roster and face a final boss at the end. Currently, the game can be played in single- and multiplayer mode on computers, game consoles, and handheld devices. The current ESRB rating is T.

Subway Surfer

In this single-player game played on mobile phones, players take on the role of a graffiti artist who must escape from authorities by running down subway tracks. In the game, play continues until the player runs into a train or other obstacle. At the same time, players are trying to increase their score by collecting coins scattered throughout the level. The goal is to collect as many coins as possible without colliding with an obstacle. There are various iterations of the game, some of them set in real-world locations, and all of the versions boast bright and cartoonlike graphics. Common Sense Media identifies this game as being appropriate for children ages nine and up.

Tetris

A puzzle game originally made in 1984 and released on the Commodore 64 home computer, *Tetris* has long been considered a classic game and remains ubiquitous to this day. A version of it has been made for almost every game console, computer operating system, and mobile device. Its mechanics are simple: players rotate and move seven different shapes, which fall from the top of the screen in a random order. The goal of the game is to line these shapes up so that they fit together with no gaps in between them. When a horizontal line across the screen is completely filled with shapes, the line is "cleared" and the player earns points. The more lines that are cleared simultaneously, the higher the score. If the shapes are aligned imperfectly and gaps are left between them, the screen begins to fill up with shapes. When it fills up completely, the game ends. While *Tetris* is usually single player, multiplayer competitive versions also exist. The current ESRB rating is E.

World of Warcraft

Released in 2004, this popular MMORPG is originally set in the fictional world of Azeroth. Upon logging into the virtual world, players choose the race, class, and gender of their character. Through this avatar, players explore the fictional world, complete quests, and engage in other in-game activities to level up their character by gaining skills, experience, currency, and so forth. Players can engage in battles with NPCs designed by the game developers or other players' avatars. The player versus player (PVP) function allows individuals as well as large and small groups of players to compete against one another. The current ESRB rating is T.

Zoo Tycoon

In this business simulation game, players manage all aspects of a zoo, including planning the zoo's layout, designing exhibits, purchasing animals, choosing vendors, and setting prices. Each animal has preferences for its exhibit, including size, decorations, shelter, and the number of animals housed there. In turn, guests have preferences for what they see in the zoo, including amenities, decorations, and most important, the types of animals. The goal of the game is to keep both the animals and the guests happy, which will yield profit and a successful zoo. Players can also complete levels that have more specific goals, such as having a certain number of animals or a minimum average happiness for the park's animals. The game was originally released for home computers, and versions have since been released for Xbox 360, Xbox One, Nintendo DS, and mobile platforms. The current ESRB rating is E.

Notes

Chapter 1: A New Perspective on Games and Families

1. Amanda Lenhart, Sydney Jones, and Alexandra Macgill, "Adults and Video Games," The Pew Internet and American Life Project, December 7, 2008, http://www.pewinternet.org/2008/12/07/adults-and-video-games/.

2. Ibid.

3. Edna Mitchell, "The Dynamics of Family Interaction around Home Video Games," *Marriage & Family Review* 8, no. 1–2 (1985): 121–135.

4. Accenture and Girls Who Code, "Cracking the Gender Code: Get 3X More Women in Computing," 2016, https://www.accenture.com/t20161018 T094638__w__/us-en/_acnmedia/Accenture/next-gen-3/girls-who-code /Accenture-Cracking-The-Gender-Code-Report.pdf.

5. Jennifer Jenson and Suzanne de Castell, "Gender, Simulation, and Gaming: Research Review and Redirections," *Simulation & Gaming* 41, no. 1 (2010): 51–71.

6. Ibid.

7. Lynn Schofield Clark, "Parental Mediation Theory for the Digital Age," *Communication Theory* 21, no. 4 (2011): 323–343.

8. Mizuko Ito et al., Hanging Out, Messing Around, and Geeking Out: Kids Living and Learning with New Media (Cambridge, MA: MIT Press, 2009).

9. Wonsun Shin and Jisu Huh, "Parental Mediation of Teenagers' Video Game Playing: Antecedents and Consequences," *New Media & Society* 13, no. 6 (2011): 945–962.

10. Lynn Schofield Clark, *The Parent App: Understanding Families in the Digital Age* (New York: Oxford University Press, 2012).

11. Cynthia Chiong, "Can Video Games Promote Intergenerational Play and Literacy Learning?" The Joan Ganz Cooney Center at Sesame Workshop, March 22, 2010, http://www.joanganzcooneycenter.org/publication/can-video-games -promote-intergenerational-play-literacy-learning/.

12. Marc Prensky, Don't Bother Me, Mom, I'm Learning!: How Computer and Video Games Are Preparing Your Kids for 21st Century Success and How You Can Help! (St. Paul, MN: Paragon House, 2006).

13. Amy I. Nathanson, "Mediation of Children's Television Viewing: Working toward Conceptual Clarity and Common Understanding," *Annals of the International Communication Association* 25, no. 1 (2001): 115–151.

14. Alexandra Ossola, "The Surprising Amount of Time Kids Spend Looking at Screens," *The Atlantic*, January 22, 2015, https://www.theatlantic.com /education/archive/2015/01/the-surprising-amount-of-time-kids-spend-looking -at-screens/384737/.

15. Donald Shifrin et al., "Growing Up Digital: Media Research Symposium," Rosemont, IL, May 2–3, 2015, https://www.aap.org/en-us/Documents/digital _media_symposium_proceedings.pdf.

16. Christopher J. Ferguson, "The School Shooting/Violent Video Game Link: Causal Relationship or Moral Panic?" *Journal of Investigative Psychology and Offender Profiling* 5, no. 1–2 (2008): 25–37.

17. Erik Kain, "As Video Game Sales Climb Year over Year, Violent Crime Continues to Fall," *Forbes*, April 19, 2012, https://www.forbes.com/sites/erikkain /2012/04/19/as-video-game-sales-climb-year-over-year-violent-crime-continues -to-fall/.

18. Craig A. Anderson and Brad J. Bushman, "Effects of Violent Video Games on Aggressive Behavior, Aggressive Cognition, Aggressive Affect, Physiological Arousal, and Prosocial Behavior: A Meta-analytic Review of the Scientific Literature," *Psychological Science* 12, no. 5 (2001): 353–359.

19. Christopher J. Ferguson, "Violent Video Games and the Supreme Court: Lessons for the Scientific Community in the Wake of *Brown v. Entertainment Merchants Association*," *American Psychologist* 68, no. 2 (2013): 57.

20. Paul J. C. Adachi and Teena Willoughby, "The Effect of Violent Video Games on Aggression: Is It More Than Just the Violence?" *Aggression and Violent Behavior* 16, no. 1 (2011): 55–62.

21. See the ESRB website: http://www.esrb.org/ratings/faq.aspx#2.

22. "Crime: Japan and United States Compared," NationMaster, accessed March 12, 2017, http://www.nationmaster.com/country-info/compare/Japan /United-States/Crime/.

23. Christopher J. Ferguson, Claudia San Miguel, and Richard D. Hartley, "A Multivariate Analysis of Youth Violence and Aggression: The Influence of Family, Peers, Depression, and Media Violence," *The Journal of Pediatrics* 155, no. 6 (2009): 904–908.

24. Douglas Gentile, "Pathological Video Game Use among Youth 8 to 18: A National Study," *Psychological Science* 20, no. 5 (2009): 594–602.

25. Daria J. Kuss and Mark D. Griffiths, "Online Gaming Addiction in Children and Adolescents: A Review of Empirical Research," *Journal of Behavioral Addiction* 1, no. 1 (2012): 3–22.

26. Victoria J. Rideout, Ulla G. Foehr, and Donald F. Roberts, "Generation M^2 Media in the Lives of 8- to 18-Year-Olds," Henry J. Kaiser Family Foundation, January 20, 2010, http://kff.org/other/event/generation-m2-media-in-the-lives-of/.

27. Gentile, "Pathological Video Game Use."

28. Richard Wood, "Problems with the Concept of Video Game 'Addiction': Some Case Study Examples," *International Journal of Mental Health and Addiction* 6, no. 2 (2008): 169–178.

29. Sharon B. Wyatt, Karen P. Winters, and Patricia M. Dubbert, "Overweight and Obesity: Prevalence, Consequences, and Causes of a Growing Public Health Problem," *American Journal of the Medical Sciences* 331, no. 4 (2006): 166–174.

30. Ibid.

31. Rideout, Foehr, and Roberts, "Generation M^2."

32. Linda A. Jackson et al., "Internet Use, Videogame Playing, and Cell Phone Use as Predictors of Children's Body Mass Index (BMI), Body Weight, Academic Performance, and Social and Overall Self-Esteem," *Computers in Human Behavior* 27, no. 1 (2011): 599–604.

33. Britt MacArthur et al., "Active Videogaming Compared to Unstructured, Outdoor Play in Young Children: Percent Time in Moderate- to Vigorous-Intensity Physical Activity and Estimated Energy Expenditure," *Games for Health Journal* 3, no. 6 (2014): 388–394.

34. Sherry Turkle, Alone Together: Why We Expect More from Technology and Less from Each Other (New York: Basic Books, 2012).

35. Catherine Steiner-Adair and Teresa H. Barker, The Big Disconnect: Protecting Childhood and Family Relationships in the Digital Age (New York: Harper, 2013).

36. Reed Stevens, Tom Satwicz, and Laurie McCarthy, "In-game, In-room, In-world: Reconnecting Video Game Play to the Rest of Kids' Lives," in *The Ecology of Games: Connecting Youth, Games, and Learning*, ed. Katie Salen (Cambridge, MA: MIT Press, 2008), 41–66.

37. The White House, "Games That Can Change the World," December 13, 2013, https://obamawhitehouse.archives.gov/blog/2013/12/13/games-can -change-world/.

38. Mizuko Ito, Engineering Play: A Cultural History of Children's Software (Cambridge, MA: MIT Press, 2012).

39. Douglas Thomas and John Seely Brown, "Learning for a World of Constant Change: *Homo Sapiens*, *Homo Faber*, & *Homo Ludens* Revisited," Paper presented at the 7th Glion Colloquium, 2009.

40. Library of Congress, "Children's Lives at the Turn of the Twentieth Century," accessed March 15, 2017, http://www.loc.gov/teachers/classroommaterials /primarysourcesets/childrens-lives/pdf/teacher_guide.pdf.

41. Joe L. Frost, A History of Children's Play and Play Environments: Toward a Contemporary Child-Saving Moment (New York: Routledge, 2010).

42. Susan Sutherland Isaacs, The Nursery Years: The Mind of the Child from Birth to Six Years (London: Routledge, 1932).

43. Justine Howard, "Eliciting Young Children's Perceptions of Play, Work and Learning using the Activity Apperception Story Procedure," *Early Child Development and Care* 172, no. 5 (2002): 489–502.

44. Lisa A. Wing, "Play Is Not the Work of the Child: Young Children's Perceptions of Work and Play," *Early Childhood Research Quarterly* 10, no. 2 (1995): 223–247.

45. Henry Jenkins et al., Confronting the Challenges of Participatory Culture: Media Education for the 21st Century (Cambridge, MA: MIT Press, 2009).

46. Douglas Thomas and John Seely Brown, A New Culture of Learning: Cultivating the Imagination for a World of Constant Change (Lexington, KY: CreateSpace, 2011), 47–48.

47. Lindsay Davis, Elizabeth Larkin, and Stephen B. Graves, "Intergenerational Learning through Play," *International Journal of Early Childhood* 34, no. 2 (2002): 42–49.

48. Janet Murray, "Toward a Cultural Theory of Gaming: Digital Games and the Co-evolution of Media, Mind, and Culture," *Popular Communication* 4, no. 3 (2006): 185–202.

49. Kenneth R. Ginsburg, "The Importance of Play in Promoting Healthy Child Development and Maintaining Strong Parent-Child Bonds," *Pediatrics* 119, no. 1 (2007): 182–191.

50. Sarah M. Coyne et al., "Game On . . . Girls: Associations between Co-playing Video Games and Adolescent Behavioral and Family Outcomes," *Journal of Adolescent Health* 49, no. 2 (2011): 160–165.

51. Heather A. Horst, "Silicon Valley Families," in *Hanging Out, Messing Around, and Geeking Out: Kids Living and Learning with New Media*, edited by Mizuko Ito et al. (Cambridge, MA: MIT Press, 2010), 149–194.

52. Pål André Aarsand, "Computer and Video Games in Family Life: The Digital Divide as a Resource in Intergenerational Interactions," *Childhood* 14, no. 2 (2007): 235–256.

53. Seymour Papert, *The Connected Family: Bridging the Digital Generation Gap* (Atlanta, GA: Longstreet Press, 1996).

Chapter 2: Strengthening Family Relations

1. Amanda L. Williams and Michael J. Merten, "iFamily: Internet and Social Media Technology in the Family Context," *Family and Consumer Sciences Research Journal* 40, no. 2 (2011): 150–170.

2. Ibid.

3. Andreas Krapp, "Interest, Motivation and Learning: An Educational-Psychological Perspective," *European Journal of Psychology of Education* 14, no. 1 (1999): 23–40.

4. Mary Ainley, Suzanne Hidi, and Dagmar Berndorff, "Interest, Learning, and the Psychological Processes That Mediate Their Relationship," *Journal of Educational Psychology* 94, no. 3 (2002): 545.

5. Ibid.

6. Suzanne Hidi and K. Ann Renninger, "The Four-Phase Model of Interest Development," *Educational Psychologist* 41, no. 2 (2006): 111–127.

7. Ibid.

8. Mizuko Ito et al., *Connected Learning: An Agenda for Research and Design*, The Digital Media and Learning Research Hub Reports on Connected Learning, 2013. https://dmlhub.net/wp-content/uploads/files/Connected_Learning_report.pdf.

9. Luther Elliott et al., "The Contribution of Game Genre and Other Use Patterns to Problem Video Game Play among Adult Video Gamers," *International Journal of Mental Health and Addiction* 10, no. 6 (2012): 948–969.

Chapter 3: Family Learning and Video Games

1. Lev Vygotsky, *Mind in Society: The Development of Higher Psychological Processes* (Cambridge, MA: Harvard University Press, 1978).

2. Barbara Rogoff, *Apprenticeship in Thinking: Cognitive Development in Social Context* (New York: Oxford University Press, 1992).

3. Ibid.

4. John Dewey, *Experience and Education* (New York: Kappa Delta Pi, 1938).

5. Jean Lave, *Cognition in Practice: Mind, Mathematics and Culture in Everyday Life* (Cambridge: Cambridge University Press, 1988).

6. Entertainment Software Association, "Games: Family Life," 2014, http://www.theesa.com/wp-content/uploads/2014/11/Games_Familes-11.4.pdf.

7. James Paul Gee, *What Video Games Have to Teach Us about Learning and Literacy* (New York: Palgrave Macmillan, 2013).

8. Rideout et al., *Generation M²*, 2.

9. Patricia A. Alexander, "Reading Into the Future: Competence for the 21st Century," *Educational Psychologist* 47, no. 4 (2012): 259–280.

10. Constance Steinkuehler, "Massively Multiplayer Online Gaming as a Constellation of Literacy Practices," *E-Learning and Digital Media* 4, no. 3 (2007): 297–318.

11. Beverly J. Dodici, Dianne C. Draper, and Carla A. Peterson, "Early Parent-Child Interactions and Early Literacy Development," *Topics in Early Childhood Special Education* 23, no. 3 (2003): 124–136.

12. Gabrielle A. Strouse, Katherine O'Doherty, and Georgene L. Troseth, "Effective Coviewing: Preschoolers' Learning from Video after a Dialogic Questioning Intervention," *Developmental Psychology* 49, no. 12 (2013): 2368–2382.

13. Frederick Zimmerman et al., "Teaching by Listening: The Importance of Adult-Child Conversations to Language Development." *Pediatrics* 124, no. 1 (2009): 342–349.

14. Adriana G. Bus, "Joint Caregiver-Child Storybook Reading: A Route to Literacy Development," in *Handbook of Early Literacy Research*, vol. 1, eds. Susan B. Neuman and David K. Dickson (New York: Guilford Press, 2001), 183–184.

15. Andrea A. Zevenbergen and Grover J. Whitehurst, "Dialogic Reading: A Shared Picture Book Reading Intervention for Preschoolers," in *On Reading Books to Children: Parents and Teachers*, eds. Anne van Kleeck, Steven A. Stahl, and Eurydice B. Bauer (New York: Routledge, 2003), 171–172..

16. Betty Hart and Todd R. Risley, *Meaningful Differences in the Everyday Experience of Young American Children* (Baltimore: Paul H. Brookes Publishing, 1995), 180–181.

17. Vygotsky, *Mind in Society*.

18. Barbara Rogoff and William Gardner, "Adult Guidance of Cognitive Development," in *Everyday Cognition: Its Development in Social Context*, eds. Barbara Rogoff and Jeanne Lave (Cambridge, MA: Harvard University Press, 1984), 95–116.

19. Brigid Barron, Caitlin Kennedy Martin, Lori Takeuchi, and Rachel Fithian, "Parents as Learning Partners in the Development of Technological Fluency," *International Journal of Learning and Media* 1, no. 2 (2009): 55–77.

20. John H. Falk and Lynn D. Dierking, *The Museum Experience Revisited* (New York: Routledge, 2016).

21. Gee, *Video Games*.

22. See Sarah Brin, "Games and Play at the Museum," San Francisco Museum of Modern Arts (SFMOMA), September 2015, https://www.sfmoma.org/read /games-and-play-museum/.

23. Gaea Leinhardt, Kevin Crowley, and Karen Knutson, Preface to *Learning Conversations in Museums*, eds. Gaea Leinhardt, Kevin Crowley, and Karen Knutson (New York: Routledge, 2002), ix.

24. David H. Jonassen, "Toward a Design Theory of Problem Solving," *Educational Technology Research and Development* 48, no. 4 (2000): 63–85

25. Constance Steinkuehler and Sean Duncan. "Scientific Habits of Mind in Virtual Worlds," *Journal of Science Education and Technology* 17, no. 6 (2008): 535.

26. Murray, "Cultural Theory of Gaming."

27. John D. Bransford and Daniel L. Schwartz, "Rethinking Transfer: A Simple Proposal with Multiple Implications," in Vol. 24 of *Review of Research in Education,* ed. Asghar Iran-Nejad and P. David Pearson (Washington, DC: American Educational Research Association, 1999): 61–100.

28. Brian N. Verdine et al., "Deconstructing Building Blocks: Preschoolers' Spatial Assembly Performance Relates to Early Mathematical Skills," *Child Development* 85, no. 3 (2014): 1062–1076.

29. Dylan Arena, "Commercial Video Games as Preparation for Future Learning" (PhD dissertation, Stanford University, 2012).

30. Jessica Hammer and John Black, "Games and (Preparation for Future) Learning," *Educational Technology* 49, no. 2 (2009): 29.

Chapter 4: Understanding Oneself, Each Other, and the World

1. Armand D'Angour, "Plato and Play: Taking Education Seriously in Ancient Greece," *American Journal of Play* 5, no. 3(2013): 293–307.

2. Rideout, "Generation M²."

3. Johan Huizinga, "Nature and Significance of Play as a Cultural Phenomenon," in *Ritual, Play, and Performance: Readings in the Social Sciences/Theater*, ed. Richard Schechner and Mady Schuman (New York: Seabury Press, 1976), 46–66.

4. Gregory Bateson, "A Theory of Play and Fantasy," in *The Game Design Reader: A Rule of Play Anthology*, ed. Katie Salen and Eric Zimmerman (Cambridge, MA: MIT Press, 2006), 314–329.

5. D'Angour, "Plato and Play."

6. Jean Piaget, *Play, Dreams and Imitation in Childhood* (New York: The Norton Library, 1962).

7. Ibid.

8. Vygotsky, "Mind in Society," 100.

9. Ageliki Nicolopoulou, "Worldmaking and Identity Formation in Children's Narrative Play-Acting," in *Sociogenetic Perspectives on Internalization*, ed. Brian D. Cox and Cynthia Lightfoot (Mahwah, NJ: Lawrence Erlbaum Associates, 1997), 158.

10. Erik Erikson, *Childhood and Society* (New York: Norton, 1995).

11. Eliana Gil, *The Healing Power of Play* (New York: Guilford Publications, 1991).

12. Eliana Gil, *Play in Family Therapy* (New York: Guilford Publications, 1994).

13. Gee, "What Video Games Have to Teach Us."

14. Elinor Ochs, Ruth Smith, and Carolyn Taylor, "Detective Stories at Dinnertime: Problem-Solving through Co-narration," *Cultural Dynamics* 2, no. 2 (1989): 238–257.

15. Diane Hughes et al., "Parents' Ethnic–Racial Socialization Practices: A Review of Research and Directions for Future Study," *Developmental Psychology* 42, no. 5 (2006): 747–770.

16. Ibid.

17. Lisa Kiang and Andrew J. Fuligni, "Ethnic Identity and Family Processes among Adolescents from Latin American, Asian, and European Backgrounds," *Journal of Youth and Adolescence* 38, no. 2 (2009): 228–241.

18. Ibid.

19. Bill Bigelow, "On the Road to Cultural Bias: A Critique of the *Oregon Trail* CD-ROM," *Language Arts* 74, no. 2 (1997): 84–93.

20. Joshua H. Nadel, *Fútbol! Why Soccer Matters in Latin America* (Gainesville: University Press of Florida, 2014).

21. Ibid.

22. FIFA, "Fact Sheet: FIFA Host Countries Overview 1930–2022," March 6, 2011, http://www.fifa.com/mm/document/fifafacts/mencompovw/51/99/03/133485-factsheet-fifahostcountriesoverview1930-2022.pdf.

23. Arturo Figueroa, "Community Identity and Sports: A Social History of Soccer in Salinas, California," *Culture, Society and Praxis* 2, no. 1 (2003).

24. Laurence Steinberg and Susan B. Silverberg, "The Vicissitudes of Autonomy in Early Adolescence," *Child Development* 57, no. 4 (1986): 841–851.

25. Jacquelynne S. Eccles et al., "Development during Adolescence: The Impact of Stage-Environment Fit on Young Adolescents' Experiences in Schools and in Families," *American Psychologist* 48, no. 2 (1993): 90.

26. Laurence Steinberg, "Autonomy, Conflict, and Harmony in the Family Relationship," in *At the Threshold: The Developing Adolescent*, ed. S. Shirley Feldman and Glen R. Elliott (Cambridge, MA: Harvard University Press, 1990), 255–276.

27. Rand D. Conger and Xiaojia Ge, "Conflict and Cohesion in Parent-Adolescent Relations: Changes in Emotional Expression from Early to Midadolescence," in *Conflict and Cohesion in Families: Causes and Consequences*, ed. Martha J. Cox and Jeanne Brooks-Gunn (Mahwah, NJ: Erlbaum, 1999), 185–206.

28. Ibid.

29. Dacher Keltner et al., "Teasing in Hierarchical and Intimate Relations," *Journal of Personality and Social Psychology* 75, no. 5 (1998): 1231–1247.

30. Ibid.

31. Ibid.

32. Étienne Wenger, *Communities of Practice: Learning, Meaning, and Identity* (Cambridge: Cambridge University Press, 1998).

33. Mary Flanagan, *Critical Play: Radical Game Design* (Cambridge, MA: MIT Press, 2009).

34. David R. Michael and Sandra L. Chen, *Serious Games: Games That Educate, Train, and Inform* (Boston: Thomson Course Technology, 2005).

35. Edward Castronova, *Synthetic Worlds: The Business and Culture of Online Games* (Chicago: University of Chicago Press, 2008).

36. Leon C. Kuczynski, Melanie Parkin, and Robyn Pitman, "Socialization as Dynamic Process," in *Handbook of Socialization: Theory and Research*, eds. Joan E. Grusec and Paul D. Hastings (New York: Guilford Press, 2015), 135–157.

37. Clark, *The Parent App*.

Chapter 5: Developing a Learning Culture through Gaming

1. Papert, *The Connected Family*, 79.

2. Seymour Papert, *Mindstorms: Children, Computers, and Powerful Ideas* (New York: Basic Books, 1980).

3. Papert, *The Connected Family*, 80.

4. Papert, *The Connected Family*, 81.

5. Papert, *The Connected Family*, 85.

6. Susan H. Landry, Karen E. Smith, and Paul R. Swank, "Responsive Parenting: Establishing Early Foundations for Social, Communication, and Independent Problem-Solving Skills," *Developmental Psychology* 42, no. 4 (2006): 627–642.

7. Lisa S. Freund, "Maternal Regulation of Children's Problem-solving Behavior and Its Impact on Children's Performance," *Child Development* 61, no. 1 (1990): 113–126.

8. Kevin Crowley and Melanie Jacobs, "Building Islands of Expertise in Everyday Family Activity," in *Learning Conversations in Museums*, ed. Gaea Leinhardt, Kevin Crowley, and Karen Knutson (New York: Routledge, 2002): 333–356.

9. Barron et al., "Parents as Learning Partners."

10. Charles Desforges and Alberto Abouchaar, *The Impact of Parental Involvement, Parental Support and Family Education on Pupil Achievement and Adjustment: A Literature Review*, vol. 433 (Nottingham, UK: DfES Publications, 2003).

11. Vikki S. Katz, *Kids in the Middle: How Children of Immigrants Negotiate Community Interactions for Their Families* (New Brunswick, NJ: Rutgers University Press, 2014).

12. Ibid.

13. Marcel M. Robles, "Executive Perceptions of the Top 10 Soft Skills Needed in Today's Workplace," *Business Communication Quarterly* 75, no. 4 (2012): 453–465.

14. Thomas and Brown, *A New Culture of Learning*.

15. Ibid.

16. Chip Espinoza and Mick Ukleja, *Managing the Millennials: Discover the Core Competencies for Managing Today's Workforce* (New York: John Wiley & Sons, 2016).

17. Ron Zemke, Claire Raines, and Bob Filipczak, *Generations at Work: Managing the Clash of Veterans, Boomers, Xers, and Nexters in your Workplace* (New York, NY: Amacom, 2000).

18. Pew Research Center, *The State of American Jobs* (Washington, DC: Pew Research Center, 2016).

19. Anna Rosefsky Saavedra and V. Darleen Opfer, "Learning 21st-century Skills Requires 21st-century Teaching," *Phi Delta Kappan* 94, no. 2 (2012): 8–13.

20. Thomas and Brown, *A New Culture of Learning*.

21. Jean Lave and Étienne Wenger, *Situated Learning: Legitimate Peripheral Participation* (Cambridge: Cambridge University Press, 1991).

22. Lave and Wenger, *Situated Learning*, 98.

23. Étienne C. Wenger and William M. Snyder, "Communities of Practice: The Organizational Frontier," *Harvard Business Review* 78, no. 1 (2000): 139–146.

24. Ibid.

25. Martin Oliver and Diane Carr, "Learning in Virtual Worlds: Using Communities of Practice to Explain How People Learn from Play," *British Journal of Educational Technology* 40, no. 3 (2009): 444–457.

26. Mark G. Chen, "Communication, Coordination, and Camaraderie in *World of Warcraft*," *Games and Culture* 4, no. 1 (2009): 47–73.

27. Oliver and Carr, "Learning in Virtual Worlds."

28. Wenger, *Communities of Practice*, 6.

29. Rogoff, *Apprenticeship in Thinking*.

30. Barbara H. Fiese et al., "A Review of 50 Years of Research on Naturally Occurring Family Routines and Rituals: Cause for Celebration?" *Journal of Family Psychology* 16, no. 4 (2002): 381.

31. Ernesto R. Ramirez et al., "Adolescent Screen Time and Rules to Limit Screen Time in the Home," *Journal of Adolescent Health* 48, no. 4 (2011): 379–385.

32. Michael J. Jacobson, and Uri Wilensky, "Complex Systems in Education: Scientific and Educational Importance and Implications for the Learning Sciences," *The Journal of the Learning Sciences* 15, no. 1 (2006): 11–34.

33. Jenkins et al., *Challenges of Participatory Culture*.

34. Ibid.

35. S. Craig Watkins, *The Young and the Digital: What the Migration to Social Network Sites, Games, and Anytime, Anywhere Media Means for Our Future* (Boston: Beacon Press, 2009).

36. Katie Salen, "Gaming Literacies: A Game Design Study in Action," *Journal of Educational Multimedia and Hypermedia* 16, no. 3 (2007): 301–322.

Chapter 6: Designing for Intergenerational Play

1. Ito et al., *Connected Learning*.

2. Barbara Rogoff, Carolyn Goodman Turkanis, and Leslee Bartlett, *Learning Together: Children and Adults in a School Community* (New York: Oxford University Press, 2001).

3. President's Council of Advisors on Science and Technology (US), *Prepare and Inspire: K–12 Education in Science, Technology, Engineering, and Math (STEM) for America's Future: Executive Report* (Washington, DC: Executive Office of the President, President's Council of Advisors on Science and Technology, 2010).

4. Amy Wilson-Lopez et al., "Latino/a Adolescents' Funds of Knowledge Related to Engineering," *Journal of Engineering Education* 105, no. 2 (2016): 278–311.

5. Laurence F. Johnson et al., *Challenge-Based Learning: An Approach for Our Time* (Austin, TX: The New Media Consortium, 2009).

6. Jonassen, "Toward a Design Theory of Problem Solving."

7. Daniel L. Schwartz and John D. Bransford, "A Time for Telling," *Cognition and Instruction* 16, no. 4 (1998): 475–522.

8. René Weber, Katharina-Maria Behr, and Cynthia DeMartino, "Measuring Interactivity in Video Games," *Communication Methods and Measures* 8, no. 2 (2014): 79–115.

9. Brigid Barron and Linda Darling-Hammond, "Powerful Learning: Studies Show Deep Understanding Derives from Collaborative Methods," *Edutopia* (October 2008), accessed March 17, 2017, https://www.edutopia.org/inquiry -project-learning-research/.

10. Melissa Gresalfi et al., "Virtual Worlds, Conceptual Understanding, and Me: Designing for Consequential Engagement," *On the Horizon* 17, no. 1 (2009): 21–34.

11. Chunka Mui, "Five Dangerous Lessons to Learn from Steve Jobs," *Forbes*, October 17, 2011, https://www.forbes.com/sites/chunkamui/2011/10/17/five -dangerous-lessons-to-learn-from-steve-jobs/.

Bibliography

Aarsand, Pål André. "Computer and Video Games in Family Life: The Digital Divide as a Resource in Intergenerational Interactions." *Childhood* 14 (2) (2007): 235–256.

Accenture and Girls Who Code. "Cracking the Gender Code: Get 3X More Women in Computing." 2016. Accessed March 6, 2017. https://www.accenture.com/t20161018T094638__w__/us-en/_acnmedia/Accenture/next-gen-3/girls-who-code/Accenture-Cracking-The-Gender-Code-Report.pdf.

Adachi, Paul J. C., and Teena Willoughby. "The Effect of Violent Video Games on Aggression: Is It More Than Just the Violence?" *Aggression and Violent Behavior* 16 (1) (2011): 55–62.

Ainley, Mary, Suzanne Hidi, and Dagmar Berndorff. "Interest, Learning, and the Psychological Processes That Mediate Their Relationship." *Journal of Educational Psychology* 94 (3) (2002): 545.

Alexander, Patricia A. "Reading Into the Future: Competence for the 21st Century." *Educational Psychologist* 47 (4) (2012): 259–280.

Anderson, Craig A., and Brad J. Bushman. "Effects of Violent Video Games on Aggressive Behavior, Aggressive Cognition, Aggressive Affect, Physiological Arousal, and Prosocial Behavior: A Meta-analytic Review of the Scientific Literature." *Psychological Science* 12 (5) (2001): 353–359.

Arena, Dylan. "Commercial Video Games as Preparation for Future Learning." PhD dissertation, Stanford University, 2012.

Barron, Brigid, and Linda Darling-Hammond. "Powerful Learning: Studies Show Deep Understanding Derives from Collaborative Methods." *Edutopia* (October 2008). Accessed March 17, 2017. https://www.edutopia.org/inquiry-project-learning-research/.

Barron, Brigid, Caitlin Kennedy Martin, Lori Takeuchi, and Rachel Fithian. "Parents as Learning Partners in the Development of Technological Fluency." *International Journal of Learning and Media* 1 (2) (2009): 55–77.

Bateson, Gregory. A Theory of Play and Fantasy. In *The Game Design Reader: A Rule of Play Anthology*, edited by Katie Salen and Eric Zimmerman. 314–329. Cambridge, MA: MIT Press, 2006.

Bigelow, Bill. "On the Road to Cultural Bias: A Critique of the *Oregon Trail* CD-ROM." *Language Arts* 74 (2) (1997): 84–93.

Bransford, John D., and Daniel L. Schwartz. Rethinking Transfer: A Simple Proposal with Multiple Implications. In *Review of Research in Education*, vol. 24, edited by Asghar Iran-Nejad and P. David Pearson. 61–100. Washington, DC: American Educational Research Association, 1999.

Brin, Sarah. "Games and Play at the Museum." San Francisco Museum of Modern Arts (SFMOMA). September 2015. https://www.sfmoma.org/read/games-and-play-museum/.

Bus, Adriana G. Joint Caregiver-Child Storybook Reading: A Route to Literacy Development. In *Handbook of Early Literacy Research*, vol. 1, edited by Susan B. Neuman and David K. Dickson. 179–191. New York: Guilford Press, 2001.

Castronova, Edward. *Synthetic Worlds: The Business and Culture of Online Games*. Chicago: University of Chicago Press, 2008.

Chen, Mark G. "Communication, Coordination, and Camaraderie in *World of Warcraft*." *Games and Culture* 4 (1) (2009): 47–73.

Chiong, Cynthia. "Can Video Games Promote Intergenerational Play and Literacy Learning?" The Joan Ganz Cooney Center at Sesame Workshop. March 22, 2010. http://www.joanganzcooneycenter.org/publication/can-video-games-promote-intergenerational-play-literacy-learning/.

Clark, Lynn Schofield. "Parental Mediation Theory for the Digital Age." *Communication Theory* 21 (4) (2011): 323–343.

Clark, Lynn Schofield. *The Parent App: Understanding Families in the Digital Age*. New York: Oxford University Press, 2012.

Conger, Rand D., and Xiaojia Ge. Conflict and Cohesion in Parent-Adolescent Relations: Changes in Emotional Expression from Early to Midadolescence. In *Conflict and Cohesion in Families: Causes and Consequences*, edited by Martha J. Cox and Jeanne Brooks-Gunn, 185–206. Mahwah, NJ: Erlbaum, 1999.

Coyne, Sarah M., Laura M. Padilla-Walker, Laura Stockdale, and Randal D. Day. "Game On . . . Girls: Associations between Co-playing Video Games and Adolescent Behavioral and Family Outcomes." *Journal of Adolescent Health* 49 (2) (2011): 160–165.

"Crime: Japan and United States Compared," NationMaster. Accessed March 12, 2017. http://www.nationmaster.com/country-info/compare/Japan/United-States/Crime/.

Crowley, Kevin, and Melanie Jacobs. Building Islands of Expertise in Everyday Family Activity. In *Learning Conversations in Museums*, edited by Gaea Leinhardt, Kevin Crowley, and Karen Knutson, 333–356. New York: Routledge, 2002.

D'Angour, Armand. "Plato and Play: Taking Education Seriously in Ancient Greece." *American Journal of Play* 5 (3) (2013): 293–307.

Davis, Lindsay, Elizabeth Larkin, and Stephen B. Graves. "Intergenerational Learning through Play." *International Journal of Early Childhood* 34 (2) (2002): 42–49.

Desforges, Charles, and Alberto Abouchaar. *The Impact of Parental Involvement, Parental Support and Family Education on Pupil Achievement and Adjustment: A Literature Review*, vol. 433. Nottingham, UK: DfES Publications, 2003.

Dewey, John. *Experience and Education*. New York: Kappa Delta Pi, 1938.

Dodici, Beverly J., Dianne C. Draper, and Carla A. Peterson. "Early Parent-Child Interactions and Early Literacy Development." *Topics in Early Childhood Special Education* 23 (3) (2003): 124–136.

Eccles, Jacquelynne S., Carol Midgley, Allan Wigfield, Christy Miller Buchanan, David Reuman, Constance Flanagan, and Douglas Mac Iver. "Development during Adolescence: The Impact of Stage-Environment Fit on Young Adolescents' Experiences in Schools and in Families." *American Psychologist* 48 (2) (1993): 90.

Elliott, Luther, Geoffrey Ream, Elizabeth McGinsky, and Eloise Dunlap. "The Contribution of Game Genre and Other Use Patterns to Problem Video Game Play among Adult Video Gamers." *International Journal of Mental Health and Addiction* 10 (6) (2012): 948–969.

Entertainment Software Association. "Games: Family Life." 2014. http://www.theesa.com/wp-content/uploads/2014/11/Games_Familes-11.4.pdf.

Erikson, Erik. *Childhood and Society*. New York: Norton, 1995.

Espinoza, Chip, and Mick Ukleja. *Managing the Millennials: Discover the Core Competencies for Managing Today's Workforce*. New York: John Wiley & Sons, 2016.

Falk, John H., and Lynn D. Dierking. *The Museum Experience Revisited*. New York: Routledge, 2016.

Ferguson, Christopher J. "The School Shooting/Violent Video Game Link: Causal Relationship or Moral Panic?" *Journal of Investigative Psychology and Offender Profiling* 5 (1–2) (2008): 25–37.

Ferguson, Christopher J. "Violent Video Games and the Supreme Court: Lessons for the Scientific Community in the Wake of *Brown v. Entertainment Merchants Association*." *American Psychologist* 68 (2) (2013): 57.

Ferguson, Christopher J., Claudia San Miguel, and Richard D. Hartley. "A Multivariate Analysis of Youth Violence and Aggression: The Influence of Family, Peers, Depression, and Media Violence." *Journal of Pediatrics* 155 (6) (2009): 904–908.

Fiese, Barbara H., Thomas J. Tomcho, Michael Douglas, Kimberly Josephs, Scott Poltrock, and Tim Baker. "A Review of 50 Years of Research on Naturally Occurring Family Routines and Rituals: Cause for Celebration?" *Journal of Family Psychology* 16 (4) (2002): 381.

FIFA. "Fact Sheet: FIFA Host Countries Overview 1930–2022." March 6, 2011. http://www.fifa.com/mm/document/fifafacts/mencompovw/51/99/03/133485-factsheet-fifahostcountriesoverview1930-2022.pdf.

Figueroa, Arturo. "Community Identity and Sports: A Social History of Soccer in Salinas, California." *Culture, Society and Praxis* 2 (1) (2003).

Flanagan, Mary. *Critical Play: Radical Game Design*. Cambridge, MA: MIT Press, 2009.

Freund, Lisa S. "Maternal Regulation of Children's Problem-solving Behavior and Its Impact on Children's Performance." *Child Development* 61 (1) (1990): 113–126.

Frost, Joe L. *A History of Children's Play and Play Environments: Towards a Contemporary Child-Saving Moment*. New York: Routledge, 2010.

Gee, James Paul. *What Video Games Have to Teach Us about Learning and Literacy*. New York: Palgrave Macmillan, 2013.

Gentile, Douglas. "Pathological Video Game Use among Youth 8 to 18: A National Study." *Psychological Science* 20 (5) (2009): 594–602.

Gil, Eliana. *The Healing Power of Play*. New York: Guilford Publications, 1991.

Gil, Eliana. *Play in Family Therapy*. New York: Guilford Publications, 1994.

Ginsburg, Kenneth R. "The Importance of Play in Promoting Healthy Child Development and Maintaining Strong Parent-Child Bonds." *Pediatrics* 119 (1) (2007): 182–191.

Gresalfi, Melissa, Sasha Barab, Sinem Siyahhan, and Tyler Christensen. "Virtual Worlds, Conceptual Understanding, and Me: Designing for Consequential Engagement." *On the Horizon* 17 (1) (2009): 21–34.

Hammer, Jessica, and John Black. "Games and (Preparation for Future) Learning." *Educational Technology* 49 (2) (2009): 29.

Hart, Betty, and Todd R. Risley. *Meaningful Differences in the Everyday Experience of Young American Children*. Baltimore: Paul H. Brookes Publishing, 1995.

Hidi, Suzanne, and K. Ann Renninger. "The Four-Phase Model of Interest Development." *Educational Psychologist* 41 (2) (2006): 111–127.

Horst, Heather A. Silicon Valley Families. In *Hanging Out, Messing Around, and Geeking Out: Kids Living and Learning with New Media*, edited by Mizuko Ito et al. 149–194. Cambridge, MA: MIT Press, 2010.

Howard, Justine. "Eliciting Young Children's Perceptions of Play, Work and Learning using the Activity Apperception Story Procedure." *Early Child Development and Care* 172 (5) (2002): 489–502.

Hughes, Diane, James Rodriguez, Emilie P. Smith, and Deborah J. Johnson. "Parents' Ethnic–Racial Socialization Practices: A Review of Research and Directions for Future Study." *Developmental Psychology* 42 (5) (2006): 747–770.

Huizinga, Johan. Nature and Significance of Play as a Cultural Phenomenon. In *Ritual, Play, and Performance: Readings in the Social Sciences/Theatre*, edited by Richard Schechner and Mady Schuman. 46–66. New York: Seabury Press, 1976.

Isaacs, Susan Sutherland. *The Nursery Years: The Mind of the Child from Birth to Six Years*. London: Routledge, 1932.

Ito, Mizuko. *Engineering Play: A Cultural History of Children's Software*. Cambridge, MA: MIT Press, 2012.

Ito, Mizuko, Sonja Baumer, Matteo Bittanti, danah boyd, Rachel Cody, Becky Herr-Stephenson, Heather A. Horst, Patricia G. Lange, Dilan Mahendran, Katynka Z. Martínez, C. J. Pascoe, Dan Perkel, Laura Robinson, Christo Sims, and Lisa Tripp. *Hanging Out, Messing Around, and Geeking Out: Kids Living and Learning with New Media.* Cambridge, MA: MIT Press, 2009.

Ito, Mizuko, Kris Gutiérrez, Sonia Livingstone, Bill Penuel, Jean Rhodes, Katie Salen, Juliet Schor, Julian Sefton-Green, and S. Craig Watkins. *Connected Learning: An Agenda for Research and Design.* The Digital Media and Learning Research Hub Reports on Connected Learning. January 2013. https://dmlhub.net/wp-content /uploads/files/Connected_Learning_report.pdf.

Jackson, Linda A., Alexander Von Eye, Hiram E. Fitzgerald, Edward A. Witt, and Yong Zhao. "Internet Use, Videogame Playing, and Cell Phone Use as Predictors of Children's Body Mass Index (BMI), Body Weight, Academic Performance, and Social and Overall Self-Esteem." *Computers in Human Behavior* 27 (1) (2011): 599–604.

Jacobson, Michael J., and Uri Wilensky. "Complex Systems in Education: Scientific and Educational Importance and Implications for the Learning Sciences." *Journal of the Learning Sciences* 15 (1) (2006): 11–34.

Jenkins, Henry, Ravi Purushotma, Margaret Weigel, Katie Clinton, and Alice J. Robison. *Confronting the Challenges of Participatory Culture: Media Education for the 21st Century.* Cambridge, MA: MIT Press, 2009.

Jenson, Jennifer, and Suzanne de Castell. "Gender, Simulation, and Gaming: Research Review and Redirections." *Simulation & Gaming* 41 (1) (2010): 51–71.

Johnson, Laurence F., Rachel S. Smith, J. Troy Smythe, and Rachel K. Varon. *Challenge-Based Learning: An Approach for Our Time.* Austin, TX: The New Media Consortium, 2009.

Jonassen, David H. "Toward a Design Theory of Problem Solving." *Educational Technology Research and Development* 48 (4) (2000): 63–85.

Kain, Erik. "As Video Game Sales Climb Year over Year, Violent Crime Continues to Fall." *Forbes.* April 19, 2012. https://www.forbes.com/sites/erikkain/2012 /04/19/as-video-game-sales-climb-year-over-year-violent-crime-continues-to-fall/.

Katz, Vikki S. *Kids in the Middle: How Children of Immigrants Negotiate Community Interactions for Their Families.* New Brunswick, NJ: Rutgers University Press, 2014.

Keltner, Dacher, Randall C. Young, Erin A. Heerey, Carmen Oemig, and Natalie D. Monarch. "Teasing in Hierarchical and Intimate Relations." *Journal of Personality and Social Psychology* 75 (5) (1998): 1231–1247.

Kiang, Lisa, and Andrew J. Fuligni. "Ethnic Identity and Family Processes among Adolescents from Latin American, Asian, and European Backgrounds." *Journal of Youth and Adolescence* 38 (2) (2009): 228–241.

Krapp, Andreas. "Interest, Motivation and Learning: An Educational-Psychological Perspective." *European Journal of Psychology of Education* 14 (1) (1999): 23–40.

Kuczynski, Leon C., Melanie Parkin, and Robyn Pitman. Socialization as Dynamic Process. In *Handbook of Socialization: Theory and Research*, edited by Joan E. Grusec and Paul D. Hastings, 135–157. New York: Guilford Press, 2015.

Kuss, Daria J., and Mark D. Griffiths. "Online Gaming Addiction in Children and Adolescents: A Review of Empirical Research." *Journal of Behavioral Addictions* 1 (1) (2012): 3–22.

Landry, Susan H., Karen E. Smith, and Paul R. Swank. "Responsive Parenting: Establishing Early Foundations for Social, Communication, and Independent Problem-Solving Skills." *Developmental Psychology* 42 (4) (2006): 627–642.

Lave, Jean. *Cognition in Practice: Mind, Mathematics and Culture in Everyday Life*. Cambridge: Cambridge University Press, 1988.

Lave, Jean, and Étienne Wenger. *Situated Learning: Legitimate Peripheral Participation*. Cambridge: Cambridge University Press, 1991.

Leinhardt, Gaea, Kevin Crowley, and Karen Knutson. Preface to *Learning Conversations in Museums*, edited by Gaea Leinhardt, Kevin Crowley, and Karen Knutson, ix. New York: Routledge, 2002.

Lenhart, Amanda, Sydney Jones, and Alexandra Macgill. "Adults and Video Games." The Pew Internet and American Life Project. December 7, 2008. http://www.pewinternet.org/2008/12/07/adults-and-video-games/.

Library of Congress. "Children's Lives at the Turn of the Twentieth Century." Accessed March 15, 2017. http://www.loc.gov/teachers/classroommaterials/primarysourcesets/childrens-lives/pdf/teacher_guide.pdf.

MacArthur, Britt, Dawn Coe, Allison Sweet, and Hollie Raynor. "Active Videogaming Compared to Unstructured, Outdoor Play in Young Children: Percent Time in Moderate- to Vigorous-Intensity Physical Activity and Estimated Energy Expenditure." *Games for Health Journal* 3 (6) (2014): 388–394.

Michael, David R., and Sandra L. Chen. *Serious Games: Games That Educate, Train, and Inform*. Boston: Thomson Course Technology, 2005.

Mitchell, Edna. "The Dynamics of Family Interaction around Home Video Games." *Marriage & Family Review* 8 (1–2) (1985): 121–135.

Mui, Chunka. "Five Dangerous Lessons to Learn from Steve Jobs." *Forbes*. October 17, 2011. https://www.forbes.com/sites/chunkamui/2011/10/17/five-dangerous-lessons-to-learn-from-steve-jobs/.

Murray, Janet. "Toward a Cultural Theory of Gaming: Digital Games and the Co-evolution of Media, Mind, and Culture." *Popular Communication* 4 (3) (2006): 185–202.

Nadel, Joshua H. *Fútbol! Why Soccer Matters in Latin America*. Gainesville: University Press of Florida, 2014.

Nathanson, Amy I. "Mediation of Children's Television Viewing: Working toward Conceptual Clarity and Common Understanding." *Annals of the International Communication Association* 25 (1) (2001): 115–151.

Nicolopoulou, Ageliki. Worldmaking and Identity Formation in Children's Narrative Play-Acting. In *Sociogenetic Perspectives on Internalization*, edited by Brian D. Cox and Cynthia Lightfoot, 158. Mahwah, NJ: Lawrence Erlbaum Associates, 1997.

Ochs, Elinor, Ruth Smith, and Carolyn Taylor. "Detective Stories at Dinnertime: Problem-Solving through Co-narration." *Cultural Dynamics* 2 (2) (1989): 238–257.

Oliver, Martin, and Diane Carr. "Learning in Virtual Worlds: Using Communities of Practice to Explain How People Learn from Play." *British Journal of Educational Technology* 40 (3) (2009): 444–457.

Ossola, Alexandra. "The Surprising Amount of Time Kids Spend Looking at Screens." *The Atlantic.* January 22, 2015. https://www.theatlantic.com/education /archive/2015/01/the-surprising-amount-of-time-kids-spend-looking-at-screens /384737/.

Papert, Seymour. *The Connected Family: Bridging the Digital Generation Gap.* Atlanta, GA: Longstreet Press, 1996.

Papert, Seymour. *Mindstorms: Children, Computers, and Powerful Ideas.* New York: Basic Books, 1980.

Pew Research Center. *The State of American Jobs.* Washington, DC: Pew Research Center, 2016.

Piaget, Jean. *Play, Dreams and Imitation in Childhood.* New York: The Norton Library, 1962.

Prensky, Marc. *Don't Bother Me, Mom, I'm Learning!: How Computer and Video Games are Preparing Your Kids for 21st Century Success and How You Can Help!* St. Paul, MN: Paragon House, 2006.

President's Council of Advisors on Science and Technology (US). *Prepare and Inspire: K–12 Education in Science, Technology, Engineering, and Math (STEM) for America's Future: Executive Report.* Washington, DC: Executive Office of the President, President's Council of Advisors on Science and Technology, 2010.

Ramirez, Ernesto R., Gregory J. Norman, Dori E. Rosenberg, Jacqueline Kerr, Brian E. Saelens, Nefertiti Durant, and James F. Sallis. "Adolescent Screen Time and Rules to Limit Screen Time in the Home." *Journal of Adolescent Health* 48 (4) (2011): 379–385.

Rideout, Victoria J., Ulla G. Foehr, and Donald F. Roberts. "Generation M^2: Media in the Lives of 8- to 18-Year-Olds." Henry J. Kaiser Family Foundation. January 20, 2010. http://kff.org/other/event/generation-m2-media-in-the-lives -of/.

Robles, Marcel M. "Executive Perceptions of the Top 10 Soft Skills Needed in Today's Workplace." *Business Communication Quarterly* 75 (4) (2012): 453–465.

Rogoff, Barbara. *Apprenticeship in Thinking: Cognitive Development in Social Context.* New York: Oxford University Press, 1992.

Rogoff, Barbara, and William Gardner. Adult Guidance of Cognitive Development. In *Everyday Cognition: Its Development in Social Context*, edited by Barbara Rogoff and Jeanne Lave. Cambridge, MA: Harvard University Press, 1984.

Rogoff, Barbara, Carolyn Goodman Turkanis, and Leslee Barlett. *Learning Together: Children and Adults in a School Community*. New York: Oxford University Press, 2001.

Saavedra, Anna Rosefsky, and V. Darleen Opfer. "Learning 21st-Century Skills Requires 21st-Century Teaching." *Phi Delta Kappan* 94 (2) (2012): 8–13.

Salen, Katie. "Gaming Literacies: A Game Design Study in Action." *Journal of Educational Multimedia and Hypermedia* 16 (3) (2007): 301–322.

Schwartz, Daniel L., and John D. Bransford. "A Time for Telling." *Cognition and Instruction* 16 (4) (1998): 475–522.

Shifrin, Donald, Ari Brown, David Hill, Laura Jana, and Susan K. Flinn. "Growing Up Digital: Media Research Symposium." Rosemont, IL, May 2–3, 2015. https://www.aap.org/en-us/Documents/digital_media_symposium_proceedings .pdf.

Shin, Wonsun, and Jisu Huh. "Parental Mediation of Teenagers' Video Game Playing: Antecedents and Consequences." *New Media & Society* 13 (6) (2011): 945–962.

Steiner-Adair, Catherine, and Teresa H. Barker. *The Big Disconnect: Protecting Childhood and Family Relationships in the Digital Age*. New York: Harper, 2013.

Steinkuehler, Constance. "Massively Multiplayer Online Gaming as a Constellation of Literacy Practices." *E-Learning and Digital Media* 4 (3) (2007): 297–318.

Steinkuehler, Constance, and Sean Duncan. "Scientific Habits of Mind in Virtual Worlds." *Journal of Science Education and Technology* 17 (6) (2008): 530–543.

Steinberg, Laurence. Autonomy, Conflict, and Harmony in the Family Relationship. In *At the Threshold: The Developing Adolescent*, edited by S. Shirley Feldman and Glen R. Elliott, 255–276. Cambridge, MA: Harvard University Press, 1990.

Steinberg, Laurence, and Susan B. Silverberg. "The Vicissitudes of Autonomy in Early Adolescence." *Child Development* 57 (4) (1986): 841–851.

Stevens, Reed, Tom Satwicz, and Laurie McCarthy. In-game, In-room, In-world: Reconnecting Video Game Play to the Rest of Kids' Lives. In *The Ecology of Games: Connecting Youth, Games, and Learning*, edited by Katie Salen, 41–66. Cambridge, MA: MIT Press, 2008.

Strouse, Gabrielle A., Katherine O'Doherty, and Georgene L. Troseth. "Effective Coviewing: Preschoolers' Learning from Video after a Dialogic Questioning Intervention." *Developmental Psychology* 49 (12) (2013): 2368–2382.

Thomas, Douglas, and John Seely Brown. "Learning for a World of Constant Change: *Homo Sapiens, Homo Faber* & *Homo Ludens* Revisited." Paper presented at the 7th Glion Colloquium, 2009.

Thomas, Douglas, and John Seely Brown. *A New Culture of Learning: Cultivating the Imagination for a World of Constant Change*. Lexington, KY: CreateSpace, 2011.

Turkle, Sherry. *Alone Together: Why We Expect More from Technology and Less From Each Other*. New York: Basic Books, 2012.

Verdine, Brian N., Roberta M. Golinkoff, Kathryn Hirsh-Pasek, Nora S. Newcombe, Andrew T. Filipowicz, and Alicia Chang. "Deconstructing Building Blocks: Preschoolers' Spatial Assembly Performance Relates to Early Mathematical Skills." *Child Development* 85 (3) (2014): 1062–1076.

Vygotsky, Lev. *Mind in Society: The Development of Higher Psychological Processes*. Cambridge, MA: Harvard University Press, 1978.

Watkins, S. Craig. *The Young and the Digital: What the Migration to Social Network Sites, Games, and Anytime, Anywhere Media Means for Our Future*. Boston: Beacon Press, 2009.

Weber, René, Katharina-Maria Behr, and Cynthia DeMartino. "Measuring Interactivity in Video Games." *Communication Methods and Measures* 8 (2) (2014): 79–115.

Wenger, Étienne. *Communities of Practice: Learning, Meaning, and Identity*. Cambridge: Cambridge University Press, 1998.

Wenger, Étienne C., and William M. Snyder. "Communities of Practice: The Organizational Frontier." *Harvard Business Review* 78 (1) (2000): 139–146.

The White House. "Games That Can Change the World." December 13, 2013. https://obamawhitehouse.archives.gov/blog/2013/12/13/games-can-change-world/.

Williams, Amanda L., and Michael J. Merten. "iFamily: Internet and Social Media Technology in the Family Context." *Family and Consumer Sciences Research Journal* 40 (2) (2011): 150–170.

Wilson-Lopez, Amy, Joel Alejandro Mejia, Indhira Hasbún, and G. Sue Kasun. "Latino/a Adolescents' Funds of Knowledge Related to Engineering." *Journal of Engineering Education* 105 (2) (2016): 278–311.

Wing, Lisa A. "Play Is Not the Work of the Child: Young Children's Perceptions of Work and Play." *Early Childhood Research Quarterly* 10 (2) (1995): 223–247.

Wood, Richard. "Problems with the Concept of Video Game 'Addiction': Some Case Study Examples." *International Journal of Mental Health and Addiction* 6 (2) (2008): 169–178.

Wyatt, Sharon B., Karen P. Winters, and Patricia M. Dubbert. "Overweight and Obesity: Prevalence, Consequences, and Causes of a Growing Public Health Problem." *American Journal of the Medical Sciences* 331 (4) (2006): 166–174.

Zemke, Ron, Claire Raines, and Bob Filipczak. *Generations at Work: Managing the Clash of Veterans, Boomers, Xers, and Nexters in Your Workplace*. New York: Amacom, 2000.

Zevenbergen, Andrea A., and Grover J. Whitehurst. Dialogic Reading: A Shared Picture Book Reading Intervention for Preschoolers. In *On Reading Books to Children: Parents and Teachers*, edited by Anne van Kleeck, Steven A. Stahl, and Eurydice B. Bauer, 177–200. New York: Routledge, 2003.

Zimmerman, Frederick J., Jill Gilkerson, Jeffrey A. Richards, Dimitri A. Christakis, Dongxin Xu, Sharmistha Gray, and Umit Yapanel. "Teaching by Listening: The Importance of Adult-Child Conversations to Language Development." *Pediatrics* 124 (1) (2009): 342–349.

Index